The Virginia Tech Massacre

Developmental Perspectives In Psychiatry

SERIES EDITOR

James C. Harris, M.D.
Johns Hopkins University

BOOKS IN THE SERIES

Tuberous Sclerosis Complex, Third Edition
Manual Rodríguez Gómez, M.D., Julian R. Sampson, D.M., and Vicky Holets Whittemore, Ph.D.

Neurodevelopmental Disorders: Recognition and Treatment
Randi Hagerman, M.D.

Demystifying Anorexia Nervosa: An Optimistic Guide to Understanding and Healing
Alexander R. Lucas, M.D.

Intellectual Disability: Understanding Its Development, Causes, Classification, Evaluation, and Treatment
James C. Harris, M.D.

The Virginia Tech Massacre: Strategies and Challenges for Improving Mental Health Policy on Campus and Beyond
Edited by Aradhana Bela Sood, M.D., MSHA, and Robert Cohen, Ph.D.

The Virginia Tech Massacre

Strategies and Challenges

for Improving Mental Health

Policy on Campus and Beyond

Edited by Aradhana Bela Sood

and

Robert Cohen

OXFORD
UNIVERSITY PRESS

Oxford University Press is a department of the University of
Oxford. It furthers the University's objective of excellence in research,
scholarship, and education by publishing worldwide.

Oxford   New York
Auckland   Cape Town   Dar es Salaam   Hong Kong   Karachi
Kuala Lumpur   Madrid   Melbourne   Mexico City   Nairobi
New Delhi   Shanghai   Taipei   Toronto

With offices in
Argentina   Austria   Brazil   Chile   Czech Republic   France   Greece
Guatemala   Hungary   Italy   Japan   Poland   Portugal   Singapore
South Korea   Switzerland   Thailand   Turkey   Ukraine   Vietnam

Oxford is a registered trademark of Oxford University Press
in the UK and certain other countries.

Published in the United States of America by
Oxford University Press
198 Madison Avenue, New York, NY 10016

Library of Congress Cataloging-in-Publication Data
The virginia tech massacre : strategies and challenges for improving mental health policy on campus
and beyond / edited by Aradhana Bela Sood, Robert Cohen. — 1 Edition.
pages cm. — (Developmental perspectives in psychiatry)
Includes bibliographical references and index.
ISBN 978-0-19-539249-4 (hardback)
1. College students—Mental health—United States.   2. College students—Mental health
services—United States.   3. Virginia Tech Shootings, Blacksburg, Va., 2007.   I. Sood, Aradhana
Bela, editor of compilation.   II. Cohen, Robert, 1941- editor of compilation.
RC451.4.S7D48 2014
616.89—dc23
2014014462

1 3 5 7 9 8 6 4 2
Printed in the United States of America
on acid-free paper

For my Mother
Sushila Avasthy
and
For my Sister
Neeharika Naidu
Two women who gave me
The courage to notice injustice
The will to be an (un)tempered radical with
an optimism to believe in the possibility of change
—B.S.

For Katherine Cohen-Filipic and Alison Moritz
and
To the memory of
Ronald Townes and Frank Palumbo,
Who knew too well our mental health care system
—R.C.

CONTENTS

Foreword by James C. Harris ix

Acknowledgments xiii

About the Editors xv

Contributors xvii

PART ONE: LESSONS FROM VIRGINIA TECH

1. The Tragedy at Virginia Tech 3

   Aradhana Bela Sood

2. An Unchecked Descent into Madness: The Life of Seung-Hui Cho 13

   Hollis Stambaugh and Aradhana Bela Sood

3. Insights from Interviews and Other Firsthand Accounts 33

   Aradhana Bela Sood and Hollis Stambaugh

4. Getting into the Mind of the Killer: A Psychological Autopsy
   of Seung-Hui Cho 45

   Aradhana Bela Sood

PART TWO: MENTAL HEALTH CARE ON CAMPUS

5. Failures in Campus Mental Health Systems: Lessons from Virginia Tech 65

   Aradhana Bela Sood and Adele L. Martel

6. Best Practices and Resources: National Models for College Student
   Mental Health 93

   Adele L. Martel and Aradhana Bela Sood

7. Predicting Violence in Public Places 127

   Cheryl S. Al-Mateen, Sala S. Webb, and Aradhana Bela Sood

**PART THREE: THE MENTAL HEALTH CARE SYSTEM
IN THE UNITED STATES**

8. Mental Health Services in the United States: Problems
   and Promising Approaches 157

   Aradhana Bela Sood and Robert Cohen

9. Global Perspectives on Mental Health Care 179
Robert Cohen and Aradhana Bela Sood

10. Toward More Responsive Systems of Care: Challenges and Strategies 195
Robert Cohen and Aradhana Bela Sood

Conclusion: Closing Thoughts 215
Aradhana Bela Sood

Postscript 229

Appendix 231

References 235

Index 255

FOREWORD

The Virginia Tech Massacre: Strategies and Challenges for Improving Mental Health Policy on Campus and Beyond is the first book-length examination of this tragic event by one of the principal members of the investigating commission. It is strengthened by being a first-person account and a continuing reflection on what happened at the time of the event and what has transpired since then. This case study of the perpetrator, Seung-Hui Cho, provides a lens through which to examine the current state of college mental health and provide recommendations to avert future campus disasters.

The events at Virginia Tech spawned an extensive reevaluation of the origins, roles, importance, and availability of mental health services on college campuses; the prevalence of mental disorders in youth transitioning into adulthood (emerging adults aged 18–25); individual rights and privacy issues for college students and their families; needed changes in privacy laws; and, inevitably, the continuing role of stigma and cultural beliefs regarding mental health in students' decision to utilize available services. This book is a welcome examination of how the tragedy came about, what lessons can be learned, and what changes in college mental health policy and reforms to mental health systems have been initiated and those that still need to be instituted to prevent other such tragedies.

The lead author and her team are well qualified to write this book because of their special knowledge of what happened at Virginia Polytechnic Institute and State University (Virginia Tech). As the psychiatrist on the Virginia governor's commission, Dr. Bela Sood had personal access to family members, faculty, administrators, and state officials. As a commission member she was intimately involved in the discussions that led to new legislation, policy changes, and recommendations made in regard to the mental health system. Within a year after the disaster the Virginia legislature improved the emergency mental health evaluation process, modified criteria for involuntary commitment, tightened procedures for assisted outpatient treatment, and increased state funding for community mental health services. This book examines the effectiveness and implementation of these changes and asks: Has there been meaningful change?

Throughout the book the authors continually refer back to the Seung-Hui Cho case as they examine college mental health, mental health practices more broadly in the United States, and mental health practices globally. The authors contrast best mental health practices with limited or unsuccessful ones. They wonder at the many lost opportunities for change that have occurred in the years since the tragedy unfolded. Narrowly they find some progress. There is greater attention to threat reduction procedures, improved crisis stabilization programs and public safety alerts on many college campuses, and better understanding of how privacy laws in place at Virginia Tech proved detrimental to communication. There, individual rights trumped public safety rights, as the authors note, with disastrous results. Yet the larger, necessary goals of enhancing mental health services on college campuses and developing effective preventive mental health programs have not been met, as mental health practitioners and policy-makers continue to search for ways to protect the public from future incidences of gun violence on college campuses. The authors of this book propose solutions and discuss work that still needs to be done to prevent future crises.

The reader is quickly alerted to how red flags were missed and warning signs were ignored. The authors specifically review the events and aftermath of the April 16, 2007, tragedy when a severely mentally disturbed 23-year-old Virginia Tech student, Seung-Hui Cho, murdered 27 fellow students and 5 faculty members and then killed himself. They discuss whether campus security at Virginia Tech acted appropriately to alert the campus population when the first killings occurred and how family members were notified about the killings by the school administration. They discusses how Cho legally obtained the semiautomatic handguns he used to commit these murders, as well as his mental state and psychiatric diagnosis during his time as a student at Virginia Tech before he obtained the guns and before he used them. They reveal that Seung-Hui Cho, an immigrant who came to the United States at age 8 years, had lifelong mental problems with social anxiety and selective mutism. At age 13 he was referred for mental health services because of depression with suicidal ideation and homicidal preoccupation with the Columbine High School killings (April 1999). Subsequently, Cho responded to psychotherapy, pharmacotherapy, and special classroom accommodations throughout his high school years. These interventions allowed him to excel academically despite his continued social anxiety. Yet none of this past history was revealed to his college, and no special accommodations were provided at Virginia Tech.

In particular, the authors ask how a student who had been adjudicated as mentally ill and referred for mental heath follow-up, who had had previous disturbing encounters on campus, and who explicitly expressed violent themes in his coursework was not disciplined, evaluated, or dismissed from school before the crisis. They examine how protections offered by the federal Americans with Disability Act, Family Educational Rights Privacy Act (FERPA), and Health Insurance Portability and Accountability Act (HIPAA) for persons with both mental and physical disabilities, developed to protect from discrimination and ensure individual rights, were misinterpreted. These anti-discrimination laws were designed to protect many thousands of students from college expulsion based on their mental status. Virginia law prevents its public colleges and universities from expelling students for attempting suicide or requesting help for suicidal thoughts or attempts. Thus colleges are conflicted about dismissing students with mental health problems.

Anti-discrimination and privacy provisions under the Family Educational Rights Privacy Act, designed to prevent disclosure of educational records without written consent, have exceptions that allow disclosure when there is a health or safety emergency. Yet the defining of an emergency is left to the discretion of officials at a university. Investigation into the Virginia Tech shootings revealed considerable confusion at Virginia Tech, and around the country, about what can and cannot be disclosed. For example, Cho's family was never alerted that he had been involuntarily committed to a hospital for suicidal thoughts and referred for outpatient treatment.

The Virginia Tech Massacre: Strategies and Challenges for Improving Mental Health Policy on Campus and Beyond is a comprehensive examination in three parts. Following the initial discussion of lessons learned from Virginia Tech, the authors move on to review mental health care on college campuses, with a detailed discussion of the increasing diversity of the college-age population and increasing prevalence of mental disorders among college students. This leads to a discussion of suicide prevention on campuses and programs that deal with threats toward others. The authors examine various approaches to college mental health, as well as successful approaches and barriers to providing care. They move then to more broadly examine how mental health care is delivered in the United States and globally, in an effort to find solutions to better recognition of and care for those with mental disorders and, importantly, to underscore the need for preventative care. Finally, the authors conclude by emphasizing the importance of policy-makers taking seriously and acting on what is known about evidence-based treatments, about harm from complications of mental illness, and about prevention strategies. There must be continuous vigilance in monitoring well-thought-out programs and policies to ensure that, once enacted, they remain in place and are adequately funded.

No combination of legal maneuvers can fully protect society from an individual intent on harming others. Yet others can be protected from being victims of firearms. Continuing reviews of the availability of firearms, more restrictive gun laws nationally and in states, and routine reporting to authorities of individuals with mental impairments who are at risk to themselves or others are essential. A reconsideration of laws that lead institutions to inaction toward potentially dangerous people in their midst is required.

Despite the national attention paid to Virginia Tech, there have followed other episodes of gun violence—in Tucson, Aurora, and Sandy Hook—that involved people with major mental illnesses. In retrospect, red flags were present for these individuals, too, indicating their need for treatment. It is hoped that this consummate examination of a terrible tragedy and the detailed solutions recommended in this book will lead to lasting change. It is a book that should reach a large audience and be read by policy-makers, college mental health administrators, practitioners, students, and their families and, more broadly, by the general population.

James C. Harris, M.D.
Professor of Psychiatry and Behavioral Sciences,
Mental Health and History of Medicine
The Johns Hopkins University School of Medicine

ACKNOWLEDGMENTS

I would like to acknowledge Dudley Olsson for editing the manuscript, Dana Schultz and Sharon Scott for help in preparing the document, and my wife Nancy for her continuous encouragement and support.

—Robert Cohen

As I have learned, an author is assisted by so many: some provide actual contribution to the effort, and some simply their presence.

In the first category I would like to acknowledge my wonderful assistant, Sharon Scott, who I discovered has a great eye for detail and dealt with my ineptitude at editing with much fortitude and forgiveness, and Dudley Ollson, who got Bob and me on a good start.

In the latter category I would like to acknowledge the men in my life: my three delightful sons—Rishi, Shawn, and Ashvin—who have been the light of my eyes; my husband Rakesh for his encouragement; and Milan Naidu, my true brother. My women friends have been treasured supports through times both difficult and luminous: Claire Patrick—you were there through Tech and much more; thanks to my other sister, Kamini Pahuja, Kusum Jain, Sunita Talegaonkar, Olga Wilkins, Ting Xu, Suzanne Schilling, Sue Dubuque, Ann Maust, and to all my book club buddies; to my new daughter-in-law, Nitika, who is fast becoming a friend; and to Mariel Slater. Finally, I thank my mentor, Robert Cohen, who did his job so well that I believe I can fly solo.

—Bela Sood

ABOUT THE EDITORS

Aradhana Bela Sood, M.D., Senior Professor of Child Mental Health Policy and Professor of Psychiatry and Pediatrics at Virginia Commonwealth University Health System (VCUHS), is immediate past Chair of Child and Adolescent Psychiatry and Medical Director of Virginia Treatment Center for Children (VTCC) at Virginia Commonwealth University, Richmond, VA. She is also the former Training Director of the Child Psychiatry Fellowship Program. Dr. Sood completed her MD in Gwalior, India, her residency at the University of Missouri in Kansas City, and a child psychiatry fellowship at Ohio State University. She is a 2002 Fellow of the Executive Leadership in Academic Medicine (ELAM) through Drexel University. She completed a Masters of Science in Health Administration from the Health Administration Program at VCU. Dr. Sood has served on the Committee on the Status of Women and Minorities (COSOWAM) and the Presidential Task Force on Campus Safety. She served as President of Women in Science, Dentistry, and Medicine (WISDM) from 2003 to 2006, and on the national Residency Review Committee for Psychiatry from 2003 to 2009. She was elected Councilor at Large for a three-year term on the American Academy of Child Psychiatry's Executive Council and is now Secretary of AACAP. She was appointed by Governor Warner to the State Board of Social Services and served an eight-year term from June 2005 to 2013 including two years as chair. She was in the 2006 class for LEAD Virginia, an executive leadership group for the economic growth of Virginia. In 2007, Dr. Sood was appointed by Governor Tim Kaine as the mental health expert to the blue-ribbon panel that investigated the VA Tech massacre of 2007. Her special interests lie in the training of an adequate work force in child mental health, mental health policy, reduction of stigma around mental health issues, outcomes research, mood disorders, and ADHD. Specifically she is focused on finding ways to provide optimal mental health care to the children of Virginia, and on using innovative technology such as telemedicine to bring such care to rural areas of the state.

Dr. Sood has advocated for the American Academy of Child and Adolescent Psychiatry's (AACAP) Work Force initiative in Washington, DC and nationally. She has been involved in systems of care reform in child mental health and early intervention programs in Virginia, and she champions involvement of families in the development of child mental health policy. In 2007 she received the YWCA Award for Women in Sciences and the Professional Achievement Award from WISDM. Dr. Sood received the VCU University Distinguished Service Award in 2008, and the Heroes in the Fight Award from Lilly, for distinguished work in child mental health. She has been on the Best Doctors list for Richmond and for the United States from 1996 through 2014.

Robert Cohen, Ph.D., is an independent policy and program development consultant and visiting scholar at Northern Arizona University. Dr. Cohen has been involved in the development, implementation, and evaluation of children's mental health and youth violence prevention policy and programs from a comprehensive, systems-based eco-logical perspective for the past 45 years. His work has focused on taking into account contextual forces (political, social, economic, cultural factors) as well as technical components (e.g., treatment, prevention strategies). He previously served as Associate Commissioner for Program Development and Policy Analysis in the New York State Office of Mental Health, and Director of the Virginia Treatment Center for Children and professor of psychiatry at Virginia Commonwealth University. His books include *Chiseled in Sand: Perspectives on Change in Human Services Organizations* (Wadsworth, 2000), *Beyond Suppression: Global Perspectives on Youth Violence* (Praeger, 2011), and *Witness to a Transformation: Virginia's Bold Attempt to Establish and Sustain a Comprehensive System of Care for At-Risk Youth* (in preparation). He has also published *Hammond's Choice* (Brandylane, 2008), a mystery novel that draws attention to prob-lems in the children's mental health system.

CONTRIBUTORS

Cheryl S. Al-Mateen, M.D., FAACAP, FAPA
Associate Professor, Psychiatry and Pediatrics
Virginia Commonwealth University School of Medicine
Richmond, VA

Adele L. Martel, M.D., Ph.D., FAACAP
Associate Professor of Psychiatry Clinical Scholar Track
Ann & Robert H. Lurie Children's Hospital of Chicago
Northwestern University, Feinberg School of Medicine
Chicago, IL

Hollis Stambaugh
President, HS Management Consulting
Fairfax, VA

Sala S. Webb, M.D.
Assistant Professor, Psychiatry and Pediatrics
Virginia Commonwealth University School of Medicine
Richmond, VA

PART ONE

Lessons from Virginia Tech

1

THE TRAGEDY AT VIRGINIA TECH

Aradhana Bela Sood

It has been several years since senseless violence erupted on April 16, 2007, at Virginia Polytechnic Institute and State University, better known as VA Tech, situated in the sylvan Roanoke/Blacksburg area of Virginia. The attack left 33 dead, including the perpetrator himself, student Seung-Hui Cho. The event received exhaustive media coverage and scrutiny, and shortly after the perpetrator was identified, Virginia's then-governor Timothy Kaine appointed an independent blue-ribbon panel to investigate and report on how such a tragedy could have been allowed to happen.

As information regarding the perpetrator began to surface, the possibility arose that mental health problems were connected to the homicides. As such, stakeholders in mental health such as advocacy groups, providers of mental health services, and families of those suffering from mental health problems looked to the governor's panel to generate a coherent debate on system gaps in mental health services and to effect meaningful change that would not only prevent such horrific violence in the future but permanently improve delivery of mental health services in general. The panel report had the potential to impact policy at the state and perhaps federal levels as it grappled with complex mental health issues.

This book uses the Virginia Tech tragedy as a lens through which to examine the mental health system in university settings and beyond in the United States and, more specifically, its failures, and how we can and should address them. Part I describes the specific events at Virginia Tech related to Seung-Hui Cho and the lessons learned from the Virginia Tech panel's thorough investigation into this tragedy. Part II covers the current understanding of and response by universities throughout the nation to issues related to the mental health of their students and to the predictors of violence. Part III takes a broader perspective, scrutinizing gaps in mental health services delivery across the United States. The U.S. approach is compared with what is done in other countries, and policy recommendations are offered.

I am a child and adolescent psychiatrist. I chair an academic division of child psychiatry at Virginia Commonwealth University in Richmond, Virginia, and serve as the medical director of a psychiatric hospital. I train child psychiatrists and other mental health providers and treat a large number of children and their families in an outpatient clinical practice.

The 16th of April, 2007, started out as an average Monday morning. My mind flitted on how to gracefully marry the gardening mania that besets me each spring with the many professional projects I had on hand. Those thoughts quickly receded into the background as news of the shooting on the Virginia Tech campus trickled through the office grapevine. Colleagues had picked up the news on a television in one of the hospital units while chatting with a patient. Gradually the grisly details flooded the media. At the center of the tragedy was a Korean-born U.S. citizen who had gone on a rampage across the university campus, killing 32 students and faculty and wounding another 17. Being the mother of three sons, two of whom were in college, and sensitized by the media overload and vicarious traumatization that followed the terrorist attacks on 9/11, that evening saw me steeling myself against exposure to the news. I had learned from the past that members of the media, enthralled with the chronicling of any such event, have no concept of how the graphic and horrific images displayed again and again on television impact an audience, let alone the survivors of those killed. That week I decided to limit my viewing of TV news to once a day.

I was vaguely aware of the reaction of President Bush and the response to the disaster from the governor of Virginia. I had also heard of the governor's plan to investigate the tragedy, but nothing prepared me for the phone call on the afternoon of April 19th from Timothy Kaine's chief of staff, asking if I would be willing to serve on a panel the governor was pulling together to investigate the tragedy. To say that I was in shock at this invitation would be an understatement. Surely this was a mistake; surely the panel required someone who had expertise in forensic psychiatry. I recall wondering whether I had the appropriate training and why I had avoided forensic work throughout my career. I had significant confidence in my clinical ability as it pertained to my everyday work, but what would it mean to serve on this investigative panel, where I would certainly feel out of my element professionally?

Eventually it would turn out that expertise in forensic psychiatry was not a prerequisite for the work, and my imposter syndrome gradually waned. At the time, however, my brain wrestled with an array of questions and doubts. I felt I was at a disadvantage, having not followed the news after the deliberate decision I had made earlier. I mused about whether missing important information conveyed by the media as the tragedy unfolded would hamstring me. Would I be able to do an adequate and well-informed assessment? Would the self-imposed shielding actually be an asset by preserving my neutrality? What would the time commitment be? How long would the process take to unfold?

Looking back, I realize I did not have the presence of mind then to seriously address these questions. The lack of reflective capability may have been fortunate; knowledge of the challenges that lay ahead in the ensuing months may have made me decline the request. My emergent hospital duties as an attending psychiatrist at a 15-bed residential treatment center, along with existing responsibilities as chair of an academic medical division with 19 faculty members, medical director of a 54-bed hospital, and training director for the post-residency fellowship would have made my participation in this investigation a difficult task. Nonetheless, I recall simultaneous panic and excitement about the challenge that lay ahead. I gradually began to view participation on the panel as an opportunity to push myself, to learn and perhaps contribute in a particularly meaningful way to Virginia and to my field.

The panel convened within days: eight members, each chosen from a different professional background to bring the expertise needed for the task. Law enforcement was represented by retired state police superintendent Colonel Gerald Massengill, who led Virginia's law enforcement response to the September 11, 2001, attack on the Pentagon as well as to the 2002 Beltway sniper shootings. The Federal Bureau of Investigation was represented by forensic expert Roger Depue, Ph.D., who served as the first administrator of the FBI's National Center for the Analysis of Violent Crime. Gordon Davies, Ph.D., former director for the State Council of Higher Education for Virginia, represented higher education. I represented mental health. Other panel members were Carroll Ann Ellis, a victim assistance expert from the Fairfax County Police Department in Northern Virginia; Dr. Marcus Martin, assistant dean for the School of Medicine at the University of Virginia and an authority on emergency medical response; and the Honorable Diane Strickland, who had served as a judge of the 23rd Judicial Circuit Court in Roanoke County and the cities of Roanoke and Salem, Virginia. The panel member who had the highest public profile and who was best known nationally was Governor Tom Ridge, the first U.S. secretary of Homeland Security. Given the diversity of the panel membership, it was clear that the governor wanted each member appointed to the panel to weigh in on different aspects of the case, based on his or her expertise.

None of the panel members had worked together previously, nor did we have specific knowledge of each other's fields. But we were all intensely aware of the suffering of the victims' families and the raw emotionality of a state and a region devastated by an event of such magnitude.

Governor Kaine was clear in his directive to the panel: He wanted us to examine the incident exhaustively, shed light on the probable causes of the massacre, and provide findings and recommendations particularly relating to campus security. We were to complete and report on the investigation before the beginning of the 2007 fall semester for Virginia universities. The specific tasks were outlined in the governor's executive order:

(1) Conduct a review of how Seung-Hui Cho committed those 32 murders and multiple additional woundings, including without limitation how he obtained his firearms and ammunition, and to learn what can be learned about what caused him to commit those acts of violence.

(2) Conduct a review of Seung-Hui Cho's psychological condition and behavioral issues prior to and at the time of the shootings, what behavioral aberrations or potential warning signs were observed by students, faculty, and/or staff at Westfield High School or Virginia Tech. This inquiry should include the response taken by Virginia Tech and others to note psychological and behavioral issues, Seung-Hui Cho's interaction with the mental health delivery system, including without limitation judicial intervention, access to services, and communication between mental health services system and Virginia Tech. It should include a review of educational, medical, and judicial records documenting his condition, the services rendered to him, and his commitment hearing.

(3) Conduct a review of the timeline of events from the time that Seung-Hui Cho entered West Ambler Johnston dormitory until his death in Norris Hall. Such review shall include an assessment of the response to the first murders and efforts to stop the Norris Hall murders once they began.

(4) Conduct a review of the response of the Commonwealth, all its agencies, and the relevant local and private providers following the death of Seung-Hui Cho for the purpose of providing recommendations for the improvement of the Commonwealth's response in similar emergency situations. Such review shall include an assessment of the emergency medical response provided for the injured and wounded, the conduct of the postmortem examinations and the release of remains, on-campus actions following the tragedy, and the services and counseling offered to the victims' families and those affected by the incident. In doing so the panel shall to the extent required by federal or state law (i) protect the confidentiality of any individual or family member's personal or health information; and (ii) make public or publish information and findings only in summary or aggregate form without identifying personal or health information related to any individual or family member that specifically permits the panel to disclose that person's health or personal information.

(5) Conduct other enquiries as may be appropriate in the panel's discretion otherwise consistent with its mission and authority as provided herein.

(6) Based on these inquiries, make recommendations on appropriate measures that can be taken to improve the laws, policies, procedures, systems, and institutions of the Commonwealth and the operation of public safety agencies, medical facilities, local agencies, private providers, universities, and mental health services delivery system. (Virginia Tech Review Panel, 2007a, p. A-4–A-5)

The constraints on the panel were enormous. The media coverage was extreme, with all panel interactions occurring in public because of the Freedom of Information Act. A discussion about VA Tech by more than two panel members was not permitted without inviting members of the media. Most of us were unaccustomed to being at the center of such a frenzy.

Despite knowing the task assigned to us, the panel had difficulty conceptualizing how to begin its work. This was exacerbated by the relative lack of familiarity and connectedness among members of the panel. From the outset we worked hard to gel as a group, and over time we developed considerable respect and camaraderie.

To me, it was vital that mental health be maintained as a focal point. Issues such as gun control or liberalization of gun laws were not to be considered in the deliberations as they could be potential distractions for the panel. As such, educating the panel about mental health issues was an ongoing task. It involved exploring and explaining the cultural background of Seung-Hui Cho's family, particularly the Cho family's attitude toward Seung-Hui; how standard psychiatry is practiced, including the prerequisites of a good psychiatric assessment and the importance of collateral data in developing prediction of risk; and cultural attitudes about mental health in a university or community setting.

At the beginning, very little was known about the perpetrator Seung-Hui Cho, other than his name, age, cultural background, and a few facts regarding his Virginia Tech academic record. We did know that he had been committed to inpatient psychiatric treatment at some point, but nothing more had been disclosed about his mental health history, ostensibly because of privacy issues.

As a child psychiatrist, I began to sketch out for my fellow panel members all the information that we would need to gather in order to piece together the psychological makings of the perpetrator. For the other panel members I developed a diagrammatic roadmap that demonstrated how mental health professionals tackle the task of conducting a psychiatric assessment. I began with Cho's intrauterine period and proceeded through all of the phases of Cho's development and functioning until the time of his death. I explained why each piece of information was important.

Professional ethics demanded that I avoid playing the armchair psychiatrist by ascribing a diagnosis based on half-truths and then speculating to and with the media. Without having examined Cho in a physician–patient relationship myself, any assessment I made as a physician would be speculative at best. Although it was tempting to hypothesize about the diagnosis most appropriate for Seung-Hui, this would have caused more points of dissension within the larger mental health community. Furthermore, it would have been distracting for the panel and counterproductive.

The decision not to diagnose Seung-Hui initially was based on the assumption that information on him would be spare and incomplete. It was a priority to ensure that the expert mental health opinion be as objective as possible. On a personal front, I began to mentally make notes of my own professional strengths and weaknesses so that I could seek expert help from colleagues where I lacked the skill set required for this task.

Deliberating over who should be my mentor in this process, I knew that my contribution to the panel's work would need to represent a mosaic of expertise. I was not simply acting as Bela Sood, the child psychiatrist, but needed instead to become a representative of wisdom from across my entire specialty. In other words, my voice should be reflective of the best thinking in the field of psychiatry.

Within a week I developed a plan to pull together additional psychiatrists who were professionally qualified to assist me in formulating suitable questions to explore in our investigation of Seung-Hui Cho. The assumption was that if we chose the right questions we would steer the process of enquiry along the right path. Over the course of the next month, the panel began conducting telephone conferences with relevant experts to outline an approach to understand Seung-Hui Cho and his motives leading up to the massacre.

For instance, the panel invited the chair of the College Mental Health Committee of the American Psychiatric Association (APA) to educate us on the current status of and problems related to college mental health and mental health care. Chairs of various other APA committees, including the Diversity Committee, were also consulted, and they provided valuable insights (Virginia Tech Review Panel, 2007b). All of these conversations helped with the formulation of the panel's questions. Involving other experts from the mental health field was a pivotal decision.

Serendipitously, at the bidding of Judge Leroy Hassell, chief justice of the state's supreme court, the state of Virginia had already begun work on revamping its mental health commitment laws in 2006. A 30-member Commission on Mental Health Law Reform was directed to "conduct a comprehensive examination of Virginia's mental health laws and services and to study ways to use the law more effectively to serve the needs of people with mental illness, while respecting the interests of their families and communities" (Commission on Mental Health Law Reform, 2009). This was relevant to the panel's work because it had emerged that Seung-Hui Cho had been committed to a hospital in southwest Virginia about a year and a half before his death.

Almost immediately after being appointed to the panel I also made contact with the chair of the Commission on Mental Health Law Reform, University of Virginia law professor Richard Bonnie. Speaking to Professor Bonnie seemed like an appropriate first step, as he was positioned at the interface between law and mental health and understood the complexities when these systems became involved with one other.

In particular, Professor Bonnie was able to weigh in on the complexities of our current commitment laws. Commitment laws are notorious for being cumbersome for consumers and practitioners alike. What did Virginia's commitment laws have to do with Cho's actions? Commitment to treatment suggests that the incident leading to Cho being hospitalized was of a serious nature. The commitment as an event becomes a public record, accessible to a set of individuals that in this instance could have taken action to prevent the tragedy.

The Virginia Tech panel strived to consider each piece of information with a high level of neutrality and objectiveness. In such a situation, naturally filled with emotions, individual and community grief, and loss, there was an ever-present fear that facts could become blurred by opinion. Information was only deemed credible by the panel if it was obtained firsthand and if the source was verified.

Each panel member had strong opinions. Each panelist spoke his or her mind boldly. We were not looking for consensus if the cost was to lose out on accuracy.

An additional duty of the panel was to not only uncover information but also make that information available to the public, to help comfort, even if minimally, grieving family members. Caroll Ann Ellis, the panel's victim assistance expert, met periodically with the families and provided them with information. She also brought their concerns to the governor when appropriate. This transparency and timeliness in communication was perceived as helpful and comforting by the bereaved families.

Astonishingly, due to Virginia's educational and health privacy laws, at first the panel itself was unable to obtain information about Cho from VA Tech, the hospital where he had been committed, or his high school. Because this so severely crippled our ability to accomplish our goals, approximately four weeks after the panel convened for the first time, the governor issued an executive order to allow release of pertinent information and retained for the panel the services of an independent law firm, Skadden, Arps, Slate, Meagher & Flom, to distance it from the state attorney general's office. The firm served pro bono. The governor also named TriData, a company with experience in covering staffing of disasters such as Hurricane Katrina and the shooting at Columbine, to assist in our investigation.

The panel visited each scene of the crime at Virginia Tech and conducted debriefings with police, leadership of Virginia Tech, staff where Cho had been briefly committed, the special justices (trained attorneys appointed by the circuit court judges to handle either adult or juvenile civil commitment hearings), and the local mental health agencies in the region, known as community service boards (CSBs). These debriefings ran several days at a time. The panel held one- and two-day meetings over the next four months, hearing expert testimony, perusing more than 1,000 pages of documents, and conducting interviews with families and Cho's dormitory suite mates. The panel also spoke with members of the Office of the Inspector General for Virginia's Department of Mental Health, Mental Retardation and Substance Abuse Services to compare their findings with those of the panel. Aware of the threat of retaliation, Hollis Stambaugh of TriData, Roger Depue of the FBI, and I interviewed Cho's immediate family under great secrecy, in a home in Northern Virginia. Seung-Hui Cho's sister served as interpreter for her parents. The interview was organized by an attorney and family friend of the Chos. Their shame and the grief they felt both for themselves and for all the families who had lost children and spouses were apparent. They were dignified, courteous, and cooperative.

What we discovered from this process were startling gaps in both the university's policies and in its handling of the terrible events of April 16, 2007. We also pinpointed substantive flaws in the state's mental health service delivery system that contributed significantly to the tragedy. But Governor Kaine had been clear in his directive to the panel: We were to focus on the incident itself, and not on other related issues that might arise during the course of our investigation. He wanted to limit the focus of the investigation so that this incident would receive the attention it required without being diluted by other related but tangential issues, such as gaps in the state mental health system and gun control. The subtext of the directive, in my view, was also that the state wanted to avoid any findings that might have liability implications. The specter of possible litigation was ever-present.

Based on the testimony provided by Virginia Tech administrators, our initial impression was that the university had reasonable policies in place to address disruptive student behavior, and that it had a responsive counseling center. However, a different picture, one of significant lapses in multiple areas, began to emerge as we delved further into the tragedy and the events that preceded it. As the time came to finalize the report and our recommendations, I became aware that as the sole mental health expert on the panel, mine was the lone voice insisting that although not directly related to the Tech tragedy, the panel report should acknowledge not just the gaps in the delivery of mental health services that contributed in part to Cho's actions, but also those we uncovered within the system overall. I felt that the report's recommendations should include ways to improve mental health care, thereby reducing the probability of a similar event occurring. As this went against the governor's directive to address only the gaps in Seung-Hui's care that lead to the tragedy, my argument caused a brief but palpable tension within the panel.

I was surprised when these men and women, who had been colleagues and had heard and soundly backed me on most of the issues I had pointed out, invoked the governor's original mandate to focus only on the incident itself. For example, other panel members pushed to limit our examination of the public mental health system to just the New River Valley CSB (responsible for the commitment of Seung-Hui Cho), rather than examining the public mental health system within the entire commonwealth.

At this point I was faced with a dilemma: Should I give in or stand firm? I began to understand better what happens in the political arena where policies are debated. In order to survive collective consensus building and be allowed to weigh in on issues, it is often necessary to obtain caucus support and retain one's place in the hierarchy of the group. Sometimes this means arguments have to be finessed to the point of being so politically correct that little substance remains; facts have to be disguised to the point where the original premise is unrecognizable; compromises have to be crafted to a degree that makes one want to abandon the debate altogether.

In this instance, I could understand my colleagues not wanting to put the governor in a precarious position legally by exposing a dangerously fragmented mental health system. Although the experience allowed me to appreciate what politicians and lawmakers face when confronted with the challenge of voting on complex bills on a General Assembly floor, I was also aware that the reputation of the panel as an independent and ethical body would be at risk if we did not point out what we had discovered as obvious shortcomings of the system. It implied that we were being influenced by external forces. With time, it became more and more clear to me that truth and reason in politics are all relative terms, and when the stakes are high, they can be compromised.

To stand up and insist on being heard is difficult, especially in a group of bright, powerful individuals. Asserting a minority position requires significant confidence in one's argument, courage of one's convictions, and the ability to walk away if one believes the outcome is fatally flawed. In this instance, I decided to stand firm. The final report had 70 recommendations, many relating to mental health. The mental health findings and recommendations in Chapter IV of the panel report were the most frequently quoted sections after the panel's work was released. There were also no challenges to the findings or recommendations in Chapters IV and V by the bereaved families, the public, the media, or mental health professionals.

The case at Virginia Tech, and the ongoing work of the Commission and the Office of the Inspector General, brought to light many of the problems that contribute to our flawed mental health system: a paucity of providers; long waiting lists of individuals needing care; threadbare mental health resources allocated to universities to prepare sufficiently qualified mental health professionals; restrictive and confusing Health Insurance Portability and Accountability Act (HIPAA) and Family Educational

Rights and Privacy Act (FERPA) laws that prevent sharing of confidential data; fear of litigation obscuring medical decision making; poor follow-through both with referral sources and with patients to assess compliance with treatment recommendations; and the frequent use of emergency rooms as default mental health service–gap fillers.

Were these issues addressed? Have we fixed our broken system? Did this tragedy transform either the campus mental health system or the government's attitude toward mental health service delivery? Seven years after the event, this book is a response to these questions. In addition to scrutinizing the tragedy and how the university responded to this troubled student, Seung-Hui Cho, the authors of the chapters herein offer examples of best practices in providing campus mental health services and suggest changes in laws related to mental health and campus safety. In reviewing the overall system of mental health care in this country, we assess the impact of political and economic forces, and offer examples of exemplary efforts in the United States and abroad. Finally, we provide recommendations for legislators and other policy-makers on how to use finite resources in a manner that is smart and cost-effective and that responds to those in need, leading to better health outcomes.

2

AN UNCHECKED DESCENT INTO MADNESS
THE LIFE OF SEUNG-HUI CHO

Hollis Stambaugh and Aradhana Bela Sood

The developmental history of Seung-Hui Cho provided here was obtained by the panel from the Center for Multicultural Human Services, where he was first evaluated in 1997 at age 13 and where he received therapy for approximately four years. This information was confirmed during our interview with his parents after his death.

Seung-Hui Cho was an intensely withdrawn loner with a history of emotional problems. Born in Korea on January 18, 1984, he had a sister who was three years older than him, as well as extended family on both his father's and his mother's side. Although many people in Korea suffered from economic adversity following the Korean conflict, Seung-Hui's parents were able to provide for their children.

Seung-Hui had numerous illnesses as a young boy. Before he was a year old he developed whooping cough, followed by pneumonia. He was hospitalized. Records indicate the doctors diagnosed Seung-Hui as having a hole in his heart or a heart murmur, though this could not be confirmed. Regardless, when Seung-Hui was three, doctors conducted cardiac tests to examine the inside of his heart. He reportedly suffered emotional trauma from that procedure and from then on did not like to be touched. Overall, he was perceived as frail. He cried a lot and was frequently ill. In the early years of his life, Seung-Hui made a few friends who sometimes came over to his house to play. He was extremely quiet and introverted, but, according to his parents, had a sweet nature. Culturally, the Korean society in which he was raised valued calmness and frowned upon noisiness. A quiet person was perceived as more scholarly—a highly desired attribute in Korea. Thus, a shy child who spoke little would not necessarily be a reason for concern. Even so, Seung-Hui's introversion was so extreme that his parents worried about him. Other family members would comment about his reluctance to speak or be engaged in his surroundings.

Seung-Hui's father had a sister who had already immigrated to the United States, settling in Maryland. She encouraged Seung-Hui's family to do the same, citing the educational opportunities that were available. In fact, the Chos' motivation to immigrate was typical of most families that move to the United States: They wished to provide their children with better opportunities. In 1992 the family left Korea and moved to Maryland. The transition was difficult because no one in the family spoke English. Seung-Hui's mother went to work outside the home for the first time, to help make ends meet. Seung-Hui and his sister felt isolated but began learning English in school. Korean was spoken at home, but Seung-Hui never learned to write or read Korean.

Eighteen months later, when Seung-Hui was nine years old and in the middle of third grade, his family relocated to Virginia. His parents continued their hard work and long hours in the dry-cleaning business and the children continued their school studies and their acquisition of English language skills. Sometimes, other students made fun of Seung-Hui and his sister. In our interview with her, she remembered taking it in stride, thinking that was just the way things were, citing that all students were teased at one time or another. Seung-Hui never complained of being teased, though he did experience it into his high school years. The wisecracks mostly took aim at his refusal to speak and interact with others, more than at his appearance or ethnicity. Northern Virginia is a culturally rich area, and the school district where the Chos lived had students from dozens of countries who spoke equally as many languages.

Mr. and Mrs. Cho worked six days a week. Time with their children was limited and there were few extra luxuries. They had only one car, which they used to get to and from work. The parents had a goal of owning their own home and were saving for the down payment. They accomplished this goal within a few years, and, when Seung-Hui was in sixth grade, they moved to a townhouse development next to the school Seung-Hui attended so he could easily commute to his classes.

Seung-Hui was an obedient son. He was not a disciplinary problem, nor did he engage in acting-out behavior—no tantrums or outbursts. His only responsibilities were to do his homework and keep his room clean. He kept to himself.

Seung-Hui's parents continued to be frustrated and concerned, however, that their son would not communicate. He talked to his sister a little bit about general things, but avoided discussing his feelings or his experiences in school. He hardly talked to his parents and he avoided eye contact. His mother encouraged him to "open up" and "have more courage," knowing this would help him become better adjusted (Virginia Tech Review Panel, 2007c, p. 33). Seung-Hui's parents urged him to get involved in activities and sports, but transportation was a problem and it was difficult for him to take part in such programs, although for a short time he was able to take Tae Kwon Do classes. He had to wait a long time for rides or public transportation in order to participate in anything.

The only real friendship of Seung-Hui's that his parents were aware of at this time was with a neighborhood boy who sometimes went swimming with their son, but mostly he watched TV and played video games with nonviolent themes, like Sonic the Hedgehog. Seung-Hui developed an interest in basketball and would shoot hoops by himself or occasionally with other boys in pick-up games.

As a special-needs child, Seung-Hui generated a high level of stress within the family. The family dynamic that evolved in the Cho household to cope with this stress was to rescue him and perhaps coddle him in an attempt to break through to a son and brother who was unreachable emotionally. The situation with Seung-Hui's self-imposed isolation was an ongoing source of frustration for the family, and probably caused more than a modicum of embarrassment. When visitors came to the house Seung-Hui was expected to be respectful and greet the company; instead, he would freeze, become pale, develop sweaty palms, and sometimes cry. When guests asked him questions, Seung-Hui would only nod his head. His father had a quiet nature himself and was less insistent that Seung-Hui be outgoing, but his mother pushed him to try harder. Nothing seemed to affect his dislike of talking and socializing. Eventually, Seung-Hui's parents had no choice but to leave the issue alone and stop pressuring him to change.

At school, teachers noted that "Seung-Hui would not interact socially, communicate verbally, or participate in group activities" (Virginia Tech Review Panel, 2007c, p. 33). A few teachers believed his withdrawn personality was caused by emotional problems rather than by language barriers. Mr. and Mrs. Cho were asked to meet with the school to discuss the problem. Seung-Hui's mother brought an interpreter with her. At the parent–teacher conference the school recommended that the family look into therapy for Seung-Hui, and they advised that the Chos obtain a psychoeducational assessment. Mrs. Cho resolved to help her son find friends. She enrolled him in a one-week basketball camp over the summer and tried to give him extra attention.

During that summer (between Seung-Hui's sixth- and seventh-grade years), Mr. and Mrs. Cho also took him to a well-regarded special resource center that offered mental health treatment, psychological evaluations, and testing to English-limited immigrants and low-income individuals. The center, located in Falls Church, Virginia, was about 20 miles away from the Cho home. For Seung-Hui to keep appointments there, one of his parents had to take time off from work, drive him to his sessions, and then return to the town where they worked. It should be noted that, from a cultural perspective, the Chos' willingness to seek this help for their son was unusual. In their native country, mental or emotional problems were stigmatized and associated with shame and guilt. Pursuing counseling or other forms of treatment for such problems was not a widespread practice.

The records noted that Seung-Hui appeared to be a much younger person than his actual age, indicating social immaturity and lack of verbal skills, but no retardation. His IQ score was above average. Mr. and Mrs. Cho requested that Seung-Hui see a

Korean counselor, but it was not a good fit, so he began working with another specialist who was trained in art therapy. Art therapy is typically used with very young children whose language and cognitive skills make verbally centered therapies less effective. For Seung-Hui, who would not speak, it was thought that art therapy might have a chance of getting to the heart of how he was feeling and what he was thinking within his closed-off world.

During the therapy, Seung-Hui modeled houses out of clay that had no windows or doors. Sometimes, as the therapist explained to Seung-Hui what his creations represented, he would get tears in his eyes. Eventually he began to make actual eye contact with his therapist, a sign that he had started to develop rapport with her, a prerequisite for using therapy effectively.

Despite his art therapy sessions, Seung-Hui maintained his withdrawal and isolation. In middle school he had no reported behavioral problems, but in the spring of eighth grade, Seung-Hui's therapist observed a change in him that was alarming. In addition to certain themes of darkness in his art, he began to show symptoms of depression. He looked more withdrawn and disengaged. When asked, he denied having thoughts of suicide or homicide, but his therapist drew up a contract with him anyway, spelling out that he would do no harm to himself or to others, and that he would communicate with someone if he had any thoughts about violence.

The following month, which was April of 1999, Seung-Hui upheld the promise he had made with the contract, albeit indirectly, by revealing his dark thoughts in a short paper submitted to his teacher. The murders at Columbine High School had just occurred. Seung-Hui made a drawing and wrote words expressing generalized thoughts of suicide and homicide and indicating that he would like to repeat what had happened at Columbine. He did not make a direct threat or name anyone in particular, but the teacher reacted immediately and took the issue to school officials, who urged the family to have Seung-Hui undergo a psychiatric evaluation. Unknown to the school guidance counselor or the principal, he had already been in continuous therapy for several years. The intake evaluation and records from the center were sent to Seung-Hui's school, following a release signed by his parents.

Through an interpreter, Seung-Hui's mother shared with the therapist what had occurred in the school. The therapist referred Seung-Hui to an experienced child psychiatrist and family counselor. The doctor learned of the disturbing paper and was impressed by Seung-Hui's depression and withdrawal. In addition, he was told by Seung-Hui's parents of their fear that when their daughter left for college in the fall, Seung-Hui would no longer communicate with anyone. "The doctor diagnosed [Seung-Hui] with selective mutism and major depression: single episode" (Virginia Tech Review Panel, 2007c, p. 35). He prescribed an antidepressant (paroxetine 20 mg). Seung-Hui was compliant with the medication and it made a noticeable difference in him; reportedly, he smiled more and was in a good mood. A year later, and after he improved, he was taken off the medication with mutual consent and was never again prescribed an antidepressant.

One month into his sophomore year in high school, one of Seung-Hui's teachers talked to a guidance counselor about his poor participation in class. She explained that his speech was inaudible and that when he did respond to questions, he answered in the briefest manner possible—one or two words. He earned high grades and did an excellent job on homework assignments, but he would not communicate with anyone. When the guidance counselor asked him if he had received mental health or special education assistance in the past several years, Seung-Hui lied and responded that he had not. This was to be his response to all such queries for the rest of his life. He repeatedly denied having been treated for mental health problems or having had thoughts of violence. This sensitivity to the potential stigma of mental illness suggests that the involuntary hospitalization Seung-Hui would undergo later in his life would have been extremely noxious to him.

The high school's Screening Committee initiated an assessment of Seung-Hui to rule out autism as the underlying cause of his problems and to determine whether he required special educational accommodations. Through Mrs. Cho they learned that Seung-Hui was receiving counseling. She agreed to allow the school to contact his therapist, to maximize and coordinate services and monitor his progress.

The multilevel screening that Seung-Hui underwent, a part of Public Law 94-142, Section 504 (Gorn, 1997), is used to evaluate students who may qualify for special services. He was assessed on a wide range of domains: psychological, sociocultural, educational, speech/language, hearing and vision screening, and his medical condition. School officials determined that Seung-Hui was eligible for special accommodations to address emotional disability and speech and language difficulties. These accommodations primarily loosened the requirement for him to participate in oral or group presentations in class and modified the grading scale related to those aspects of academic functioning. He also was to receive in-school language therapy, but since selective mutism was the real problem and not the mechanics of language, language therapy sessions were limited to 50 minutes per month. Seung-Hui was given permission to eat lunch alone and to meet privately with a teacher to provide verbal responses in lieu of speaking in front of the whole class. For his part, Seung-Hui was urged to join a club and stay after school for extra help from teachers.

When Seung-Hui was in 11th grade, his art therapy sessions stopped. Though there had been very slight improvement in his desire to talk and interact, he insisted that there was nothing wrong with him and that he was not depressed and would like to quit the counseling, not an uncommon reaction among older teenagers. As he was going to turn 18 soon, legally he was allowed to make that decision and his family and therapist acquiesced. Other than the standard physical required to enter Virginia Tech and a few trips to the medical clinic at Virginia Tech for skin problems, Seung-Hui saw no doctors again for mental or physical illness or injury until the fall of 2005.

The high school's education plan for Seung-Hui appears to have addressed his severe social anxiety such that he could manage in school under the least restrictive environment and do well. That was the school's responsibility, and it met all the requirements. However, the emotional disability itself, the selective mutism, did not improve. Selective mutism to the degree exhibited by Seung-Hui is rare and encountered infrequently by mental and behavioral health practitioners. Many may be unfamiliar with the ramifications of this emotional disorder, including special education advisors and clinicians who conduct Section 504 evaluations. The possibility that the school did not address his problems as proactively as was perhaps needed could be explained by the nature of his illness: intense shyness and social anxiety is a visible impairment but easy to ignore. Given the limited resources within schools, unless children are overtly aggressive in a classroom, they may not be identified as needing services. In the final years of high school, Seung-Hui finished taking upper-level science and math courses, spending three to four hours a day on homework. His grades were excellent in advanced-placement and honors classes and his SAT scores were high, qualifying him for possible acceptance at Virginia Tech, the school he dreamed of attending. Seung-Hui's high school counselor and his mother tried to convince him that a smaller college closer to home was a better choice, given the transition challenges of starting college and his poor social skills. Undeterred, Seung-Hui applied to Virginia Tech and was accepted.

Overall, it appears that his mother's and the school's acknowledgement of the emotional problems that Seung-Hui had, his mother's diligence in seeking mental health services, and the availability of those services within the Northern Virginia area were pivotal to Seung-Hui's doing as well as he did in high school. This was in sharp contrast to the manner in which his problems were addressed at Virginia Tech, where he spent close to four years of his life.

The admissions staff at Virginia Tech were not aware of the exceptions made for Seung-Hui by his high school. Nor were they aware that to some degree these modifications propped up his grades. Invisible to them was the fact that Seung-Hui's functioning and good academic performance were sustained by special accommodations from school counselors and teachers. Not only did these supports disappear once he began at Virginia Tech, but the university also had no way of knowing about Seung-Hui's emotional problems, the extreme nature of his withdrawal, or that at least once he had exhibited homicidal and suicidal ideations, albeit briefly. This lack of knowledge of any aspect of the student other than academic grades is fairly typical of the college enrollment process.

The cover page accompanying Seung-Hui's high school transcripts contains a subsection in the lower right corner, entitled "Special Services Files." Six options are listed: Contract Services, ESL (English as a second language), 504 Plan, Gifted and Talented, Homebound, and Special Education. The only box checked was "ESL," even though Seung-Hui had received special education services for emotional disability.

When Seung-Hui went to Virginia Tech in the fall of 2003, he entered an environment where he had no support system in place, knew no one, and was spending nights away from home for the first time in his life. One of the registration forms he filled out asked for parent contact information; Seung-Hui left the space blank. Colleges typically will not ask parents if they are aware that their child may not have put down their contact information. He began classes with no friends and an impaired ability to make new ones. He was on no medication for depression and was not receiving therapy. Based on his academic functioning and his parents' observations during their weekly face-to-face meetings with him, the panel concluded that, other than social isolation, Seung-Hui did not have symptoms of depression at that time.

The first year at Virginia Tech went relatively well for Seung-Hui. He disliked living with his messy roommate and had his dorm assignment changed mid-year, but otherwise he kept his grades up and ended the year with a 3.0 GPA. He moved off campus in year two, sharing a condominium with a senior who was away most of the time. Seung-Hui's courses included science and math and his grades began to slip. The entry-level poetry course he had taken as a freshman had sparked an interest in writing, and he turned his attention there. He liked poetry and tried his hand at what he thought of as a novel, hoping to have it published at some point. Based on information from his sister, we know that he spent time over semester breaks writing and reading books on literature, poetry, and how to become a writer. Seung-Hui's family was thrilled that he had developed a passion about something.

In the spring semester Seung-Hui took three English courses, but his grades were below average. Based on the information obtained from the interview with his sister, it was determined that he had switched his major to creative writing and was excited about his prospects, submitting a book topic idea to a New York publishing house. It was rejected. His sister encouraged him to work at his craft longer and not lose heart. We might speculate that this event was a formative one for Seung-Hui: being faced with the rejection of his manuscript, he may have struggled with rising feelings of hostility, aggression, and low self-esteem—stressors that another person, with a more robust support network, might have shrugged off.

The fall semester of 2005 was a pivotal point in Seung-Hui's experience at Virginia Tech. From that point on, a growing number of students and faculty would become aware of his unusual conduct both in and out of class, and of hostile, even violent writings and threatening behavior.

Seung-Hui returned to the dorms that fall and lived in a suite with three other students. He piled on four English courses, having changed his major to English, and included a creative writing course in poetry. Seung-Hui's sister noticed subtle changes in her brother: he was less enthusiastic about writing and seemed even more withdrawn than usual. The family surmised that he was getting anxious about graduating the following year and what he would do after completing his education. Seung-Hui had said he did not want to get a Master's degree, so his father offered to help him get a job after graduation, but Seung-Hui was unenthusiastic about the offer. He had held no part-time jobs during high school or college, so the experience of working was unfamiliar to him.

Seung-Hui's roommates took him along with them to a couple of parties, but he would always sit alone in a corner. Once at a dorm room party, he pulled out a small knife and began stabbing the carpet. His roommates also invited Seung-Hui to eat with them, but he would never talk, so they stopped asking him to come along. As in high school, he seemed to prefer eating alone in the dining hall or lounge. He played basketball at the gym by himself. Seung-Hui would go the library to check out movies and watch them on his laptop. The themes were dark. He listened to heavy metal music and posted the lyrics on his Facebook page. Seung-Hui's strange behavior got stranger. He burned pieces of paper and left them under a sofa cushion. He started going to different study lounges and would call one of his suitemates on the phone, identifying himself as "question mark"—Seung-Hui's fictional twin brother. He used that same identity in messages he sent to his roommates via Facebook. He seemed to be acting out a different persona. The panel interviewed the resident advisor (RA) responsible for Seung-Hui's dorm during the fall semester (Virginia Tech Review Panel, 2007c, p. 45), who characterized Seung-Hui as "being strange and becoming stranger" as days passed. This information was confirmed by his suitemates and classmates through interviews conducted by panel members during the investigation. The interviews are documented in the panel report.

If Seung-Hui's behavior outside of class was strange, his behavior in some classes was no better. He could be hostile and uncooperative when told he needed to contribute more to group projects and participate in class. Since Seung-Hui had not identified himself as requiring special accommodations and educational assistance on account of his emotional disability—help he had received in high school—his professors' expectations of him were the same as those for all the other students in the classes. His poetry professor, Nikki Giovanni, asked him to make changes in pieces he wrote, but he simply presented the same pieces, unchanged, the following week.

Seung-Hui was deliberately inarticulate. He sat with his hat over his face and wore sunglasses, both of which he refused to remove when asked to do so. He frightened the other students in the poetry class when he read a paper expressing violent emotions. He accused his classmates of being "low-life barbarians" and "despicable human beings" who he predicted would turn into cannibals. In a foreshadowing of what was to come, he read aloud, "I hope y'all burn in hell for *mass murdering* and eating all those little animals (Virginia Tech Review Panel, 2007c, p. 42)." (These vicious words are curious, since Seung-Hui was not himself a vegetarian.) He also took covert pictures of other students with his camera phone. One professor offered to help him transfer to another class; when he refused, she took the matter to the head of the English Department, Dr. Lucinda Roy, insisting that Seung-Hui be removed from her class or she would resign.

Alerted to Seung-Hui's disruptive and disturbing behavior, Dr. Roy did what appeared to be a thorough job of communicating with other faculty and administrators at Virginia Tech about the situation. She contacted the dean of Student Affairs (who then contacted the director of Judicial Affairs), the Cook Counseling Center on campus, and the office of the College of Liberal Arts, sharing with each Seung-Hui's macabre writings and requesting input and a psychological evaluation of the words. She sought to find out if the unauthorized picture-taking might be an infraction of the Student Code of Conduct. Dozens of e-mails and phone calls later, and on the advice of colleagues, Dr. Roy developed and set in motion a plan to excuse Seung-Hui from the classroom and tutor him privately. University regulations required that she offer him an alternative that was equivalent to the instruction he otherwise would have received in class.

Seung-Hui agreed to the plan when he met with Dr. Roy and another faculty member. During that meeting he wore his trademark dark sunglasses and seemed very depressed. He lightly dismissed the impact his writing and readings had had on the poetry professor and class, cavalierly commenting that he thought it was funny. Seung-Hui was urged to see a counselor at the university's Cook Counseling Center, but he would not commit to doing so. He was also advised that if he took any more pictures of students without their permission the university would take it very seriously (Virginia Tech Review Panel, 2007c, p. 43). Other than referring him to the Care Team, Dr. Roy had no mechanism of ensuring that he was evaluated for mental illness and if necessary, given services through the counseling center.

Virginia Tech had established what was known as the Care Team to review cases of students who needed special attention or intervention. Key offices that dealt with Seung-Hui at one point or another—for example, Judicial Affairs, Dean of Students, Cook Counseling Center, and so forth—were represented on the Care Team either as standing members or as associate members. Campus police were not standing members. While the English Department worked out a solution for instructing Seung-Hui outside the poetry classroom, the Care Team discussed Seung-Hui and his problems at one of its meetings. Members present at that meeting were briefed on the developing plan to tutor him privately and on the reasons why this was necessary. Some members already knew the circumstances because they had been consulted about the morbid writing and Seung-Hui's behavior in class. His case, however, was never revisited or followed up by the Care Team; they believed the problem had been resolved. However, the problems with Seung-Hui were only beginning to come to light.

Dr. Roy wrote detailed reports and updates on Seung-Hui's behavior, which she distributed to at least five key administration and academic leaders. In one message she wrote that the meetings with him were going reasonably well, but that "all of his submissions so far have been about shooting or harming people because he's angered by their authority or by their behavior" (Virginia Tech Review Panel, 2007c, p. 45), and that she was very worried about him. She also noted that Seung-Hui continued to refuse her offers to accompany him to the Cook Counseling Center. There was no explicit protocol available to faculty at Virginia Tech for following up if a student refused such offers of help.

In the dormitories, Seung-Hui began a series of unwanted communications to three female students. One talked to an RA about Seung-Hui, saying he was harassing her online and twice had come to her room—once in disguise—and that she was afraid to confront him.

On November 27, 2005, an RA placed a call to campus police on behalf of a female student. The student said she had been receiving multiple instant messages from some-one who gave a false campus address and false e-mail address, called her, and then one night appeared at her door wearing a disguise and identifying himself as "question mark." The student said she thought it was Seung-Hui. Police officers immediately went to his dorm room, read him his Miranda rights, and questioned him. They warned him to stay away from the young woman and informed him that they were going to file a judicial referral, which they did. Around the same time, Seung-Hui's roommates found a large knife in his desk and threw it away. The same RA also passed along her concerns over Seung-Hui's behavior—including his possession of the knife—to a Residence Life staff member. However, this information was not shared with campus police, even though that type of knife would have been considered a weapon, possession of which was a violation of school policy. Communication was consistently lacking between all these interacting systems—campus police, academic professionals, and the students who interfaced with Seung-Hui.

Finally, on November 30, 2005, Seung-Hui called Cook Counseling Center and requested an appointment with the licensed clinical psychologist who had been rec-ommended by Dr. Roy. The intake staff person conducted a brief telephone triage per standard procedures (obtaining race, gender, age) and scheduled Seung-Hui for an appointment on December 12. Seung-Hui failed to keep the appointment, but later on the afternoon of December 12 he called back and was triaged again on the phone, this time by the psychologist. No additional information was obtained. It is unclear why the phone triage was conducted again; perhaps this reflects another lack of communication within the system.

The morning of that same day, Seung-Hui had gone to a third woman's dorm room and written an excerpt from *Romeo and Juliet* on the white board attached to the outside of her door. The quote was, in fact, the second he had posted, having gone there the night before to write the first message. The quote was:

> *By a name*
> *I know not how to tell thee who I am*
> *My name, dear saint is hateful to myself*
> *Because it is an enemy to thee*
> *Had I it written, I would tear the word*

When the woman returned from class that morning and discovered the additional writing, she called campus police. She suspected Seung-Hui because she was fairly certain he was the one who had been sending her instant messages and Facebook postings throughout the semester. The series of messages had not been threatening in and of themselves (they were mostly self-deprecating), but when the woman wrote back to try to make him feel better and asked if it were Seung-Hui to whom she was responding, he would only say, "I do not know who I am." Her dorm room was where Seung-Hui had brought out a knife and jabbed the carpet.

No one at Cook Counseling Center was made aware of this series of events. It is noteworthy that the Office for Judicial Affairs was made aware of Seung-Hui's "odd" and "stalking" behavior on December 6, yet despite this intimation, and inconsistent with their policy on stalking behavior, they did not advise the female student who had been threatened as to her rights. Overall, the telltale signs of a mind unraveling were observed by students and faculty, but there was no coherent action from the institution to provide to Seung-Hui much needed psychiatric attention.

In response to the woman's call, campus police officers emailed Seung-Hui and went to his room, but he was not there so they left a message for him to contact them. Police met with him the following day, December 13, and told him to leave the woman alone. She did not file criminal charges, and though the incident was communicated to staff and administrators—the Residence Life Administrator on call, the Director of Residence Life, and the Assistant Director of Judicial Affairs—none of these individuals brought it to the attention of the Care Team.

Later on December 13 and despondent after the visit from police—the second in two weeks—Seung-Hui sent an instant message to one of his suitemates, saying he might as well kill himself. That threat set off a chain of events that ended with his hospitalization. Alerted by the suitemate, campus police took Seung-Hui to department headquarters to be evaluated by a pre-screener from the New River Valley Community Services Board (CSB), the local public mental health agency. The pre-screener talked to Seung-Hui, who denied any previous mental health problems or thoughts of suicide, to the police officer, and then to Seung-Hui's roommate and a suitemate by phone. The pre-screener found Seung-Hui to be mentally ill and an imminent danger to himself or others. Since he was not willing to be treated, she recommended involuntary hospitalization and contacted a magistrate to request a temporary detention order. Shortly after 10:00 P.M that night, the magistrate issued the order and campus police officers transported Seung-Hui to St. Albans Behavioral Health Center of the Carillion New River Valley Medical Center. Ativan was administered to Seung-Hui for anxiety and he stayed at the hospital that night.

Early the following morning, December 14, a St. Albans staff member explained to Seung-Hui that there would be a mental health hearing that day. Pursuant to Virginia law, an independent evaluation was conducted, resulting in a finding that Seung-Hui was not imminently dangerous and did not require involuntary hospitalization. Just prior to the scheduled hearing, the attending psychiatrist also evaluated Seung-Hui. His assessment concurred with that of the independent evaluator. Neither practitioner gathered any supplementary information about Seung-Hui—for instance, no attempt was made to get additional data from his suitemates, who had initiated the call to the Virginia Tech Police Department (VTPD). As labile mood or erratic behavior can often stabilize briefly in a structured environment like that of a hospital, exploration of the concerns of the referring family or friends is essential to assess if the presenting problem is fleeting, innocuous, or not. But this was not done. The psychiatrist noted that privacy laws impeded further information gathering and that there was insufficient time in any case to check on Seung-Hui's medical history before the required hearing. Seung-Hui himself denied to the psychiatrist that he had had any previous mental health treatment or problems, and the psychiatrist was not in a position to verify whether this was the truth. The psychiatrist suggested outpatient treatment for Seung-Hui with counseling, but prescribed no medications and made no primary diagnosis.

Seung-Hui was then taken to meet with an attorney. At the hearing, the attorney read the pre-screener's report, and the special justice read what the independent evaluator and the psychiatrist had written. It is noteworthy that the special justice had a background in social work, before going into the practice of law, which made him particularly aware of the signs of mental health problems. Seung-Hui answered a couple of questions monosyllabically in a nearly inaudible voice, and in the special justice's opinion, was ruled as presenting an imminent danger to himself as a result of mental illness. Although the psychiatrists that day had opined there was no danger, the justice believed that Seung-Hui's denial of suicidal intentions the day prior masked a different reality. The special justice ordered Seung-Hui to obtain outpatient treatment. Before he left the hospital, the hospital representative placed a call to Cook Counseling Center to schedule an appointment, but the scheduler insisted that Seung-Hui speak with her directly so they could be sure it was a voluntary appointment (Cook Counseling Center did not accept involuntary patients). Seung-Hui made an appointment for 3:00 that afternoon.

The hospital representative notified the New River Valley Community Services Board of the outcome of the hearing and then faxed the psychiatrist's discharge summary, the physical evaluation findings, and the recommendation from the justice to the Cook Counseling Center on campus before Seung-Hui's appointment time. The discharge summary called for Cook Counseling Center to provide the follow-up and after-care, and the physical evaluation report noted that the St. Alban's psychiatrist was to treat Seung-Hui and that therapy would help his mood disorder.

When Seung-Hui appeared for his appointment at the campus counseling center that afternoon, he was again triaged (data on gender, age, race, and symptoms were obtained), though this time in person. Winter break was about to begin, and the record indicates that Seung-Hui had said there was a doctor back home that he could see during vacation. No one from Cook Counseling Center followed up after the break on whether he did or did not see this alleged private physician, nor did Seung-Hui ever return to Cook Counseling Center to begin therapy there. Since he was a "voluntary patient," Cook Counseling Center was not required to notify the Community Services Board, the court, St. Albans, or Virginia Tech officials about whether he ever followed up with outpatient treatment. Nor did Cook Counseling Center follow up on Seung-Hui after winter break in early 2006, despite the fact that he had recently been committed to a hospital for suicidal ideations. Finally, as no one had called his parents to tell them about Seung-Hui's suicide threat, his hospitalization for mental illness, his conflicts with professors, his stalking behavior, or his episodes with police, the Chos had no idea how seriously troubled their son had become.

The hospitalization marked the period when Seung-Hui went underground, so to speak. From the spring semester of 2006 until April 16, 2007, no official interventions took place with Seung-Hui on campus or elsewhere. Ironically, when Seung-Hui's former art therapist at the Northern Virginia counseling center recognized danger signs in the emotional tunnels and underground passages he had begun creating, she had insisted he promise to communicate with someone if he developed any ideas about hurting himself or others. The critical point here is that since Seung-Hui did not talk, that communication would have had to take place through art or the written word—and during his time at Virginia Tech he produced multiple writings in which he revealed his true nature and possible intentions. However, the emphasis placed on free expression in a university setting relegated his repeated dire warnings of what was to come to that of acceptable, though troubling, speech and artistic choice. Those who were disturbed by his writing in the English Department and who did raise the alarm were not successful at convincing him to seek help, nor did they have the authority to mandate it. The option of dismissing Seung-Hui from school until he was treated was not acted upon. Obvious opportunities for assessment and intervention were missed.

No further documentation or evidence exists of Seung-Hui's ever again stalking female students or talking about suicide. Residence advisors where he lived his senior year were aware of Seung-Hui's behavior in previous years, but they encountered no problems with him themselves. His classroom behavior of sitting silently and not answering questions or contributing verbally, however, did not improve. Angry, violent themes appeared in more writings. In a fiction workshop class the semester after his hospitalization, Seung-Hui's stories reflected rage, and violent content appeared in other English class compositions as well. Professors noted that Seung-Hui's creative writing skills were below average and his grammar—verb tenses and articles—was flawed. Seung-Hui loudly confronted one professor who told him that his work was unsatisfactory and his topics were unacceptable. Seung-Hui dropped the class. Yet another professor perceived Seung-Hui as depressed and in need of help—encouraging him to consider counseling.

Seung-Hui's most telltale writing took the form of a play that foreshadowed the setting and nature of the April 16, 2007, attack. In the play, Seung-Hui describes a protagonist wearing black jeans, a black vest with many pockets, and large sunglasses. He screams about hating his life, saying "[t]his is when you damn people die with me" (Virginia Tech Review Panel, 2007c, p. 50). The character has guns, goes to empty halls and then to an arbitrary classroom, but leaves, later telling a girl in the story: "I'm nothing. I'm a loser. I can't do anything. I was going to kill every…person in this damn school…but I…couldn't" (Virginia Tech Review Panel, 2007c, p. 50). One now can see the clear signs of an unraveling mind. The professors did read the play but chose not to take any administrative action, such as informing the department hierarchy. His English professors (from spring 2006 on) were not aware of Seung-Hui's earlier problems with Professors Giovanni and Roy.

The earlier, overt signs or "cries for help" in the fall of 2005 were, by the spring of 2006 and later, replaced by writings indicating intense resentment and anger toward society and toward the people who seemed to Seung-Hui to belong and live comfortably in that society. Perhaps these feelings arose from the cataclysmic jolt to his ego caused by the involuntary hospitalization. It appears that he rejected his parents' offer of help after graduation, possibly already planning a dramatic exit from the world. He may have seen his "talent" in writing as having been rejected both at Virginia Tech and by the New York publishing house.

Beginning in the spring semester of 2007, Seung-Hui started to purchase weapons and ammunition. He went to a shooting range and practiced. He also rented a van and, as was discovered later, video-recorded himself brandishing guns and voicing his fury. The taping of his diatribe, which he mailed to a major news network, indicates a premeditated plan of action, one which stemmed from immense self-hate and rage toward the world. Uncharacteristically, he failed to show up for some of his classes. The deterioration of his mental state was invisible to his family. The night before Seung-Hui carried out the murders, he called his parents per their usual Sunday night arrangement. He told them that, no, he did not need any money. They ended the conversation with "I love you." Those were the last words they would ever say to him.

On the face of it, it is hard to understand why the English Department at Virginia Tech did not lobby for Seung-Hui to be removed from the school unless and until there was proof of his receiving mental health treatment. It may be they knew such a position would not be well received, or they may have underestimated the threat he represented. After all, Seung-Hui's professors did not know that there were stalking complaints about Seung-Hui, nor that there had been other examples of aberrant behavior. They did not know Seung-Hui had been detained and taken to a mental hospital. No one group, office, or person had access to the whole picture over time—this was one of the fundamental flaws in the university's handling of this situation.

The Virginia Tech tragedy poses questions about warning signs. Many accumulated over the years, but never once were they considered all together, and they were not adequately heeded. The underlying failure was that pieces of information about Seung-Hui's aberrant behavior, trouble with law enforcement, social isolation and refusal to speak, suicide threat, and ongoing violent writings with homicidal fantasies were not pulled together into a comprehensive profile of a young man's increasingly dangerous emotional and behavioral state. As such, the seriousness of each red flag contributing to a worsening pattern of disturbing and threatening behavior was underestimated, discounted by the individuals who witnessed it in the absence of all the other warning signs. No one could know for sure that Seung-Hui was no longer safe and that others were not safe around him—in class and in residence at Virginia Tech.

It would be inaccurate to imply that no one shared any information about Seung-Hui during his years at Virginia Tech. In particular: Dr. Nikki Giovanni, Dr. Lucinda Roy, students and RAs in Seung-Hui's junior-year dormitory, campus police the day he mentioned suicide, and the pre-screener from the New River Valley Community Services Board all reported their findings to others in some attempt to right the situation. These individuals understood that Seung-Hui's abnormal behavior was worrisome. They perceived him to be dangerous to himself and others, recognizing that his denials of problems and of previous treatment for mental health issues might be distortions of the truth. They took action, exhorting Seung-Hui to seek counseling and passing their concerns up the chain of command.

In other instances, though, information about Seung-Hui was not adequately shared, out of concern for privacy laws, specifically the Health Insurance Portability and Accountability Act (HIPAA; Office for Civil Rights, 2003), Family Educational Rights & Privacy Act (FERPA; 2010), and the Virginia Health Records Privacy statute (VA Code § 32.1-127.1:03). The finding of a separate panel, appointed by President Bush in the wake of the Virginia Tech massacre to investigate the causes of the tragedy, indicated that educators and mental health practitioners typically default to a position of not sharing information under any circumstances when considering privacy rights and the potential for liability if those rights are abridged (Leavitt, Gonzales, & Spellings, 2007, p. 7; Family Educational Rights & Privacy Act, 2008, p. 4).

To err on the side of caution and interpret laws narrowly is natural for bureaucracies that are legally liable in instances of improper disclosure. Usually when such information is not shared it is out of deference to the law and what is believed to be sacrosanct; however, sometimes a decision not to share information is due to a desire to divert responsibility onto another person or institution, because it is easier not to comply with a request for information, or because it provides a convenient excuse for purposefully withholding information. Seung-Hui is a textbook example of individual rights trumping public safety rights, with disastrous results.

The Virginia Tech panel's examination of the information privacy laws governing mental health, law enforcement, and educational records and information revealed a "widespread lack of understanding, conflicting practice, and laws that were poorly designed" (Virginia Tech Review Panel, 2007c, p. 63). Chapter V of the Panel report explains that while privacy laws do block some opportunities to share information, there exist acceptable circumstances under which it is proper and permitted to disclose information. Unfortunately, these circumstances are not straightforward; often they are so complex and hard to understand that they are not explored. Usually information related to privacy laws falls within the purview of risk management departments of institutions such as hospitals or universities (Virginia Tech Review Panel, 2007c, p. 50; see Chapter 5 for details on what types of information can be shared as laid out by HIPAA and FERPA, and the circumstances for such disclosures, as well as what must be withheld).

So, exactly what information was shared and what was not shared about Seung-Hui during the most critical period leading up to April 17, 2006? Table 2.1 highlights some of the most important red flags and who was given access to information about those events.

Table 2.1 Red flags Regarding Seung-Hui Cho's Potential for Harm and Who Knew About Them

Aberrant Behavior or Event: / Reported To: ⟹	Chair of English Dept.	Student Affairs	Residence Life	Judicial Affairs	Campus Police	Seung-Hui's Family	Cook Counseling Center	Community Services Board	St. Albans Hospital	Court
1. Disruption/picture-taking and violent writing read to class (Dr. Giovanni)	✓									
2. Plan to remove Seung-Hui from poetry class and assessment of Seung-Hui's actions (Dr. Roy)	✓	✓		✓	✓		✓			
3. Care Team review of situation	✓	✓					✓			
4. Various disturbing behaviors in dorm (knife at party, masquerading as his "twin," isolation, violent lyrics on website, etc. (students and RA)			✓	✓						
5. Stalking of 3 females (victims)			✓		✓					
6. Campus police investigate stalkings				✓	✓					
7. Large knife found in Seung-Hui's room (students)		✓	✓				✓			
8. Seung-Hui initiates calls to counseling center							✓			
9. Seung-Hui talks of suicide (roommate)					✓					
10. Police respond to suicide threat. Temporary detention order					✓			✓	✓	

(continued)

Table 2.1 Continued

Aberrant Behavior or Event:	Chair of English Dept.	Student Affairs	Residence Life	Judicial Affairs	Campus Police	Seung-Hui's Family	Cook Counseling Center	Community Services Board	St. Albans Hospital	Court
11. Seung-Hui treated at St. Albans								✓	✓	✓
12. Seung-Hui's hearing before special justice and release from St. Albans								✓	✓	✓
13. Seung-Hui makes appointment at Cook Counseling							✓		✓	
14. Violent stories in Fiction Workshop class	✓									
15. Seung-Hui won't cooperate with assignments in Technical Writing class; submits one on serial killings; confronts professor and drops class										
16. Fall 2006—Advanced Fiction Workshop professor checks with dean about whether Seung-Hui is safe and tries to help him										
17. Seung-Hui submits violent play foreshadowing homicides of April 16, 2007										

Table developed by Hollis Stambaugh.

Research into Seung-Hui Cho's life revealed dozens of critical points at which warning signs should have been recognized, assessed, and acted upon. Reflecting on how these warning signs were missed may help other organizations examine and improve their own systems, to prevent and reduce the potential for similar violence on campuses and at workplaces. Rethinking privacy laws and health-related information sharing, with the goal of improving health and safety, should be a priority and will be discussed in later chapters. Progress also will rely on an honest and open debate about the balance between protecting public safety and protecting free speech when that speech (or writing) indicates a pattern of dark thoughts and violent content, targeted or not. Stigma surrounding treatment for mental health must also be addressed, and adequate funding for mental health services must be provided in every community.

Finally, it would appear that we need to know more about how Seung-Hui's emotional and mental health problems played into this event, and perhaps use this tragedy as a means of understanding the extent to which the combined psychiatric diagnoses of selective mutism, depression, and anxiety turned him into a premeditated murderer. Was schizophrenia, which was bandied around as a possible diagnosis by various lay and professional entities soon after the event, a possibility in Seung-Hui Cho? What is the range of severity of selective mutism, and what treatments are effective? What causes it and can it be prevented? How frequently is major depression associated with selective mutism and how does one approach counseling with an individual who chooses to be silent and reveals practically nothing to others? Is intervening early in the disease process helpful in averting serious downstream problems? Are school accommodations, such as those provided to Seung-Hui in high school, the right answer for success, or do they in fact help perpetuate the underlying problem? For mental health practitioners and researchers, a full agenda of topics must be confronted and resolved.

Mental health and interventions for mental illness are no longer just a concern for affected families, providers, or advocates. In the past six years since the Virginia Tech massacre, incidents in which human casualties have been linked to mental instability in the perpetrator continue to occur with disturbing frequency. For lawmakers, the importance of tackling gaps in mental health screening, assessment, and treatment has become a topical and relevant issue.

3

INSIGHTS FROM INTERVIEWS AND OTHER FIRSTHAND ACCOUNTS

Aradhana Bela Sood and Hollis Stambaugh

Interviews with people involved in the case provided the panel with details that were not captured in a newspaper article, an e-mail, a case file, or a court record. It was these conversations—with victims' parents; Seung-Hui's family, high school counselor, professors, therapists, and doctors; student paramedics; campus police; university administrators; and others—that put the facts into context and gave a face to the story of Seung-Hui Cho and Virginia Tech. The interviews conducted by the panel provide a unique and personal view of the event, as seen through the eyes of pivotal figures in the Seung-Hui Cho history; interview subjects' opinions were not included in the panel report—only facts as they reported them. The insights offered by these interviews help us to appreciate the gaps in communication and the system failures discussed in Chapter 2 that contributed to the massacre, and how each of these shortcomings point to larger systemic gaps in mental health delivery in the United States.

In this chapter, we relate salient information obtained from these interviews in order to address some of the critical questions raised about this horrific event. Additional information was obtained from Virginia Tech professor Lucinda Roy's 2009 book, *No Right to Remain Silent*. Specifically, we will look at the experience of the families following the shooting rampage, the perspectives of faculty at Virginia Tech in relation to the incident, and the response of the university administration. We will also share the perspectives of Seung-Hui Cho's family. Instead of lengthy transcripts of interviews conducted by the panel, we have chosen to recount here in our own words what was told to us by the interview subjects.

FAMILIES OF THE VICTIMS

The task of positively identifying victims and notifying their next of kin after a mass fatality event is daunting. The first two victims, slain in the West Ambler Johnston dormitory, were freshman resident Emily Hilscher and resident assistant Ryan Clark. They were identified by 8:15 A.M. on April 16, but we learned from a later interview with a member of Emily's family that no official notified her parents that she had been seriously wounded and was in the hospital undergoing emergency treatment, nor that another student in the room had been killed. Word had come instead from the mother of Emily's boyfriend, who called the Hilschers and informed them of the shooting, though he did not know where Emily had been taken. Desperate with worry, Emily's parents tried every avenue to locate their daughter, but hospital personnel to whom they spoke did not want to disclose information over the phone. The Hilschers lived hours away, so they could not get to the hospital quickly to ask after their daughter in person. Emily had also been transferred from one hospital to another, further complicating the situation. Had the Hilschers been contacted right away by someone at the university they might have had the opportunity to talk to the emergency department doctors and place a call to Emily so that she at least could have heard the voices of her family. But no one from Virginia Tech or from the hospital contacted them before Emily died.

Death notifications are nearly always conducted by law enforcement officers trained in handling this part of a murder case. Whether campus police thought that Virginia State Police or possibly the paramedics or hospital staff would take care of notifying Emily Hilscher's parents, we do not know. Apparently none of the executives in the university administration's Policy Group (comprised of the president, vice-presidents, and other officials) made sure that the victims' parents were contacted in a timely manner.

The failure to communicate quickly with the Hilschers was a harbinger of things to come. Delayed notification to the campus community about the attack in the dorm and then major problems notifying and sharing information with the Norris Hall victims' families aggravated the grief these families experienced. Controlled, official communication was virtually nonexistent. This fueled anger and led to mistrust, which consequently resulted in liability issues for the university. On that day, family members needed an official, university-run and organized assistance site at which to congregate and obtain timely information and communicate with others, a place protected from media intrusions and rumors.

The Inn at Virginia Tech

The university did attempt to provide such a site. Unfortunately, though, The Inn at Virginia Tech did not function as the safe haven it should have. Family members were instructed by the university administration to go The Inn, and it immediately became their meeting place and supposedly a place where information following the Norris Hall shooting was to be shared. In interviews with the panel several weeks and months after the event, families of the deceased students and professors discussed their experiences at The Inn. According to those who were interviewed, the scene there was chaotic. When they arrived, loved ones and friends encountered a cacophony of voices frantically reporting inconsistent and unconfirmed information. Some families were approached and offered counseling, but what they desperately needed was news of their loved ones. One mother who went to The Inn on the day of the killings was approached in the elevator by a member of the clergy who offered his condolences over her child's death—the first she had heard about the outcome of her child's wounds.

Other family members learned of their loved ones' deaths under similarly tragic circumstances. In one interview conducted by the panel members, the wife of a professor said she knew her husband was dead when she looked out her living room window and saw a phalanx of reporters heading up her driveway. In one of the worst infractions of decency, a member of the press, pretending to be from the university, went to the local airport to intercept and interview a family arriving to learn the status of their child.

The Medical Examiner's Office

Exacerbating the difficulty of notifying the families of those injured and killed was the difficulty of identifying the victims after the killings at Virginia Tech. University officials encountered problems accounting for each student who had been in Norris Hall. Early that day it was not clear who had been killed and who had been seriously wounded, whether victims had transported themselves to the hospital or been transported, or even which hospital they had gone to. Hence, identifying the deceased by name with certainty was impossible. Some people with minor injuries were able to transport themselves or were driven by friends to medical facilities. Others, either deceased or injured, were transported to various hospitals by a variety of different means, such as ambulances and police vehicles. Meanwhile, back on campus, students' identification remained in backpacks and purses strewn throughout the carnage in the affected classrooms. The crime scene at Norris Hall contained scattered personal effects such that it was not possible to determine what belonged to whom.

To further complicate matters, in order to prevent misidentification of the deceased, in general, many medical examiner's (ME's) offices require scientific proof of identification (e.g., through dental records, finger prints, or DNA) and do not allow presumptive identification, such as with birthmarks or ID found on the deceased's person. Within hours of Seung-Hui's rampage, the Office of the Medical Examiner of Virginia was faced with identifying 32 victims. Given the chaos that existed, they did a commendable and scientifically accurate job of this task, with assistance from state police and the families of victims who provided dental records and clothing or other items from which DNA samples could be taken. However, the ME's insistence on scientific procedures meant that even though family members might be able to identify their loved ones by eye and hair color, a scar, or other significant feature, the identities could not be officially confirmed until the other physical evidence proved who the victims were.

In contrast to its performance in identifying victims, as reported by those interviewed by the panel, the ME's office did a poor job of communicating with families, who by and large did not understand why presumptive evidence would not suffice, nor why they were not being allowed to view the remains. Upon enquiry by the panel, the ME's office indicated that there was inadequate space to complete their work and that their regulations required that all remains be taken to a funeral home or a facility designated by the families for viewing before they could actually let the family have access to the remains. Although autopsies were completed as quickly as possible, the period that elapsed between death and notification felt too long to families. Their grief was made worse by lack of information about the laws, the process, and, eventually, the logistics of retrieving their loved ones' belongings. Many of the family members who were interviewed said they suffered additional trauma because of the unavailability and insensitivity of the ME's office in handling their questions and in helping them understand the process.

Given the constraints that operational regulations imposed on the ME's office with regard to communication with families, the lack of an experienced public information officer (PIO) who could have served as a liaison between the ME's field office and the families at The Inn was glaring (Virginia Tech Review Panel, 2007d, p. 140). Based on interviews conducted by the panel with families of victims and survivors, the PIO provided at The Inn was unresponsive to many of the questions the families had or did not respond in a timely fashion. This added to the widespread perception (by families, the panel, and faculty interviewed) of Virginia Tech's mismanagement of the period immediately following the tragedy (Virginia Tech Review Panel, 2007d, p. 140).

The Media and Unauthorized Volunteers

The media was oppressively present on campus and in Blacksburg; reporters aggressively pursued chances to talk with victims' families. During our interviews with these families, they spoke of how disturbing it was to thread their way through lines of cameras, reporters, and microphones in order to gain access to The Inn. As mentioned earlier, the spouses of slain faculty members encountered the press near or at their homes. There was no visible attempt by the local or campus police to protect the faculty from such intrusions.

A problem reported by more than a few families of victims was the interference of unauthorized persons who approached them with offers of counseling or salvation. Dozens of trained mental health workers from around Virginia volunteered their time and provided enormous help to the campus community at a moment when so many people were grieving and trying to cope with the sheer magnitude of the attacks. Nearly all of the families of the shooting victims who worked with personnel assigned by the university expressed gratitude for their assistance. At the same time, difficult to avoid were various self-styled "experts" and others who lacked training in handling disasters and assisting victims of violent crime. The lesson from this has been that it is important to specify the qualifications required of volunteers in such situations and to check the credentials of all who offer help, especially people who claim a competence and intention that may not be genuine.

Emergency Preparedness at Virginia Tech

At first, the double homicide at West Ambler Johnston could not officially be linked to the slaughter at Norris Hall. Once the evidence confirmed that the same shooter was responsible for both crime scenes, questions spewed forth concerning when Virginia Tech's Policy Group had learned about the first shooting and whether it had acted appropriately to inform the campus community. The panel and others who studied and speculated about the tragedy in the months following attempted to answer the underlying question: Could any of the Norris Hall killings have been prevented if the campus community had been notified sooner of the West Ambler Johnston attacks?

On campus and in the news, the spotlight was trained on why the campus community had not been alerted immediately following the dormitory shooting, and why the warning that eventually was released contained so little specific information about the crime and about the precautions to be taken with a killer on the loose. Although Virginia Tech police officials believed they knew who was responsible for the dorm shooting, based on an interview with the female victim's roommate around 8:15 A.M., that suspect had not been apprehended, and a search of his vehicle on campus had come up empty. Police believed he had left campus and was no longer a threat to the university community. As it turned out, that person of interest, the young woman's boyfriend, was innocent. The panel's finding was that the focus on one suspect, without exploring other possibilities, may have contributed to the university's failure to prevent the string of events that followed.

The panel struggled with the question as to why the campus had not been locked down after the two students in the dorm had been discovered—one deceased and the other seriously wounded. Upon reflection and interviews with the leadership at Tech and the VTPD, it became clear that it was not possible to physically lock down the entire perimeter of Virginia Tech, which exceeds 2,600 acres. Entrances and buildings could be closed, but not the whole campus area. Parents of some of the deceased and others argued that a quasi-lockdown order could have been given, such as cancelling classes and asking students to remain in their dorms.

Officials fielded pointed inquiries about the decisions they made during the time between the dorm shootings (7:20 A.M.) and the shootings in Norris Hall (9:40 A.M.) and the reasons for those decisions. Based on the interviews conducted by the panel members, for some people, the university's answers—conveyed through President Charles Steger and the communications director, Larry Hincker—adequately explained why there had been a delayed alert after the shooting in the dormitory. No one could have known that the worst was yet to come in terms of the number of victims. To others, particularly the families of the victims, these answers led to more questions and a growing anger over how the situation had been handled. Many individuals wondered why people on campus and en route to campus had not been informed via the university's e-mail alert system, and whether the media had been informed about the first shootings. This would have allowed individuals to decide for themselves whether to avoid campus, opt out of attending class that morning in favor of staying in their place of residence until someone was arrested, or, at a minimum, be alert for signs of danger. Indeed, when Seung-Hui began shooting faculty and students in the first Norris Hall classroom, the sound of his gunfire was initially mistaken by some in the building as noise from nearby construction work. The thought of a weapon discharging was incongruent with the setting; building occupants knew nothing about the earlier murders and were not on guard for a possible shooter.

Some victims' families interviewed by the panel were distressed also because they wanted President Steger to apologize for not communicating information about the first shooting quickly enough. The warning was disseminated at 9:26 A.M., almost exactly two hours after police found the victims at West Ambler Johnston. Seung-Hui began his assault at Norris Hall around 9:40 A.M., and it lasted until he committed suicide at 9:51 A.M. President Steger spoke of his sorrow about the terrible tragedy, but many families were looking for someone to take responsibility for failing to warn their spouse or child sooner that danger might be lurking in their midst. They anguished over whether their loved ones might have avoided going to the classrooms where they died, had they received notice *before* 9:05 A.M., when classes began in Norris Hall, that a double homicide had occurred and that no one had yet been arrested. If they had been alerted to the possibility of a shooter in the area, would more students and faculty have considered the sound of Seung-Hui's guns to be a shooting in progress? Would they perhaps have reacted more quickly to block Seung-Hui from getting through their classroom doors?

The resentment and mistrust of the university among many family members was the reason for the appointment of Carroll Ann Ellis, the director of the Fairfax County Police's Victim Assistance Program, as the primary liaison between the panel and the families. The panel offered many opportunities for families to provide input, through personal interviews (which many chose to do), speaking opportunities at the four public hearings held around the state, letters, and phone calls. Often the panel members (and staff to the panel) answered questions raised by those who had lost someone in the tragedy.

The Cho Family

During an interview with Seung-Hui's parents and their daughter, his parents said that they wanted the world to know that their grief over the losses of April 16, 2007, will be with them forever. They carry the unimaginable sorrow of having lost a beloved son while also knowing that he took 32 sons, daughters, husbands, and wives from other families. The young man they knew bore no resemblance to the killer on campus that day. Unaware of Seung-Hui's episodes with professors, campus police, and the women he stalked, and ignorant of the emergency hospitalization and the fact that he had purchased guns and ammunition, his family worried about him when news of the shooting first circulated. By evening they were scared that he might have been injured because they could not reach him, and so they planned to leave in the morning for Blacksburg to find him.

Around midnight, Virginia State Police came to the Cho home with the news that Seung-Hui was dead and that he had been the one responsible for the tragedy. Certain that the police officers were mistaken, the Chos argued that it must have been another Asian male. Nothing about the crime and the details that were beginning to emerge bore any resemblance to their child. They had just spoken to him the night before. Nothing was wrong. He seemed fine.

After a few hours, the Chos were forced to accept the truth. Agents from the Federal Bureau of Investigation sequestered the Chos at an undisclosed location out of concern for potential acts of retaliation and a media determined to find and photograph them.

Over the next days and weeks, Seung-Hui's family participated in multiple interviews with law enforcement officers from different agencies. They also agreed to meet with two members of the Virginia Tech panel and a co-director of the panel staff. The Chos authorized the release of their son's health and educational records to help with the investigation. Their willingness to cooperate contributed significantly to the body of information on the life of Seung-Hui described throughout this volume.

Virginia Tech Faculty

Some of the earliest interviews conducted were with members of the Virginia Tech faculty in the English Department. English was Seung-Hui's major and it was in English classes that the first serious problems with his violent themes were recognized. The vast majority of interviews were conducted in May through July—a time when many professors are away from campus unless they are teaching summer courses. This impacted who was interviewed. For example, Dr. Nikki Giovanni, the poetry professor who refused to allow Seung-Hui to remain in her class because of what he wrote and how he frightened the other students, was traveling overseas and the panel was unable to interview her.

The faculty members who were interviewed were unanimous in how they described Seung-Hui. As discussed in Chapter 2, he wore sunglasses, avoided eye contact, and sat slumped in his chair with a cap pulled low. He did not work well in groups and did not contribute his share. His voice was rarely heard, except for occasions such as when he read his angry composition in Dr. Giovanni's poetry class, or argued with a professor over an assignment. Seung-Hui often chose topics on which he could expound using violent content, regardless of the topic parameters set forth by the professors.

In her book, *No Right to Remain Silent: The Tragedy at Virginia Tech*, Dr. Lucinda Roy describes Seung-Hui as follows:

> Each time he walks into my office, I am seized with the desire to fill the void he creates. There is something melodramatic about his entrance. He knows what impression he is creating and it seems to give him satisfaction....Sometimes it's like talking to an inanimate object with limbs and an attitude. The core of his identity is impenetrable, his gaze strangely neutered, as if he has spent his entire life ridding it of expression....His egotism and insecurity create a dangerous combination because then he can ridicule everything that intimidates him. It is a character combination that is essentially dismissive of others. He is uncomfortable when challenged about his ideas, and yet he seems to yearn to be challenged, hoping that someone will topple the despair that colors what he sees. (Roy, 2009, p. 46)

None of the faculty interviewed said that Seung-Hui was an excellent writer. Despite this, he received some A's, though other professors assigned him C's or D's. Seung-Hui reportedly did complete all his assignments and regularly attended classes.

Two professors who recognized that Seung-Hui was very troubled mentioned in interviews that they urged him multiple times to take advantage of the campus mental health services at Cook Counseling Center. In retrospect, it is questionable how much progress could have been made with Seung-Hui through counseling since he denied any previous need for treatment of mental or emotional problems. Nevertheless, attempts were made to intervene and guide Seung-Hui to resources that were available. Lucinda Roy in particular repeatedly asked the sullen and alarmingly quiet Seung-Hui to talk to a counselor; she even contacted a therapist at the Cook Counseling Center on his behalf.

Unless a student voluntarily sought help, intervening with a troubled student at Virginia Tech was difficult, according to Dr. Roy. This was especially true if the concern arose from something the student had written, as First Amendment issues became involved—a reality on many college campuses. Several English Department faculty were certainly aware that Seung-Hui's consistently violent themes and his passive-aggressive behavior were cause for concern, but as discussed earlier, they were unaware of his problems elsewhere on campus and of his interactions with police. This probably caused them to downplay the seriousness of what they observed.

To some of the panel members and staff it seemed that some of the faculty were uncomfortable answering the questions that the panel asked. A few had been interviewed by federal law enforcement officers, reporters, or others, so there was a sense of weariness and wariness about participating in yet another round of questions. And while no one refused to speak with Virginia Tech panel members and staff, some faculty were guarded in their answers. University officials and legal counsel encouraged everyone to cooperate, but at the same time signaled concern over what and how much should be said. This was evidenced by the manner in which interviews with panel members were handled by the university. The associate university counsel, Mary Beth Nash, was present at scheduled faculty interviews. Once, when a small group of professors and deans were being interviewed by telephone, legal counsel interrupted before one of the group could answer a particularly important question. The interviewer, a co-director of the panel staff from TriData, tersely pointed out to the legal counsel that the question was not directed at her and she was not the one to answer it. Not surprisingly, little more was accomplished before the call ended. The TriData staff person immediately contacted the university's appointed liaison to the panel, Lenwood McCoy, and complained of legal counsel's preempting responses to legitimate questions, which interfered with the investigation. Later interviews proceeded without counsel's presence.

In her book, Dr. Roy states that very early after the murders, President Steger informed the press that the university had no idea that Seung-Hui was troubled: "By the end of the first week following the tragedy, President Steger and his key advisers had 'battened down the hatches,' a phrase I have often heard utilized by one of his team to describe the administration's approach to the media. This wasn't just an attempt to keep outsiders away; the hatches were battened down internally also" (Roy,

2009, p. 68). In complying with the initial request that faculty provide the police with whatever they had on record about Seung-Hui, Dr. Roy had produced pages of internal e-mails documenting her response to Dr. Giovanni's distress about Seung-Hui's behavior and chronicling weeks of e-mail correspondence with other departments—including Judicial Affairs, Student Affairs, and Cook Counseling Center—about his violent writing and unauthorized picture-taking in class. Had President Steger checked with these groups for background information on Seung-Hui, he would have known that individuals within the university had indeed had an idea that Seung-Hui was troubled.

The administration's response to unfolding events appears to have been to limit communication between university personnel and others. In her book, Dr. Roy reported that she was on the official "do-not-speak-with" list. A few long-time associates and friends of Dr. Roy's who were part of the administration admitted to her that there was a ban on communicating with her and that they stood to lose their jobs if they did not comply. To quote her again: "From Tuesday, April 17, when the identity of the shooter was confirmed up until the time of writing this book, there has been no meaningful internal investigation with regards to specific incidents related to Seung-Hui Cho. As far as I can tell, apart from the development of some guidelines about how to evaluate and refer troubled students, Cho's history at Virginia Tech has been erased from the upper administration's collective memory" (Roy 2009, p. 68). Moreover, they said if any faculty or staff were to be represented by the university's legal counsel they would be required to follow counsel's directives. Did these actions mean university officials were concerned about potential legal liability resulting from the university's handling of Seung-Hui? (Although most of the families of victims and survivors of the tragedy entered into a settlement with the state, the Virginia Supreme Court recently overturned jury awards against the Commonwealth of Virginia in two cases that went to trial. The Court ruled that even assuming that there was a special relationship between the Commonwealth [through its employees at the university] and the students of Virginia Tech, under the facts of the case, "there was no duty for the Commonwealth to warn students about the potential for criminal acts by third parties.") Did they fear they might be found to have failed to adequately address concerns brought forth by faculty in the English Department about Seung-Hui?

The information gleaned from the faculty interviews conducted by the panel further highlights the policy and procedural dilemmas faced by campus personnel when called upon to deal with the kinds of behaviors seen not only in students but also in staff and faculty.

This tragedy continues to hold the attention of university personnel across the nation as they grapple with the threat of similar incidents on their campuses. Although there have been many school shootings, the need is now greater than ever to develop coherent policy and procedures to address such realities. The overwhelming impression from the interviews conducted was that the university officials at Tech had not been successful at picking up the warning signs related to Seung-Hui Cho's mental illness and had not taken consistent steps to get him into treatment. Could notification of his parents about his condition in 2005 have averted the tragedy? Could the tragedy have been averted had the Care Team at Virginia Tech insisted that Seung-Hui be assessed and treated after hearing the English professors' concerns? The interviews revealed the distress of the victims' families and survivors over the lack of a coherent and planful response of the university within the days following the massacre. The interviews revealed how administrative and bureaucratic responses were experienced by unique players within this tragedy: parents, faculty, university leaders, and community agencies. Although distinctive and disparate in their observations, these critiques have the potential to push systems to become reflective and creative in their response to crisis and its prevention.

These observations, in part, provide the framework for Chapters 5 and 6 in this book, which relate to campus mental health services.

4

GETTING INTO THE MIND OF THE KILLER
A PSYCHOLOGICAL AUTOPSY OF SEUNG-HUI CHO

Aradhana Bela Sood

After the massacre, the foremost question in every mind was, "Why did he do it?" We need to find reason among such chaos so that the nonsensical begins to make sense, the macabre becomes human, and the inexplicable, understandable. Most importantly, only by understanding such people and such events can we hope to prevent them in the future.

At times, a neat psychiatric diagnosis (a specific medical cause for a disorder) is not possible; in the case of Seung-Hui Cho, the fundamental obstacle is the lack of data. He is no longer here to respond to questions that could reveal what was plaguing him. With the clues to what he did in his last days, offered by credit card records and wisps of remembrances from brief encounters, we can conjure up a person and his actions, but as he hardly spoke, we know little about his thinking. A psychological profile is usually developed for a person who is alive; it is based on relevant information about behavior at the point of assessment, on the events in the person's life that preceded the event, and on information about him or her from acquaintances and family and then examining how that fits in with theories of psychology. All we can construct for Seung-Hui Cho is a psychological autopsy, a profile developed after death. This procedure for investigating a person's death reconstructs what the person thought, felt, and did before death, based on information gathered from personal documents, police reports, medical and coroner's records, and face-to-face interviews with families, friends, and others who had contact with the person before the death.

In an attempt to understand his motivations, the panel members constructed several theories, and this led to considerable discussion among us. As underscored in Chapter 2, one principle that guided the work of the panel was to document facts and then allow the facts to speak for themselves. There was dissension among the panel members as we grappled with unlocking the mystery of Cho's mental health from two different angles: Dr. Depue's forensic science background and work with the FBI, and my vantage point from child psychiatry, which uses phenomenology and human development as its foundation. We agreed that developing a psychological profile was beyond the scope of the panel's work, so the panel did not publish such a profile of Seung-Hui at the conclusion of our work in August 2007. But after seven years, the question still comes up repeatedly: What was wrong with him?

I will qualify my remarks here with the statement that attempting to diagnose someone who was not a patient, and especially one who is deceased, is dangerous and unethical—too much hangs on speculation. What we can do here is review what it means to diagnose a person with a mental disorder in the abstract. We can then focus on the discussion of the possible illness or illnesses that Cho may have suffered from, even if we cannot officially diagnose him with any of them.

Armed with firsthand data from his parents and sister as well as from the people in closest proximity to Seung-Hui, his suitemates and professors, Dr. Depue and I are the only mental health professionals to come close to performing a psychological autopsy on Seung-Hui. But while wisdom in science is knowing what can be stated as theory, as relative fact and as fact based on evidence, what we provide here are theoretical hypotheses that attempt to explain why Seung-Hui did what he did. These hypotheses are based on the facts of Seung-Hui's life that were reported in Chapter 2.

PSYCHIATRIC DIAGNOSIS

The complexity of making a psychiatric diagnosis is immense, even under ordinary circumstances. Psychiatric illness may present as episodic crises or as long-term, chronic conditions. When patients complain of a problem, this subjective complaint is known as a symptom. When physicians carry out a physical and psychiatric examination based on symptoms, they elicit observed and objective problems in the body or mind, called signs. A combination of subjective symptoms and objective signs generates a medical or psychiatric diagnosis. Just as fever, lymph node enlargement, and night sweats might make an internist consider tuberculosis as a diagnosis, similarly, certain emotions in a specific combination accompanied by impairment in educational, social, and occupational functioning would make a mental health clinician consider a psychiatric diagnosis. This involves investigating the individual's abilities regarding orientation to his or her surroundings, attention span, concentration, and memory. In addition, abnormalities in perception such as hallucinations, paranoia, speed of thoughts, content of thoughts, and logical thinking are used to make the most likely diagnosis. Data from multiple sources must be elicited to construct a complete picture of what may be contributing to a person's behavior at any single point in his or her history. For a diagnosis to be accurate, reliance on precise descriptions of the problem by multiple but reliable sources, such as parents, a spouse, employer, or peers, is essential. The clinician must make sure that he or she has gathered sufficient information to piece together a plausible diagnosis for the condition the person is presenting with.

The criteria by which to make these diagnoses are spelled out in the *Diagnostic and Statistical Manual of Mental Disorders,* Fifth Edition (DSM-5; American Psychiatric Association, 2013). The problems that these diagnoses cause may be exaggerated when a person is under stress. Complicating the picture may be character traits which determine an individual's response to external events. When these responses or psychological defense mechanisms are lifelong and predominantly negative, especially under stress, they may suggest a personality disorder. Diagnosis aside, observable behavior can be viewed as a lifelong pattern of interplay between effects of life experiences, innate temperament, genetic vulnerabilities, and psychological defenses that are either helpful or destructive. As life experiences for individuals are disparate and unique, the manner in which they interact with temperament and the disease process is unpredictable.

PSYCHIATRIC EMERGENCIES

When does psychiatric illness become a psychiatric emergency? Usually emergencies are preceded by some stressor or series of stressors that overwhelm the person's normal coping mechanisms. In the face of these stressors, the individual's coping mechanisms, whether highly functional or marginally functional, weaken to the point that the person is catapulted into a psychiatric emergency. Theoretically, all of us have the capacity to decompensate to the point of looking mentally ill under the right circumstances and stressors. Protective factors may help stave off the deterioration, such as having a resilient temperament and effective social supports. In short, mental illness and its presentation are on a continuum of normalcy and illness. The dimensions of normalcy versus illness are broad, and the line (not the concept) separating the two is often arbitrary and subjective, potentially leading to confusion about what constitutes behavior that needs intervention and what can be noted but let go.

WHEN DO WE TREAT PSYCHIATRIC ILLNESS AND HOW DO WE ASSESS RISK FOR DANGER?

A general consensus exists among health care providers that the burden an illness puts on an individual and the extent to which it deranges the individual's social, occupational, and family functioning determines whether the illness should be treated or not. An individual may be overtly hallucinating, but if he or she chooses not to be treated and is not causing anyone harm he or she has every right to remain in that state. But if individuals say that they are hearing voices that tell them to kill someone (command hallucinations), then most state codes recognize as constitutional the legal need to intervene (i.e., temporary detention orders to hospitalize the person).

In a psychiatric emergency the first order of business is establishing safety. Risk assessment, therefore, requires the evaluator to estimate the dangerousness of an individual, not only in the setting of the assessment but also in the various environments to which the individual will be returning, and in the context of the psychological crisis that precipitated the psychiatric emergency. Hospitalization and continued detention for the purposes of assessment and treatment has to meet rigorous criteria. The elements of the criteria are sufficient and continued dangerousness that precludes placement in a less restrictive environment.

Who makes the assessment that there is sufficient and continued dangerousness? This decision falls on the physician clinically responsible for the patient in the hospital and an independent evaluator assigned by the court system to advise the judge hearing the case whether the individual meets these criteria or not. Assessing an individual's dangerousness, especially in the setting of an evolving psychological crisis, is often a very difficult task. A reasonably good risk assessment requires accurate knowledge of many aspects of an individual's life. Given that the patient has developed problems in the context of stressors that occurred within his or her living environment, it is risky to base judgment about safety primarily on current behavior and self-disclosure. It is of utmost importance to obtain collateral information to corroborate, clarify, or refute the information the individual has provided. Yet, the individual is usually the only one interviewed to determine the way his or her mind is functioning at that point in time. This is a flaw in the process. The individual being evaluated should not be relied on as the sole provider of information to assess safety and the formulation of the problem. As we saw with Seung-Hui, doing so can have disastrous consequences.

Current Challenges in Risk Assessment

In reality, within an episode of a hospitalization, corroborating data are often not obtained. What happened at the Carillion Hospital where Seung-Hui was hospitalized in December 2005 was typical of most clinical encounters. Indeed, the psychiatrist cited the lack of time and fear of HIPAA violations as the chief reasons for not seeking information from or providing information to parents or school officials. Although not directly related to this issue, the psychiatrist attributed the less-than-optimal post-discharge plans to the paucity of outpatient resources in the area. An opportunity was lost by not developing an effective post-discharge plan for Seung-Hui, which may have gotten him the treatment that was much needed.

A PSYCHOLOGICAL PROFILE OF SEUNG-HUI CHO BASED ON INFORMATION AVAILABLE

With all the qualifiers offered up earlier, the available information suggests something was deeply wrong with this young man. First and foremost, this was an individual who was isolated and highly anxious. He was seen as weird and withdrawn by his peers and roommates. He barely spoke to anyone. When invited to social events, he was rarely asked back again because he was unable to negotiate the situation without awkwardness. Was this painful shyness, social ineptitude, or oddness to the point of reflecting poor reality testing?

The pictures of Seung-Hui Cho painted by his family and by his peers and professors are of two people. To his parents, sister, high school counselor, and a number of faculty at Virginia Tech he was a fragile, solitary, and silent young man who inspired sympathy; indeed, a number of attempts were made to help and encourage him. To a few classmates and dorm residents, however, he was a strange, threatening, and sometimes frightening peer. One professor sized up Seung-Hui as a student who manipulated the goodwill of others to serve his own purposes and avoid responsibility. Seung-Hui's perception of himself was of a martyred victim who missed out on what the rest of the world enjoyed while he existed in a sullen, angry, and colorless world of solitude.

From a professional perspective, conclusions can be drawn about Seung-Hui's mental functioning based on data points from his middle and high school years when he was evaluated and treated by a therapist and child psychiatrist. That data are rich and well defined. Unfortunately, they are also dated and unreliable for predicting much in Seung-Hui's later life at Virginia Tech. But a history of psychiatric problems, especially those with onset in childhood, does predict future vulnerability, as such illnesses tend to be chronic.

After high school, the first point at which data about Seung-Hui's emotional health were gathered was during his brief interaction with the pre-screener from the New River Valley Community Service Board and with the psychiatrist during his hospitalization at Carillion Hospital in December 2005. The incomplete data collected by the mental health professionals at Cook Counseling Center and Carillion Hospital provide a relatively superficial picture of Seung-Hui's psychological state at that time. The outpatient files on Seung-Hui that chronicle his contacts with Cook Counseling Center at Virginia Tech (which were originally thought to be lost, but were found a year and a half later by the former counseling center director at his home) were thin and not informative. The information was threadbare, lacked depth and descriptive richness, and was lacking corroboration from collateral sources. There was no effort to pull existing data together when he was alive.

Seung-Hui had no further interaction with the mental health system after December 2005, so we are forced to piece together his background, looking for obvious stressors or an evolving mental disorder that may have caused him to descend into such a violent mindset. Examining stressors, there was no reason to suspect that he was financially strapped, or that his parents were unsupportive, or that he was overtly bullied or ostracized. He was marginalized, but this was probably because of his own desire to remain isolative, and then secondarily because of his odd behavior. Could he have felt marginalized because of his ethnicity? According to the records from high school and the reports of his peers at Virginia Tech, this was not the case. As far as an evolving psychiatric illness is concerned, although he did not behave in a bizarre manner with his peers outside of class after his hospitalization, the same could not be said about his behavior in the English Department where he was enrolled.

In the spring and fall of 2006, we see that his behavior warranted the attention of an English professor again; Seung-Hui was writing dark and aggressive material. One essay, written exactly a year before the massacre, specifically alluded to the Holocaust. These writings suggest a pent-up rage against society. He was clearly ruminating about perceived inequities. Seung-Hui posted a letter to the English Department, attacking Professor Carl Bean, with whom he argued angrily over a paper he wrote in spring 2006 (Bean judged the paper to be subpar and suggested that Seung-Hui drop the course). Next Seung-Hui wrote an essay foreshadowing closely the events of April 16, 2007. The piece describes an angry student who hates his peers, killing them and then himself. Was it coincidence or premeditated belligerence and intimidation that this writing was turned in by Seung-Hui to the English professor exactly a year before the 2007 massacre?

Though we can never know for sure, it seems that Seung-Hui was methodically planning his exit from the world in a dramatic manner. His attack was well thought out and well planned—clearly not an act of sudden passion. For instance, he purchased a firearm well in advance of the killings, in February of 2007, and stockpiled ammunition obtained from different sources (eBay, Wal-Mart) and on different dates between March and April 2007. He appears to have been attempting to avoid raising anyone's suspicions, which indicates that his thought processes were clear, not illogical or bizarre, as is often the case in psychotic illnesses like schizophrenia. He created videotapes of himself (in a rented van and in a hotel room), and patiently waited the requisite one-month period to purchase a second firearm (March 13, 2007) and hunting knife (March 31, 2007). Whatever was going on in his mind, it did not affect his ability to plan and execute the killings. The videotape diatribe Seung-Hui sent from a local post office to NBC news at 9:01 A.M. on the day of the killings is approximately 1,800 words long and was read from a script that expresses his rage, resentment, and desire to get even with oppressors. Based on a lack of evidence that he was a victim of either deliberate or accidental oppression by his peers or teachers, these rants appear delusional, suggesting psychosis, yet his previous behavior belies that.

Some have drawn a connection between Seung-Hui's actions and the film *Oldboy* (Kim, 2003), because of the manner in which he filmed himself and the pervasive theme of revenge in his script. *Oldboy* is a Korean film (South Korea's Grand Bell Awards winner, 2004) in which a middle-aged man takes vengeance after being released from 15 years of unexplained incarceration in a hotel room. The weapon used is a hammer (which Cho held in one portion of the video). However, that is where the resemblance ends. Even if he did view the movie, it would be a stretch to claim that the movie inspired him to commit the act, as he had expressed his aggression via other themes in his creative writing in the year preceding his death. Those writings indicate an inherent predisposition toward being aggressive and angry about perceived slights; *Oldboy* may have resonated with his sense of being a victim seeking revenge, but it was not a source he was "copying."

Hence, all through January 2006 through December 2006, Seung-Hui manifested this angry persona only within the English Department, where concerned professors brought his behavior to the attention of the associate dean of Liberal Arts and Human Sciences. But no action was taken—another missed opportunity to connect the dots. The stockpiling of the ammunition and buying of guns began in early 2007. Seung-Hui had practiced at a firing range and had done uncharacteristic things like stay at a motel to tape a video before the fateful day. He seems to have been not only planning the event but also deliberately trying to hide any suspicious behavior, which is in stark contrast to his actions during the fall of 2005, when he was almost certainly intentionally seeking attention by behaving erratically.

What specifically happened in the days prior to the homicide-suicide spree? Based on the interviews with his family we know that he had fairly innocuous conversations with them every Sunday that ran like scripts, with questions asked by his parents: "How are you? What did you eat? Do you need any money?" The night before the massacre was no exception. Seung-Hui made no statement to them that in retrospect would have suggested that this day was different. There were no good-byes or statements that indicated anticipatory guilt, remorse, or an emotional crisis. (The only immediate forewarning may have been a faculty member's sighting of an Asian male, probably Seung-Hui, near Norris Hall on April 14, 2007. He had remarked to another student that he saw chains on the doors of Norris Hall. Had Seung-Hui been practicing? This would be yet another indication that he was lucid, planful, and quite careful that his actions arouse no suspicion.)

How accurate was the information that the panel members obtained from the Cho family? Were they truthful? Could something have been said that night to provide a clue as to what Seung-Hui was planning? We do not know. What we learned from Seung-Hui's family has to be taken as the best possible information we have. We also have no reason to disbelieve their claim that they had no knowledge of his hospitalization or gradually worsening condition. During their interview they stated that, had they known what was going on, they would have taken Seung-Hui out of college and gotten him treatment. Based on their consistent follow-through with therapy recommendations in Seung-Hui's middle and high school years, there is no reason to doubt this.

A SPECULATIVE PSYCHOLOGICAL PROFILE OF SEUNG-HUI CHO

How do we piece together these bits of information to form a hypothesis about Seung-Hui's psychological state?

Childhood: Baseline Anxiety

From childhood, Seung-Hui was characterized as being painfully shy. Seung-Hui's parents and sister denied being aware of his being bullied extraordinarily, but his apparent high degree of social anxiety is consistent with someone who was hypersensitive to any criticism and perceived small slights as magnified. For Seung-Hui, it is possible that there was a deepening negativity, poor self-esteem, and escalating sense of marginalization that he had begun to feel coming from the world around him. Held at bay normally, it is not unlikely that all of these internalized perceptions would rise to the surface when Seung-Hui came under high stress.

As discussed earlier, Seung-Hui's friendships were minimal. It is remarkable that no one stepped forward as his friend after the slayings, even simply to garner some media attention, suggesting that he really was a loner. In college he began to display traits of avoidant behavior, wanting to be around people but as a result of anxiety avoiding social contact at all costs. This is in contrast to a schizoid personality structure, in which an individual has no desire to be around other people, preferring his or her own company and solitary activities. Avoidant behavior is generally associated with the sufferer being prone to an anxiety disorder, whereas a person with a schizoid personality may be constantly hypervigilant when around others and misperceive what is transpiring, leaning more in the direction of having a thought disorder such as paranoid schizophrenia.

Although autism and Asperger's syndrome have also been alluded to as possible diagnoses for Seung-Hui, to our knowledge there was no information in his early mental health record to suggest or support either diagnosis. Instead, he began therapy to deal with intense shyness, which was diagnosed as "social anxiety."

Stress-Induced Suicidal and Homicidal
Thoughts in Middle School

As described in Chapter 2, in the spring of 1999 Seung-Hui's therapist observed his creative work becoming more and more negative, culminating in a school essay, written after the Columbine massacre, that was homicidal and suicidal in content. The child psychiatrist who evaluated him at the resource center after he wrote the essay added a diagnosis of major depression to the existing selective mutism, which appears to be accurate given the information available to us. The diagnosis of depression was probably given because of his dark and negative statements and his dropping grades. In children, depression presents differently from in adults, with more physical symptoms, like headaches and stomachaches that "speak" for internal sad feelings. When the depression becomes more severe, the person can develop hallucinations that actively confirm that the negative self-image is accurate. The more incapable a person is of expressing feelings, the more those feelings come out in psychological metaphors or physical behaviors. As Seung-Hui was virtually incapable of expressing his feelings verbally, they appear to have come out in the form of virulent diatribes in his essays.

Depression can also be expressed as aggression. In this way, internalized distress and anger can be experienced by the recipient of the aggression. Thus the person who is depressed experiences a short period of gratification for making others "feel as bad as me."

Therapy and a selective serotonin reuptake inhibitor, paroxetine, proved to be helpful—further supporting the diagnosis of depression. The combination treatment, psychotherapy and antidepressant, produced functionality within months of initiating the medicine. Seung-Hui appeared brighter, happier, and more like himself. The drug was discontinued approximately 11 months later as both he and parents were convinced he was doing well enough to stop. Such requests are not uncommon, and unless there is good reason (previous suicide attempts, severe depression, chaotic environment), most psychiatrists will accede to them.

Was He Psychotic?

Claims that Seung-Hui was psychotic (unable to differentiate reality from fantasy, had confused thinking, would hallucinate or have thoughts that were not based in reality) from elementary through high school are not borne out by any records. However, the records do suggest that under heightening depression, the stressor that triggered his brief "out-of-the-ordinary" behavior was the Columbine shooting. His writing suggested that he identified with the aggressors and wanted to mimic their actions. This event during his school years suggests that he had the predilection for unraveling under high levels of stress. But his baseline behavior did not reflect that, under ordinary circumstances, he was the type of person who would pose a danger to himself or others. He was quiet but not aggressive toward anyone and was never suspended from school. He did not engage in self-mutilation or suicidal behaviors.

Threats and Buffers of School Years

How do we understand what was going on in Seung-Hui's mind, based on the records from school and the multicultural center where he received his therapy? He had a plethora of thoughts and feelings that he kept bottled up inside, inaccessible to everyone, including his family. He had a family environment that appeared placid and consistent with the traditional immigrant experience: parents who were toiling hard, working long hours to make a "better" life for their children, supporting their academic lives in every possible way, and hoping the children would assimilate as easily and as quickly as possible (this information was obtained in interviews).

All who came in contact with him noted that Seung-Hui was probably extraordinarily sensitive to the reactions of other people, like most children who are excessively shy. This hypervigilance can make a person highly emotionally reactive to any stressor, whether it is real or perceived. The internal set of standards against which such a person might measure an event could be highly inconsistent with how an average person might assess it. The equilibrium of day-to-day life hangs in a delicate balance for these individuals and is constantly being rocked by minor tremors caused by disappointments and perceived slights. Their defense mechanisms operate to retreat, flee, or come to a complete standstill. They hope that no one notices them, that they are left alone and that the danger shall pass.

At times, albeit rarely, hypervigilance and anxiety in such individuals can cross over to paranoia, which can build to an extraordinarily heightened sensitivity to the external world. This could be the result of a psychological vulnerability, such as depression or a real or perceived loss. Any event or perceived stressor could derail rational thought processes and precipitate a major crisis. Although with Seung-Hui there was nothing to suggest that in his day-to-day life he posed a risk of overt aggression to either himself or others, when stressed by noxious external events, his underlying inability to adjust psychologically surfaced as anger. This anger was somehow connected to Columbine, which he had personalized (identifying with the perpetrators and wishing to emulate them).

For individuals who are loners by choice or because they lack the social skills to create a network of friends, there are no external mechanisms (social, family, employment) that they can use as a sounding board, hence opportunities to correct these aberrant perceptions are scarce. The reaction of paranoid vigilance becomes pronounced and eventually acted out by an attempt to either save oneself or save others from whatever the perceived "threat" is. A normally shut-down person can be galvanized into action; the ensuing action may not be rational or functional and can be aggressive.

For Seung-Hui, we can hypothesize that the developing depression in March 1999 made him extremely vulnerable and reactive to the news of the Columbine massacre. The lens through which he may have seen the event could have led to his identifying with the perpetrators. Why? To speculate, perhaps he negatively internalized some whiff of ethnic discrimination or comments about his quietness or his family. This is merely conjecture, as he had never made comments about being sad or spoken of being bullied. Despite this, his sister did allude to him experiencing "mild bullying" and feeling "different as an Asian" in those early years of their lives. It is noteworthy that, other than this brief period, there are no allusions to aggression toward others or self-injurious behaviors, by either school personnel or family members. A possible interpretation is that this was a depressive episode that exaggerated the baseline hypervigilance and excruciating anxiety and pushed him into paranoia that spilled out into his classroom writings. With appropriate interventions, the depression melted away but left the baseline anxiety and the selective mutism intact.

Interestingly, Seung-Hui was able to obtain for himself a variety of psychological supports: a family that stood by him and took him to therapy regularly, a middle school guidance department that made the effort to invite family in and suggest therapy, and a high school that provided a number of accommodations to enable him to be successful. Even in his college years his ability to draw people into helping him was remarkable—especially for a person who brought little to the table in the way of social graces of engagement and reciprocity.

How much support can schools give to accommodate a student before the help becomes enabling, allowing the underlying problems to flourish rather than helping the student to overcome them? Was allowing him to write out his presentation and waiving all verbal presentations helpful or harmful to his developing a sense of psychological independence or confidence?

There were arguments among the Virginia Tech panel members about this issue. If Seung-Hui got so many accommodations in high school, was his 3.57 GPA really reflective of what he was capable of accomplishing? Some inferred that the school had aided and abetted the feeling of dependency and encouraged him to think that he was "special." How does that argument have clinical relevance to the evolution of Seung-Hui as a college student and the tragedy of April 16, 2007?

The decision to go to Virginia Tech, a large university, was entirely Seung-Hui's. He was warned against going to Tech by his guidance counselor, teachers, and family but chose to ignore their advice. This decision was certainly not the thought process of a person who had been subdued and made dependent. His ability to manage a 3.0 GPA at Tech at the end of his freshman year points to a good adjustment and intellectual capability, and he did so without any special accommodations. In fact, the large size of the university and the hands-off approach (in contrast to high school) probably felt more comforting to this young man, who was so excruciatingly shy. There was nothing in his behavior during this period to suggest depression. He did not make any friends, but he did not disengage from those he knew best: his family.

The problems began in his junior year. What transpired to set in motion the events that occurred that year? Information from the university health clinic indicates a pre-occupation with being infested with mites, but the only intervention was with minocycline for acne in his sophomore year, suggesting Seung-Hui was mistakenly attributing the acne to mites. Minocycline can lead to depression as a side effect, but that was never established or commented on by the treating physician in Seung-Hui's medical notes. After a fairly successful freshman and sophomore year, as evidenced by good grades and his capacity to transition between roommates and live off campus, his interest turned to writing. His family saw him writing during breaks and over the summer vacation between his sophomore and junior years. They were content that he had found a passion that would occupy him. His sister was privy to one sample of his writing and she was struck by the themes of aggression and gore. He did not share much of his writing with anyone at home. By the summer he had switched his major from the sciences to creative writing and was excited for the fall semester, again, according to his sister.

What happened during this period? Why the sudden unraveling in the next four months? While the following is speculative, it is based on facts we know and their temporal connection to behavior; a causal link between the two appears to be reasonable: It seems that the rejection of the manuscript he sent to a New York publishing house was a considerably blow to his ego, and he felt his writing career had ended even before it began.

Similar to the stressor of the Columbine incident, the stressor here was the rejection letter that threatened what he had set his sights on. Rather than being able to talk about it and come to terms with it, this feeling of rejection began to balloon into odd and paranoid behavior, not necessarily related to reality. Just as in middle school, his writing in his English course became the outlet for his thinking, giving his professors a glimpse of his unraveling mind. The writings contained numerous aggressive themes.

In other words, he was wounded, and he was showing his wounds to everyone around him in the only way he could. Some of them responded, and some did not. The chance to intervene psychiatrically was squandered by an unfortunate lack of communication between parties involved, combined with oversensitivity to various privacy and free-speech issues at the university.

What happened after that? Why did he disappear? Though a tentative hypothesis at best, it would seem that a second sentinel event fueled his aggression. This event was the commitment to Carillion Hospital, under a temporary detention order in December 2005. His mind was unraveling in the wake of perceived rejection due to legitimate feedback on his academic work. This sense of failure and the final most damning injury—being locked up in a hospital—may have led him to feel not only a loathing for himself but a loathing for all around him.

The next year was probably spent with his anger growing, until it became all encompassing. It bubbled out in his essays written for his English classes. Uncharacteristically, he had arguments with his English professors, and at least four of them were concerned enough to bring the matter to the attention of the dean.

When his parents began to question his plans for graduate school he indicated a disinterest in further education. He also refused their help in finding him a job. Culturally these themes of independence and stubborn reticence are not typical for adolescents of Korean heritage. Do these behaviors suggest that he was already planning his exit from the world? His anger continued to grow.

Having literally no friends or social network was a major factor in the escalation of his rage. Social networks allow us to float our hypotheses, both valid and irrational, to other human beings. Responses from friends, peers, and family allow correction of highly skewed views into quasi-reasonable ones. Seung-Hui had none of these supports with whom he could have shared his thoughts and feelings in his final months (except for his English professors, who were dismayed and concerned and provided critiques that he rejected).

Why did these feelings escalate to this extent? Death is an irrevocable step. Even an individual who is about to kill himself has to rationalize the suicide to his or her own self. The impetus for this action may very well have been his feeling of rejection and lost hope as a writer. His behaviors were clearly troubling to his professors and peers. It appears that he was almost begging for someone to sit up, take notice, and get him out of the cycle of rage that he had created for himself. This was followed fairly quickly by the event of being hospitalized against his wishes. This time there was no escaping the fact that he had a mental illness and was being detained for this reason. Since the concept of having a mental illness carries a relatively strong stigma in Eastern cultures he did not tell his parents about it. The hospitalization could be viewed as the erosion of his last bastion of self-esteem.

This injury caused self-doubt to turn into anger at self and also at the "perpetrators." Again, to speculate, Seung-Hui's developing fantasy was dredging up feelings of marginalization (for which he was responsible) and memories of the bullying (even minor) and racial slurs. This fantasy also triggered feelings of hopelessness associated with the family's negative immigrant experience: watching his parents toil hard for what the family had and comparing this to peers who seemingly "had it all." Hence, his diatribe and its content begin to make sense, at least to Seung-Hui. The themes of being a victim, seeking revenge, annihilating, and destroying could be viewed as overblown responses to perceived threats. The major themes of the diatribes on the NBC tapes suggest paranoia and even poor reality testing. However, from his calculated actions it is clear that he was not so impaired that he could not think lucidly. Was he hallucinating? Probably not. Was he delusional?

The material from the NBC tapes is the closest we can come to his mind and its complexities through his first-person voice. That material definitely suggests delusional thinking, a fixed false belief that cannot be explained by a person's cultural, social, or occupational background. Were the thoughts expressed in the video he created enough to warrant a diagnosis of schizophrenia? They were not; as discussed earlier, psychiatric diagnosis is an extremely complex process. It could not have been conducted on the basis of a videotape.

When is creative work autobiographical and when is it being truly created out of imagination? At what point should we be alarmed by the content of creative work and concerned about the creator? This was the dilemma that Seung-Hui's English professors dealt with throughout his time in their courses. If, for the purposes of furthering our understanding of his mind, we take into consideration his angry and horrific ramblings within his creative work in class as his own thinking and not just imagination, one could make a case for a delusional disorder. A delusional disorder (previously called paranoid disorder) is a type of serious mental illness sometimes called a "psychosis," in which a person cannot tell what is real from what is imagined.

With Seung-Hui, the question of what in his diatribe was real versus imagined is somewhat easily answered: Very little of it can be anchored to reality. Yet he was also not roaming around campus acting on command hallucinations. The main feature of a delusional disorder is the presence of unshakable beliefs in something untrue. People with delusional disorders will often experience non-bizarre delusions, which involve situations that *could* occur in real life, such as being followed, poisoned, deceived, conspired against, or loved from a distance. These delusions usually involve the misinterpretation of perceptions or experiences. In reality, however, the perceptions are either incorrect or highly exaggerated. A case has been made that the nidus of Seung-Hui's paranoia was his difference from his "well-to-do" peers, but this cannot explain *why* this was his perception. People with delusional disorder often can continue to socialize and function normally, except when focused on the subject of their delusion. They generally do not behave in an obviously odd or bizarre manner.

Seung-Hui's personality and almost muteness were lifelong characteristics and hence cannot be construed as new bizarre or odd behaviors for the period between 2005 and 2007. His mutism in the last two years of his life did not stand out as being at odds with his baseline behavior. In some cases, however, people with a delusional disorder might become so preoccupied with their delusions that their lives are disrupted.

The following various elements of a delusional disorder can be seen in Seung-Hui's behavior.

Erotomanic type: Someone with this type of delusional disorder believes that another person (often someone important or famous) is in love with him or her. The person may engage in stalking behavior, which is not uncommon. For Seung-Hui, the objects of his attention in the fall of 2005 were female peers, and he did stalk some of them in his junior year.

Persecutory type: People with this type of delusional disorder believe that they are being mistreated, or that someone is spying on them or planning to harm them. The paranoia that is evident from Seung-Hui's writings and diatribe certainly suggests a bizarre view of the world, his surroundings, and relationships.

Grandiose type: A person with this type of delusional disorder has an over-inflated sense of worth, power, knowledge, or identity. The person might believe he or she has a great talent or has made an important discovery. In Seung-Hui's writing one can glean a sense of inflated self-worth that is probably compensation for the inadequacy he really felt.

Many have questioned whether Seung-Hui could be labeled antisocial. Certainly his cold-blooded killing suggests an abysmal lack of empathy for anyone. But let's analyze his behavior further. Individuals with antisocial personality disorder (APD) repeatedly violate societal rules with little empathy for the rights, safety, or feelings of others. People with APD are overrepresented in prison populations and their actions suggest that they have no conscience, guilt, or remorse. They move through society as predators, paying little attention to the consequences of their actions. Deceit and manipulation characterize their interpersonal relationships. Men or women diagnosed with this disorder demonstrate few emotions beyond contempt for others. Their lack of empathy is often combined with an inflated sense of self-worth and a superficial charm that tends to mask an inner indifference to the needs or feelings of others. Some studies indicate that people with APD can only mimic the emotions associated with committed love relationships and friendships that most people feel naturally. These characteristics are lifelong and are often preceded by a conduct disorder in childhood, characterized by aggression, legal charges for breaking and entering, assault and battery, and truancy, among other things.

The diagnosis of APD carries extremely negative connotations, as it is poorly responsive to treatment interventions. Although Seung-Hui's last actions clearly suggest the highest degree of violating the rights of others, nowhere in the timeline of his life were there other periods when this type of behavior or thinking occurred, except episodically and that, too, in response to stress. If Seung-Hui were antisocial and manipulative, that would have been evident from school records and would have emerged as a fixed personality characteristic. We can somewhat safely assume that, although his behaviors in the end were antisocial, they were most probably unrelated to an antisocial personality disorder, which connotes a lifelong pattern of sociopathy. This long-term pattern cannot be established in Seung-Hui's case.

More likely, Seung-Hui was suffering from delusional thinking, which, sadly for all of his victims and their families, is potentially treatable. He was the type of person who would probably always have had the tendency to unravel and become aggressive in his thought processes in the face of perceived threats. If he had survived this episode he would have needed regular oversight, support, and treatment, with medications, therapy, and additional support from family, friends, and co-workers, to tamp down emerging horrific fantasies in the face of stressors.

This chapter provides a speculative profile of Seung-Hui based on available current information on him. If history reveals more data or facts through family and friends our assessment of him may change, and we need to be open to new information that may surprise us or even debunk all our notions about Seung-Hui.

Several important points emerge from this exercise. This speculative psychological profile of Seung-Hui Cho illustrates the complexity of formulating a psychiatric diagnosis, especially when the subject is no longer living. Accurate formulations within mental health are highly dependent on the richness and accuracy of corroborating data, cross-checking of facts, and an in-depth look at the individual. These require considerable time and effort.

Conversely, misevaluating human behavior may result in discounting the need for potential intervention, as was the case with Seung-Hui. Individuals at Virginia Tech, specifically at the Cook Counseling Center, did not pay adequate attention to the evolving problems with Seung-Hui, and the staff at Carillion Hospital also failed to explore reasons for Seung-Hui's behavior that had led to his suicidal statements. We also know now that his problems did not develop overnight, but were longstanding and waxed and waned under stress. He was at a critical level of distress at least a year and a half before his homicide-suicide spree, and his symptoms were obvious enough to merit a thorough follow-up. It would not be an overstatement to posit that the generally strong support for mental health and emotional needs received by Seung-Hui in his middle and high school years resulted in success for him in the academic arena and prevented potentially dangerous behavior. This period is in sharp contrast to the time Seung-Hui spent at Virginia Tech, during which the counseling services and the institution virtually ignored the disturbing aberrant behaviors that his professors and peers had witnessed. Although he did not reveal his history of mental health problems at Tech, his actions there clearly suggested abnormal functioning. These red flags went unnoticed by most; while some individuals did notice his distress, no one privy to *all* of the information and with the administrative and professional clout to connect the dots did so. Many opportunities for intervention with Seung-Hui Cho were missed at Virginia Tech.

This case illustrates the importance of identifying and treating mental illness early, to prevent crises and even tragedy. The relationship between stigma around mental illness, the lack of awareness about mental illness, and the lack of services to intervene with mental illness is central to the gaps in the manner in which mental health is delivered in our schools, colleges, and communities.

PART TWO

MENTAL HEALTH CARE ON CAMPUS

5

FAILURES IN CAMPUS MENTAL HEALTH SYSTEMS
LESSONS FROM VIRGINIA TECH

Aradhana Bela Sood and Adele L. Martel

For more than two decades, reports regarding the mental health of college-aged students have shown an increase in the number of students arriving on campuses across the country with complex psychological and behavioral problems and an increase in the number of students utilizing campus mental health services. College and university counseling centers have responded to this burgeoning clinical need in a variety of ways, including reallocation of limited resources to the more severely mentally ill, expansion of student outreach services, and implementation of mental health triage systems. College and university administrations have been forced to reconsider the institution's role in the mental health of students and how campus mental health, in general, merges with the educational mission of the school. Unfortunately, it is the high-profile cases such as those at Virginia Tech and Northern Illinois University that have brought the crisis in college student mental health to the level of a national priority and to a level of scrutiny that could potentially impact public policy.

Meeting the complex mental health needs of college students who are in the midst of a significant developmental transition presents many challenges (Kadison & DiGeronimo, 2004). The students themselves, for the first time in their lives, are responsible for dealing with their mental health needs more independently. Parents, campus mental health providers, faculty, and administrators are challenged to balance the drive toward independence and the privacy of the individual student with the need to protect the rights of the campus community in general. Peers are challenged to respect differences yet be involved in identifying and seeking help for impaired classmates. Clearly defined pathways of communication among these parties are key to establishing effective systems of care for college-aged students.

In order to comprehend and remedy recent failures in campus mental health systems of care, it is essential to first learn about the population being served and the environmental and societal context within which the services are delivered. This chapter reviews the demographics of the college student population, including its diversity and its vulnerabilities. The changing mental health needs of the population are defined, and the social, cultural, and political forces shaping those needs are discussed. A brief history of college counseling centers, their complex relationship with parents and other university constituents, and the application of privacy laws in the context of treating students as members of campus communities are also reviewed. Lastly, the Virginia Tech tragedy will be reviewed and system failures identified within the context of this background information.

AGE OF VULNERABILITY

The literature addressing the developmental tasks of adolescents and young adults is extensive. Some examples include the theory of psychosocial development, in which Erikson (1963) describes the major task (or psychosocial crisis) of adolescence as the formation of identity versus a sense of role diffusion. He presents the major task of young adulthood as the achievement of a capacity to have intimacy with adults, instead of isolation. Arnett (2000), in evaluating societal trends in industrialized countries, proposes the term "emerging adults" to describe the typical college age group—ages 18–25. He defines five essential qualities of "emerging adulthood" as the age of (1) identity exploration, (2) instability, (3) self-focus, (4) a feeling of being in-between, and (5) possibilities.

Grayson (2006) takes a different approach and categorizes the issues and tasks of the college-aged population into three overlapping developmental themes: (1) separation-individuation, (2) identity formation, and (3) achieving intimacy. His descriptions of these three stages are summarized as follows. *Separation and individuation* tasks originate in toddlerhood and are revisited in adolescence. In college, the individual is further challenged to separate from parents, be autonomous in day-to-day functioning, "and engage in campus life." Abandonment and engulfment themes can resurface as an individual negotiates separation and individuation. *Identity formation* is complex, with the overall goal being to develop a stable, "cohesive, resilient, and accurate idea of self." This self-discovery includes attainment of sexual identity, peer group identity, social identity, and cultural identity. Based on life experiences, academic performance, and innate abilities, the individual develops career ambitions and future goals. Likewise, a personal value system is refined, and the individual is able to assert his or her own views and preferences. Lastly, *achieving intimacy* involves more than achieving sexual satisfaction. The goal is to achieve more "mature and satisfying intimate relationships." In addition, increasingly substantive and discriminating and valued friendships are formed.

College students, therefore, live in a transitional world, reworking and refining tasks of adolescence and taking on tasks of early adulthood. It is a vulnerable time as students become more cognizant of their strengths and weaknesses. Away from family and longtime friends, they may wish to shed old identities and try on new ones (Eichler, 2006). For students with mental health issues, this could mean casting away their identities as patients and stopping prescribed medication. They may avoid what they perceive as dependence on yet another adult and drop out of therapy. Resistance and noncompliance with treatment can be more readily understood in the context of this life stage. In a more positive vein, "the culture of learning, self-exploration and tolerance," present on many college campuses, means that mental health issues "can be supported and normalized" (LeJeune, 2009).

Case Example: Vivien

An 18-year-old freshman with a 4.0 GPA in the first semester, Vivien began to develop crying jags and ruminative thoughts of wanting to cut herself. When a dorm-mate, an older female student, discovered her curled into a fetal position one evening, rather than ignoring the event she decided to sit with Vivien. Over coffee she shared her own difficulties with depression, encouraged Vivien to share her thoughts, and finally persuaded her to consider counseling. She pointed out that the recent death of Vivien's grandmother, an event which could throw anyone into a funk, could be connected to her feelings. She suggested that in the absence of her family, it made sense for her to seek someone she could reliably and predictably speak to.

In this case, the distressed student was away from family supports and others who may have recognized her deterioration earlier. She was aided by a peer who was not only tolerant of the situation but also normalized the distress by sharing her own experience. The peer also was aware of the treatment options on campus. A caring community culture could help to reduce the complications of a developing depression, such as academic decline and suicide.

In addition to the liabilities associated with the complex, wide-ranging developmental tasks of this stage in their lives, college students are also at an age of vulnerability for the new onset of major psychiatric disorders. Schizophrenia affects approximately 1% of the general population; the disease typically begins in early adulthood, between the ages of 15 and 25, with the average age of onset being 18 in men and 25 in women (Sham, MacLean, & Kendler, 1994). The National Comorbidity Survey Replication Study (Kessler et al., 2005), which investigated the age of onset of DSM-IV-defined anxiety disorders, mood disorders, impulse control disorders, and substance use disorders, found that 50% to 75% of these disorders emerge between the ages of 14 and 24 (Figure 5.1). Another aspect of biological vulnerability for this age group, as documented by contemporary imaging techniques (Giedd, 2004;

Age of Onset of DSM IV Disorders

% Lifetime Cases	25%	50%	75%
Anxiety D/O	Age 6	Age 11	Age 21
Mood D/O	Age 18	Age 30	Age 43
Impulse Control D/O	Age 7	Age 11	Age 15
Substance Use D/O	Age 18	Age 20	Age 27
Any Disorder	Age 7	Age 14	Age 24

FIG 5.1 Select data from Table 3 of Kessler, Bergland, Demler, Jin, and Merikangas (2005), "Lifetime Prevalence and Age-of-Onset Distributions of *DSM-IV* Disorders in the National Comorbidity Survey Replication." For the disorders studied, 50–75% emerge between the ages of 14 and 24. D/O, disorder.

Kambam & Thompson, 2009), is that the brain's center of executive reasoning, the cerebral cortex, is not fully developed until about the age of 25. Thus, many young adults who engage in risky behaviors during college are still in the process of learning to make good choices.

Case Example: Mike

A 21-year-old Caucasian male, Mike was a history major in his junior year of college. During the fall semester, he went to the counseling center accompanied by the resident assistant in his dormitory and his girlfriend, because of concerns that he had been isolating in his room and had been waking up neighboring students at night by knocking on their doors. Mike insisted that he had heard others talking about him and that his name had been called. He had also been avoiding class because he thought other students were talking about him and he was feeling very angry at them. He found it difficult to concentrate. He noted that he had been experiencing the problems for about one month, and found that trips home to visit his family on weekends seemed to calm things. Mike had made a solid transition to college and was on target to do an honors thesis in his major. He had no medical problems, did not use illicit drugs, and drank alcohol in moderation, one night per week. He had not been drinking as of late, to avoid being around others. His affect was flat, but he denied feeling depressed, and he avoided eye contact with the counselor. Mike agreed to start medication and participate in therapy at the counseling center. He gave permission for university counseling center staff to contact his parents. His parents reported that other than being a shy kid, Mike had always been a cooperative youngster who had succeeded at school and had one or two good friends. Mike partially responded to treatment and was able to finish the semester on a reduced schedule. He attended a partial hospital program during the mid-semester break and returned to school for the second semester, but had to take a medical leave of absence for an exacerbation of his symptoms. Mike was eventually diagnosed with schizophrenia. He finished college but struggled with his diagnosis and was concerned for his future.

Young adults are at an age of significant vulnerability for the emergence of major psychiatric illnesses such as schizophrenia, bipolar disorder, and major depression. Appropriate education of resident assistants and the student body in general on recognizing signs of psychiatric illness is useful. Post-identification, the access to expert assessment and treatment services for these illnesses is essential to prevent rapid and fatal deterioration.

Although 18- to 25-year-olds who are not attending college face the same developmental tasks as their college-going peers and have the same age risk-factor for being diagnosed with a new-onset psychiatric disorder, students on college campuses are frequently away from their familiar supports and structure for extended periods of time. Many first-year college students are living with a stranger and sharing a room for the first time in their lives, sometimes with little choice in the decision. They are also in an environment that promotes sleep deprivation. Academic, career, and financial pressures are high. There is reduced adult supervision and easy access to alcohol and drugs. This scenario is likely to precipitate the new onset of a psychiatric disorder or the recurrence of an old one (National Mental Health Association [NMHA] and the Jed Foundation, 2002).

DEMOGRAPHICS

Data from the National Center for Education Statistics (Snyder & Dillow, 2010) indicate that over 19 million students were enrolled in degree-granting institutions in the United States in 2008. This number includes undergraduate students, those enrolled in graduate school, and first-year professional students. Undergraduate students accounted for 16 million of those enrolled. Compared to statistics from the year 2000, this represents an increase of 4 million enrolled students, and it is projected that 21 million individuals will enroll in degree-granting institution by 2016. Based on these numbers alone, one could predict that campus counseling centers across the nation would be faced with an increased demand for services.

College students have also become an increasingly diverse group. The percentage of enrolled minority students increased from 19.6% in 1990 to 33.3% in 2008. During that time period, the percentage of Hispanic students rose from 5.7% to 11.9%; the percentage of Black students rose from 9.0% to 13.5%; and the percentage of Asian or Pacific Islander students increased from 4.1% to 6.8%. The percentage of American Indian/Alaskan Native students remained at about 1% (Snyder & Dillow, 2010).

Students with disabilities have also been participating in post-secondary education activities at higher rates, further increasing diversity on college campuses. In the National Longitudinal Transition Study-2 (Cameto, 2005; U.S. Department of

Education, 2005), a nationally representative sample of more than 11,000 youth ages 13 to 16 who were receiving special education was followed for several years. This cohort of students is now in the 21–24 age range. Compared to a similar cohort established in the late 1980s, participation in post-secondary education among the sample increased by 20%. Based on the accepted federal special education designation categories in use at that time, the percentage of emotionally disturbed (ED) students attending two-year colleges increased 10%, learning disabled (LD) students attending two-year colleges increased 20%, and LD students attending four-year colleges increased 10%.

In addition to ethnicity and educational disability status, there are other aspects of diversity present on campus. The number of foreign students enrolled in colleges in the United States reached 583,000 in 2007, a 21% increase over the prior 10-year period (Villarreal, 2008). Additional data from the National Center for Educational Statistics (Snyder & Dillow, 2010) show that although the majority of enrolled students are between the ages of 18 and 24, older students (25 and older) are substantial in number, accounting for 38% of enrolled students in 2008. Since the late 1970s and early 1980s, women have outnumbered men on college campuses, reaching 57% in 2003. Attendance status (full-time or part-time), sexual orientation, military experience, socioeconomic status, presence of a chronic medical problem, family-of-origin structure, first-generation status (Wang & Castaneda-Sound, 2008), and religious affiliation also contribute to the diversity of the student population of the 21st century.

This diversity hopefully enriches the living and learning atmosphere of institutions of higher education. However, it is precisely this diversity which presents new and significant challenges to universities and their counseling centers. Each group of students brings to campus its own distinct vulnerabilities and needs (Fauman & Hopkinson, 2010). Acculturation issues, differences in help-seeking behaviors, worries about families left behind in other countries or impoverished living situations, and post-traumatic stress reactions as a result of early sexual abuse or military experience are just some of the added concerns complicating an already stressful life transition.

Conversations about mental health may be welcomed in some families and shunned in others. In part, this is reflective of the stigma associated with mental illness and the sociocultural meaning to families of having mental illness. Behavior is an expression of the condition of the person and is understood on a continuum. It is difficult to quantify dysfunction, which is dependent on the threshold used and, to a very large extent, self-disclosure. Mental stress may be expressed in physical symptoms such as headaches and stomachaches, especially in youth of Asian background. Likewise, privacy concerns, loss of face, and non-recognition of functional impairment because of illness are expressed differently by youth from varying ethnic backgrounds (Komiya & Eells, G., 2001; Ting & Hwang, 2009; Yoo & Skovholt, 2001).

Case Example: Lauren

Lauren, a Chinese-American female being treated for major depression with psychotic features (in remission), chose to attend a prestigious university about eight hours from home. She had a close relationship with her family, who had high expectations of her. Despite referrals to the university counseling center and significant preparatory work by the home child psychiatrist, Lauren chose not to connect because of the initial euphoria of becoming independent of her family and home town. Troubles began when her symptoms of depression returned, and the fear of "losing face" with her family for poor grades made her despondent. She turned to alcohol. During one of those binges, she was raped. She could not visualize herself sharing this with anyone given her background; her failure to follow through on the advice of her doctor and "failing her family" led to guilt and a suicide attempt that eventually led to crisis intervention.

This case emphasizes that services within a university should be culturally informed (aware of the cultural issues that impact help-seeking behaviors) and culturally competent (services are offered by providers who understand cultural differences and use that knowledge to create an environment that promotes help-seeking behaviors and identity development in diverse young adults).

MENTAL HEALTH ISSUES ON COLLEGE CAMPUSES

As already noted, adding still another level of complexity to an already diverse population are the increasing numbers of students with pre-existing mental health problems present on college and university campuses (Kitzrow, 2003). In addition to the expected college student difficulties with relationships, homesickness, time management, increased academic demands, and identity concerns, these students present with anxiety, depression, impulse control disorders, learning difficulties, self-harming behaviors, and suicidal ideation. Many have already started one or more psychotropic medications and have a history of psychiatric hospitalizations (Center for Study of Collegiate Mental Health [CSCMH], 2009). Meeting the needs of this growing cohort of students has taxed most college and university counseling centers.

Documentation of the epidemiology and severity of the mental health needs of college students is derived primarily from national surveys of counseling center directors and college students. The National Survey of Counseling Center Directors began monitoring campus and counseling center trends in 1981. Each year, approximately 300 counseling center directors respond to questions about the trends in psychopathology on campus, clinical needs, systems of care, innovative programming, administrative issues, and legal/ethical concerns. The International Association of Counseling Services (IACS), the American College Counseling Association, the Association of

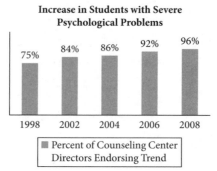

FIG 5.2 Data adapted from the National Survey of Counseling Center Directors, from 1998 to 2008. The bars represent the percentage of counseling center directors who endorsed the trend that in recent years there has been an increase in the number of students with severe psychological problems coming to campus counseling centers.

University and College Counseling Center Directors (AUCCCD), and the University of Pittsburgh have been involved in the survey. (Data from these surveys can be accessed at: http://www.iacsinc.org). In 2006, AUCCCD piloted its own survey with several expanded sections, including those on presenting concerns of clients and outcome measures being used. (Data from these surveys can be accessed at: http://www.aucccd.org).

The data depicted in Figures 5.2–5.5 (Martel, 2009) are taken from the National Survey of Counseling Center Directors, from 1998 through 2008. In 2008, nearly 100% (Figure 5.2) of counseling center directors endorsed the trend that they are seeing more students with severe psychological problems, up from 75% one decade earlier. And, consistently for the past 10 years (Figure 5.3), over 90% of directors reported an increased number of students coming in for counseling who are already on

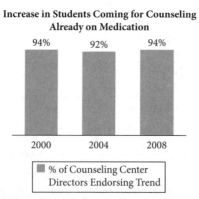

FIG 5.3 Data taken from the National Survey of Counseling Center Directors, from the years indicated. Over 90% of counseling center directors surveyed endorse the trend that the number of students arriving at counseling centers who are already taking psychotropic medication has increased.

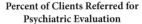

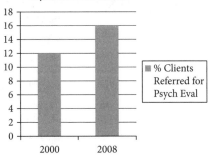

FIG 5.4 Data taken from the National Survey of Counseling Center Directors, from the years indicated. In 2008, counseling center directors estimated that 16% of clients were referred for a psychiatric evaluation, compared to 12% in 2000.

medication. Between 2000 and 2008, 25% more counseling center clients were referred for psychiatric evaluation (Figure 5.4), one indicator of illness severity. The reported percent of *current* clients taking medication increased 35% between 2000 and 2008, and 60% between 1994 and 2008 (Figure 5.5). Despite some limitations with this type of data, it is apparent that the complexity and severity of the mental health needs of students seeking services on campus has trended upward over the past decade. This has impacted the provision of services. On some campuses, there is greater demand for services than there are providers; some campus counseling centers may have part-time psychiatrists or none at all, and caseloads for therapy are often full.

Student surveys corroborate these trends and provide additional information on the numbers of students with mental health needs. The American College Health Association's (ACHA) National College Health Assessment (NCHA), conducted twice annually among a sample of randomly selected college students, provides information

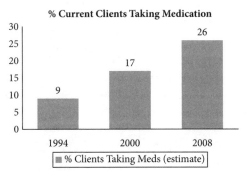

FIG 5.5 Data taken from the National Survey of Counseling Center Directors, from the years indicated. In 2008, counseling center directors estimated that 26% of current clients were on psychiatric medication, compared to 17% in 2000 and 9% in 1994.

on a broad range of student health concerns and health-related behaviors and perceptions. The original NCHA was last conducted in the spring of 2008; it polled 80,121 students on 106 campuses. In the fall of 2008, NCHA II, a revised survey with an expanded section on mental health issues, was introduced; it polled 26,685 students on 40 campuses. The generalizability and validity of these surveys are discussed on the NCHA website (http://www.acha-ncha.org/); the data from these surveys can be found there as well.

In the fall of 2008 (American College Health Association [ACHA], 2009), approximately 20% of students surveyed reported being diagnosed or treated by a professional for mental health problems within the last 12 months (NCHA II). This translates into more than 3.8 million students, based on the total population of students enrolled in degree-granting institutions in 2008 (19 million). The top five disorders reported by students were anxiety (10.4%), depression (10.2%), panic attacks (5.1%), attention-deficit/ hyperactivity disorder (ADHD; 3.6%), and insomnia (3.3%). The percentage of surveyed students reporting bipolar disorder and schizophrenia were 1.4% and 0.3%, respectively. The numbers are impressive. Furthermore, these students, with diverse backgrounds and needs, face the same developmental tasks mentioned earlier in this chapter, which are challenges even for those young adults with no prior psychiatric histories.

In reviewing the data from the 2000 through 2008 NCHA I spring surveys, it is important to note that there were 4 million more enrolled students in 2008 compared to 2000. Therefore, even when the percentage of students endorsing a problem stays essentially the same from one year to the next, the actual *number* of students across the country who have that problem, and who will potentially seek or require clinical services, continues to rise. Figures 5.6 to 5.10 (Martel, 2009) were created using the NCHA I data. In 2008, 15% of students surveyed endorsed ever having been diagnosed

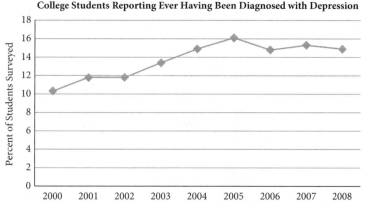

FIG 5.6 Data from consecutive years of the American College Health Association–National College Health Assessment I (ACHA-NCHA I) spring surveys.

College Student Experiences within the Last School Year

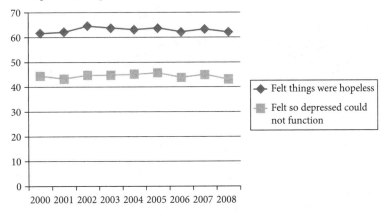

FIG 5.7 Data from consecutive years of the American College Health Association–National College Health Assessment I (ACHA-NCHA I) spring surveys. The y-axis represents the percentage of students surveyed who reported experiencing "feeling things were hopeless" or "feeling so depressed it was difficult to function" within the last school year.

with depression; this represents a 33% increase over the 2000 figure (Figure 5.6). Consistently over the nine-year period of 2000–2008, about 44% of students had felt so depressed in the past school year that it was difficult to function, greater than 60% felt hopeless one or more times (Figure 5.7), 10% had seriously considered suicide, and 1.5% had attempted suicide (Figure 5.8). In the same surveys, when students were asked about which *health conditions* they experienced in the past school year, the proportion of surveyed students experiencing depression remained fairly constant, at

College Student Experiences within the Last School Year

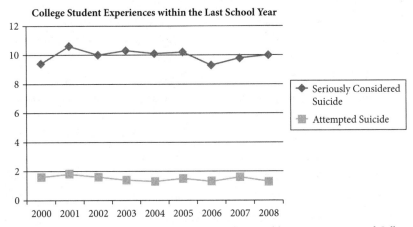

FIG 5.8 Data from consecutive years of the American College Health Association–National College Health Assessment I (ACHA-NCHA I) spring surveys. The y-axis represents the percentage of students surveyed who reported experiencing "seriously considering attempting suicide" or "attempting suicide" within the last school year.

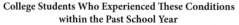

College Students Who Experienced These Conditions within the Past School Year

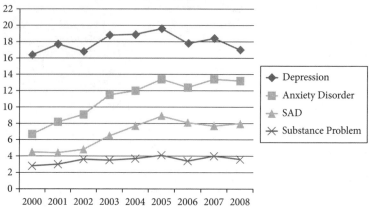

FIG 5.9 Data from consecutive years of the American College Health Association–National College Health Assessment I (ACHA-NCHA I) spring surveys. The y-axis represents the percentage of students surveyed who reported experiencing various health conditions within the last school year. SAD, social anxiety disorder.

17%, whereas those experiencing anxiety nearly doubled, from 6.7% in 2000 to 13.2% in 2008 (Figure 5.9).

Blanco and colleagues (2008) expanded on the survey data and reported that 46% of college students had met criteria for diagnosis of a psychiatric disorder in the preceding 12 months, although only 19% had sought treatment. The authors highlight that the range of psychiatric diagnoses and the prevalence of specific disorders in college students parallel that of the general U.S. population. Similarly, in a longitudinal study of students attending a large university, Zivin, Eisenberg, Gollust, and Golberstein (2009) found that mental health problems were prevalent and persistent over a two-year period and few students received treatment. These findings provide additional evidence of the complex mental health needs of significant numbers of today's college students. Thus, institutions of higher education are challenged to provide services for the full spectrum of psychiatric diagnoses, from the more common disorders of anxiety and depression to eating disorders, substance use disorders, ADHD, and psychosis.

The Healthy Minds Study (HMS) also has surveyed students from across the country but with a more focused look at mental health issues. In addition to studying the prevalence of mental health conditions on college campuses, the HMS (http://www.healthy-mindsstudy.net) is designed to look at campus attitudes toward mental health, barriers and facilitators to seeking mental health services (including stigma), and the impact of various policies, programs, and initiatives. Daniel Eisenberg, the principal investigator, is on the faculty at the University of Michigan School of Public Health and is associated with the University of Michigan Comprehensive Depression Center. The Center for

Student Studies (a division of the Survey Sciences Group) is a research partner in this endeavor. In 2007, 13 schools participated in the study, and in 2009, 15 schools participated in the study. The plan is for this survey to be conducted annually and to have more institutions of higher education participate. Findings from the HMS support and expand on the NCHA data; specific data from the HMS are cited in Chapter 6.

In the fall of 2008, a survey was piloted through the Center for the Study of Collegiate Mental Health (CSCMH), at Penn State University (CSCMH, 2009). The sample consisted of 28,000 students who were receiving services at 66 counseling centers across the country. Figure 5.10 (Martel, 2009) lists the percentage of clients in the CSCMH study endorsing mental health treatment at some time prior to starting college, as well as the percentage of clients reporting concerning behaviors prior to college. Similar, large-scale data from previous years are not available, so trends in client characteristics, from the client perspective, cannot be noted at this time. Still, these data suggest a high level of psychopathology and complexity of mental health issues among counseling center client populations. In addition to looking at the mental health histories of these students, the survey is designed to assess the impact of various protective factors (religion, spirituality, social supports, etc.) and risk factors (trauma, substance abuse) on functioning in the college environment.

To summarize, data from national surveys, in conjunction with population statistics, provide evidence that more students with severe psychopathology are present on

---

CSCMH Survey of Counseling Center Clients

Rates of Mental Health Treatment Prior to College

    Counseling experience 34%

    Psychiatric medications 21%

    Psychiatric hospitalization 6%

    Prior drug or alcohol treatment 3%

Rates of Concerning Behaviors Prior to College

    Non-Suicidal Self-Injury 18%

    Seriously Considered Suicide 19%

    Prior Suicide Attempt 6%

    Seriously considered haring another person 7%

    Intentionally harmed another person 4%

FIG 5.10 Data adapted from the Center for the Study of Collegiate Mental Health (CSCMH) Pilot Study (2009). Students seeking services at campus counseling centers were asked about mental health treatment experiences and personal history of concerning behaviors. Respondents could select only one option out of four ("never," "prior to college," "after starting college," "both"). The percentages in this table were obtained by adding the "prior to college" and "both" categories, thus capturing the percentage of respondents who endorsed mental health treatment and/or concerning behaviors at some time prior to starting college.

college campuses and are in need of services. Also, the number of students seeking counseling for the more routine relationship and adjustment issues is also on the rise. Meeting the complex and changing mental health needs of college students presents many challenges and has been referred to by some as the *crisis* in college student mental health.

POSSIBLE REASONS FOR THE TRENDS

There has been much discussion about the potential factors contributing to the increase in psychopathology and demand for services on college campuses (Grayson & Meilman, 2006; Hunt & Eisenberg, 2010; Kadison & DiGeronimo, 2004; Kitzrow, 2003). The increase in the number of 18- to 24-year olds enrolled in institutions of higher education, linked with the age of vulnerability for new diagnosis of psychiatric disorders in itself accounts for some of the increase in demand for services. Improvements in the diagnosis and treatment of mental health disorders during childhood and adolescence, such as pervasive developmental disorders, ADHD, and mood and anxiety disorders, may be one reason more students with serious disabilities are now able to attend college (Martel, 2009). Furthermore, legislation such as the Americans with Disabilities Act (1990) prohibits discrimination and mandates accommodations for those with documented disabilities, including mental health diagnoses. Transition planning requirements included in amendments to the Individuals with Disabilities Education Act (1997, 2004) have opened up opportunities for special education students, including enrollment in post-secondary education.

As mentioned earlier in this chapter, the diversity of today's college student population may account for some of the increased demand for services. International students, minority students, older students, and students with military experience present with unique vulnerabilities and needs in the context of college life. Kitzrow (2003) and Grayson and Meilman (2006) cite a variety of sociocultural issues that may account for some of the increased pathology and need for services, such as divorce, family dysfunction, instability, poor parenting skills, poor frustration tolerance, violence, early experimentation with drugs, alcohol and sex, poor interpersonal attachments, and pampered youth who lack skills of independence.

Stress has consistently been ranked the number one factor impacting academic performance (ACHA-NCHA surveys). The pervasiveness and sources of stress on college campuses have been evolving and likely impact mental health and the need for services. Increased instability in the world after 9/11, increasing financial burdens, more intense competition, and the omnipresence of technology (Jed Foundation and mtvU, 2006) contribute to the level of stress experienced by today's college students.

In response to the changing mental health needs of college students, college and university counseling centers have created outreach programs and have worked to reduce barriers to treatment (including stigma). The results of these efforts may be reflected in the increased demand for services as well. Also in a positive vein, Stone and Archer (1990) contend that despite ongoing stigma, our society in general is more psychologically sophisticated and open to seeing a mental health professional, resulting in more students seeking services on campus.

THE WORK OF COLLEGE AND UNIVERSITY COUNSELING CENTERS

College and university counseling centers (UCCs) offer a multiplicity of services including mental health treatment, academic and career counseling, consultation to campus constituents, and graduate student training within the college or university environment. The administrative structure of UCCs, the exact services provided, and the physical location of the counseling center on campus are quite variable from one school to the next. Despite this heterogeneity, there are established accreditation standards for university and college counseling centers (International Association of Counseling Services [IACS], 2000).

Several authors have written about the development and evolution of college student mental health services. Heppner and Neal (1983) provide a detailed historical account covering several decades, looking at the problems students have presented to counseling centers, the myriad forces that have shaped counseling centers, the roles counseling centers have played on campus, and trends in the various services provided. In his paper, S. Cooper (2003) more narrowly focused on historical trends in campus consultation activities and proposed an organizational consultation cube model to help prioritize consultation efforts and to understand the impact of those efforts on the campus in general. Stone and Archer (1990) produced a seminal paper on strategic planning for college and university counseling centers for the 1990's. Hodges (2001) and Kitzrow (2003) have examined the challenges facing university and college counseling centers in the 21st century. Kraft (2009) and Barreira and Snider (2010) bring the historical perspective to the present and discuss the use of evidence-based treatments and prevention strategies. Common themes from these articles are highlighted below.

Generally speaking, counseling center functions were initially carried out by school personnel such as advisors, faculty, and deans, with a focus on educational and vocational counseling. Eventually, trained professionals or clinical counselors began to focus on personal counseling in addition to vocational and academic guidance. The role of these professionals was ultimately broadened to include a more ecological approach, acknowledging that outreach programs and consultation services could expand the impact of counselors to the campus community in general. These changes were spurred by a multitude of factors both internal and external to campus communities. Heppner and Neal (1983, p. 81) best summarize this process:

> Counseling centers have the continuous task of making decisions about which of a multitude of potential roles to adopt and which services to provide at a given time. These decisions are often mediated by numerous factors: budgetary and economic factors, staff interests, political climate on the campus, changing consumer demands and needs, external professional issues in the field of counseling psychology, and national as well as world events.

With regard to the 1990s and the new millennium, the authors agree that addressing the needs of the increasing numbers of students with serious psychological problems and the rapidly growing population of minority and nontraditional students would further shape the evolution of college and university counseling centers. Paradigm shifts in the models used by counseling centers of the late 1980s would be required to meet these needs. Optimally, changes in institutional practices and attitudes would parallel the shifts in thinking and practice of UCCs.

For many years, counseling centers focused on personal counseling, addressing normal developmental issues and the transition from late adolescence into early adulthood. This developmental model, which emphasizes self-assessment, self-referral, and ease of entry into the service system, is not fully relevant to the increasingly heterogeneous student body of today (Crego, 1990). As such, many centers have been drawn into complex consultation, training, and outreach roles and have been forced to transition to a medical model with an emphasis on diagnosis and crisis intervention.

The move toward a more clinical/medical model and away from the traditional developmental approach to address the rising numbers of students with serious psychological problems has also involved several philosophical and functional shifts in UCC practice. Utilization of a diagnostic classification system, such as the *Diagnostic and Statistical Manual of Mental Disorders* (American Psychiatric Association, 2013), has become a necessity in understanding the severity and complexity with which many college students present to counseling centers. Examples of these psychiatric illnesses include major depression with psychotic features or even psychosis in which reality testing may be lost and help-seeking behavior minimized. These illnesses pose psychiatric emergencies that cannot be addressed by the usual available resources within a UCC.

In order to address the needs of a more diverse student population, counseling centers have been working to provide more culturally sensitive services and have included marginalized cohorts of students in the planning process (Berg-Cross & Pak, 2006; Crego, 1990; Hodges, 2001; Stone & Archer, 1990). Recruiting a more diverse staff and creating targeted outreach activities to minority groups on campus are two strategies that have been used. Initiatives in staff training that help counselors grasp the impact of sociocultural forces in the origin of psychological problems, coping patterns, and help-seeking attitudes have been undertaken. Smith, Baluch, Bernabei, Robohm, and Sheehy (2003) have advocated for and employed a social justice framework to college counseling center practice.

Over the past two decades, UCCs have been constantly challenged to meet the varying needs of the students and the campus communities they serve. In doing so, they have had to traverse the very complicated terrain of confidentiality laws (discussed in more detail later in this chapter). Counseling centers are challenged to maintain their clinical/therapeutic role and administrative neutrality despite requests for mandated assessments and treatment and opinions on administrative decisions about students (IACS, 2010). In the 2009 National Survey of Counseling Center Directors (Gallagher, 2009), 69% of the counseling center directors surveyed considered "keeping administration informed while protecting student's confidentiality" a present concern. The nature of the therapeutic relationship and encouraging utilization of campus mental health services by students demands that counselors carefully weigh their duties to students, administrators, and the campus in general when making decisions about breaking confidentiality. Counselors confront similar ethical, professional, and legal dilemmas in connection with the parents and families of students they treat.

At the same time, institutions of higher education, referred to here as universities, have been challenged to view campus counseling centers as effective contributors to the educational mission. They have had to reevaluate the institution's responsibility in promoting and maintaining the mental wellness of individual students and other members of the campus environment. In particular, as discussed in Chapter 10, universities are challenged to balance student independence and community safety as well as the role of the university *in loco parentis* for young adults in transition with a hands-off approach toward non-curricular elements of campus life. These issues surface at times of budgetary decisions, when student retention patterns are analyzed and, unfortunately, at times of crises.

The efforts put forth by some UCCs and universities to address mental health issues on campus should be applauded and acknowledged. It is a fact of life that resources will remain limited and choices about which programs and services should be offered at a given time will have to be made. A look at failures in campus systems of care (in the next section) and best practices (Chapter 6) may help guide some of those decisions.

LESSONS FROM VIRGINIA TECH: SYSTEM FAILURES IN COLLEGE MENTAL HEALTH

The unraveling of Seung-Hui Cho's mind during the fall of 2005, his junior year, was evident from the telltale signs of his behavior. Faculty of the English Department reported his dark writings, female peers reported his unwelcome and bizarre contacts, and his suitemates reported his worrisome behaviors. Multiple attempts were made to get Cho to the campus counseling center. Eventually, the situation reached a threshold of concern that led to his overnight commitment to a local psychiatric hospital. For the next 16 months, he received no formal follow-up or care as he went about his life as a college student. The only testimonies post-hospitalization that Cho was a young man in desperate need of help and who might become violent are his writings, which showcased the deep anger and resentment he felt and which he hid even from his parents. Sadly, Cho's story ended in a horrific tragedy.

The question remains: Who was responsible? In a system where there was no clear structure of how to handle aberrant behavior, it is difficult to ascribe clear culpability. The independent panel established to examine the events at Virginia Tech found that the Cook Counseling Center and the Care Team at Virginia Tech failed to provide needed support and services to Cho during a period in late 2005 and early 2006.

The independent panel also identified lack of communication, inadequate services, and misinterpretation of privacy laws as contributing factors in the tragic outcome. Recommendations for remedying these problems are detailed in Chapter 6.

A. Lack of Communication

On campus, students interact with peers, faculty, administrative staff, student advisors, financial aid and human resources staff; with health and mental health clinics when the need arises; and occasionally with law enforcement. Any of these entities may be privy to or gather information about a student that may have relevance to the overall educational functioning or non-educational aspects of life. Aberrant behavior may be detected, but depending on the interpretation of duties, that information may be disseminated to relevant authorities or ignored.

Overall, the Virginia Tech panel's findings state that communication at all levels of the university was faulty. There was a lack of information sharing among administrative, academic, and public safety entities. Was this because there was a concern that the administration would do nothing? Was it that the faculty had no idea what the code of conduct for the university was and did not know the course of action to take? Or was it that faculty and administrators felt that they could not share their observation and assessment of Seung-Hui with each other under confidentiality laws? As discussed in Chapter 4, which examined the chronology of events leading up to the massacre at Virginia Tech, the university lacked a culture that supported recognition of faculty and student complaints regarding aberrant behavior and did not have mechanisms in place to adequately address and communicate about such concerns.

The topic of parental notification of emergency situations involving a student and others whose safety may be threatened also is relevant to this discussion. The very people who had the biggest vested interest in Seung-Hui Cho, his parents, were not contacted when problems arose. Seung-Hui's parents had no idea that their son had talked of suicide and been hospitalized. They were not aware of his many dark compositions, possession of a knife, and stalking of three female students. It was unknown to them that campus police had had several interactions with Seung-Hui and that professors had begged him to get counseling. Virginia Tech and other colleges do notify parents if a child is caught drinking or using drugs; so what is the logic behind the lack of communication with a student's family when talk of suicide, stalking, and involuntary hospitalization take place? Should institutions of higher learning require, not make optional, that students provide to their schools upon registration the name of a trusted relative or other individual, along with that person's contact information, for use in the case of a medical or psychiatric emergency?

Not only do many universities fail to inform parents when their children face serious problems, many schools actively discourage parents from monitoring their children at college. Warnings from college admissions officers about becoming "helicopter parents" are standard during college orientation sessions. Would common sense dictate a middle-of-the-road policy, where students learn to handle the responsibilities that come with their new independence, but parents are alerted to serious problems and emergency situations so they can work with the school and the student on appropriate interventions? If not, what good does it do for colleges to develop effective threat assessment teams (see next paragraph), only to hit a brick wall or wade through time-consuming bureaucratic red tape as serious safety concerns arise and officials need collateral information immediately from parents, guardians, physicians, counselors, or others? A student's pre-college history certainly is relevant to his or her four- or five-year stint in college; in the absence of information, how are informed decisions to be made about potential threats on campus? Perhaps permission to contact a parent under exigent circumstances should be implicit in college admissions paperwork, exceptions being permitted under certain conditions, but then requiring at least one trusted agent to be named and contact information to be provided.

The 2008 General Assembly of Virginia created a law (VA Code § 23-9.2:11) requiring each public institution of higher education in Virginia to establish a violence prevention committee and a threat assessment team. Prior to Virginia Tech, universities in Virginia were not mandated to have any coherent policies to deal with campus-wide threats. The lack of communication among the various players in this tragedy led to disastrous consequences; however, whether it substantively changed the culture and stance of Virginia Tech toward information gathered regarding mental health issues remains unclear. Within eight months of the Seung-Hui Cho incident, another Tech student committed suicide after posting emotionally wrought material on his Internet site, leading to e-mails from his acquaintances to university officials. The officials at Tech did not act on this information (Sturgeon, 2009). Policies may be created, but if not followed in spirit they are of little use.

Post–Virginia Tech, there has been a significant legislative mandate from the General Assembly of Virginia to universities in the public domain in Virginia to establish policies and procedures for violence prevention (VA Code § 23-9.2:10) that include creation of threat assessment teams, crisis intervention teams (VA Code § 9.1-187), written crisis and emergency plans, and emergency notification systems (VA Code § 23-9.2:11). Universities nationwide have observed Virginia and the response of its public universities to develop systems that support sharing of necessary information without compromising student confidentiality and that reduce disasters similar to a Virginia Tech–like scenario. The issue of transferring information about special education status and accommodations and about emotional or mental disturbance or any communicable disease is a significant one and should be debated publicly. It is not uncommon for one school to overlook transferring critical records to another school as the student matures and enters a new stage of development and scholarship. Privacy laws protect most personal information, but some information must be shared—otherwise, why did Seung-Hui's transcript cover sheet include a section on special educational or health-related circumstances? Privacy regulations give the impression that records must be as mute as Seung-Hui's condition rendered him, but what *should* be the rules? It is time to reexamine information sharing with an eye toward public safety, while maintaining reasonable limitations on who can access which files in order to protect an individual's privacy. Before students can begin classes, colleges require proof of immunizations out of concern for contagious disease outbreaks on campus. But other significant threats face students beyond measles, mumps, or polio.

The Family Educational Rights and Privacy Act (FERPA) of 1974 and the regulations which interpret that law allow secondary schools to disclose educational records (including special education records) to a university, but the Americans with Disabilities Act (ADA) prohibits colleges from preadmission inquiries about an applicant's disability. This seems fair: Students should not be stigmatized or denied educational opportunities because of mental or social disability. However, once a student is admitted, perhaps these conditions should be part of the required physical examination form, signed by a physician. This practice would allow colleges to make inquiries on a confidential basis about whether special accommodations are needed or whether particular health or mental health conditions exist. According to 2011 U.S. Department of Education guidelines, students are under no obligation to inform institutions of higher learning that they have a disability, unless, of course, they wish to receive special accommodations (U.S. Department of Education, Office of Civil Rights, 2011). Seung-Hui requested none and did not disclose his emotional disability.

B. Inadequate Care

i. Lack of Assessment and Treatment Capacity

By and large, UCCs are well equipped to deal with crises relating to transition periods in a young person's life, but they are not typically staffed to handle major psychiatric illnesses. For example, a coherent path to accessing psychiatric assessment and follow-up care for these illnesses is often lacking. UCCs appear to generally operate on the assumption that they are well equipped to counsel most students, and the major psychiatric illnesses are so rare that providing staff for them is not necessary. However, it has become clear that members of this minority of the student body with major psychiatric illness may become the cause of sentinel events on campus. Problems that led up to the one at Virginia Tech may have seemed minor when first noted, but when no therapeutic attention was given, it grew into something more serious. Major psychiatric illness causes significant distress and if left untreated can lead to grave consequences.

In exploring these issues with various UCC leaders following the Virginia Tech tragedy, the general consensus is that a positive outcome of the tragedy has been that university administrators have become more attuned to the need to staff counseling centers according to national standards. They have also recognized the limits of the skill set of UCC staff and the need to identify resources within the community that can respond with a higher level of care and the more specialized skills needed to manage severe mental illness. The relationships between UCCs and local and regional resources for evaluative and treatment services vary. In the wake of the Virginia Tech tragedy, the report from the Office of the Inspector General of Virginia (Office of the Inspector General for Mental Health, Mental Retardation & Substance Abuse Services [OIG], 2007) identified a clear paucity of providers who could respond to mental health crises among both adults and children in a timely manner in Virginia.

ii. Lack of Follow-up

There is no evidence that the campus counseling center followed up on Cho after his release from the hospital. There was no attempt to make a functional connection with the home mental health provider Cho said he would see over Christmas break, nor was there follow-up when he returned to campus.

In the wake of the less-than-optimal handling of Seung-Hui Cho by the campus counseling center, the issue of privacy of the individual student and the public safety of peers has polarized university culture and raised the following question: Is it unreasonable to expect a student who is already sending distress signals to seek formal psychiatric help on his own? The usual response of counselors or providers and administrators is that they would be concerned about being paternalistic or intrusive if they approached a student without some overtures on the student's part. Furthermore, the general philosophy of mental health providers is that compliance with treatment recommendations is not optimum if treatment is coerced, forced, or involuntary. While these are relevant concerns, the stigma around mental health and the nature of mental illness (which, when severe enough, leads to suspension of logical thinking and reduces help-seeking behaviors) pose practical concerns about reaching the goal of stabilizing the student to the point that he or she can be a productive member of the student community.

Many universities are reaching out to local and regional mental health providers to expand and complete a system of comprehensive mental health services for their students. As part of this process, communication protocols and guidelines need to be proactively addressed. Improved communication between clinical staff at UCCs and mental health professionals in the community, who share in the care of students from the campus, is essential to a more responsive campus mental health care system.

iii. Inadequate Access to Outpatient Care

College students, like any other group bound together as a community, should have access to a mental health system that is responsive to them when a need arises. In the case of Seung-Hui, the Cook Counseling Center at Virginia Tech "triaged" the young man three times, based on concerns raised by various students and faculty, obtaining little more than basic demographic information in order to flesh out the reasons why the concerns were being raised. Even when his problems caused Seung-Hui to be committed to the hospital and he was brought to the notice of the counseling center, no steps were taken to inform his parents to or follow up with him on his return from Christmas break in January 2006 or throughout the entire spring semester of 2006. Cho continued to have significant difficulty in his classes, experiencing deepening anger, which was manifested in continuation of aggressive themes in his writing. It is important to note and underscore that this young man had similar problems in the wake of the Columbine shooting, which had served to trigger aggressive themes in his prose while in middle school. This was picked up by his teacher and timely treatment served to dissolve his suicidal and homicidal themes, as witnessed by his therapist and family. These were chronicled in his medical record from the center where he was treated while in middle and high school.

Post–Virginia Tech, there has been a great deal of discussion about the need for crisis stabilization units (CSUs). CSUs do have a place in the system of care as a venue for an emergency intervention, but they should not be the primary focus of reform. We would propose that while responsive to the immediate crisis, CSUs are a high-expense venture and are inappropriate as structures where continued recovery is the goal. The focus ought to be on low-end outpatient care that is visible on campus and easily accessible, and that builds on the natural resilience and strengths of the individual. UCCs must allow for the management of potential emergencies through memorandums of understanding (MOUs) with community providers who can partner with them on a contractual basis. Rather than wait lists, these MOUs should facilitate quick access to care.

Identifying contracted providers that specialize in particular illnesses can be a useful way to enhance the depth of expertise that exists within the counseling center itself, with its focus on adjustment reactions, transition assistance, and mild depression. At Virginia Commonwealth University, we forge relationships with therapists who have specific skills in areas such as cognitive-behavior therapy, trauma work, and gay and lesbian issues, and we are able to get referrals seen in an expedient way.

C. Misinterpretation of Privacy Laws

The Health Insurance Portability and Accountability Act (HIPAA) of 1996 (Office for Civil Rights [OCR], 2000, 2003) is a federal law set by the U.S. Department of Health and Human Services that governs the privacy of health information and regulates the sharing of this information from the provider to any entity. The Family Educational Rights and Privacy Act (FERPA, or the Buckley amendment), a provision set by the U.S. Department of Education (FERPA, 2010), relates to the privacy afforded to all educational records; these records cannot be released without explicit permission of the student or under certain circumstances. The overlap of both these laws is seen on college campuses and applies to a student who becomes ill. The specter of violating HIPAA or FERPA and the ensuing threat of litigation is often cited as the major reason why providers and educators have felt constrained to gather or share information about a student or patient. Although the elements of the law are not unreasonable, the myths that surround it make some providers or educators err on the side of caution and therefore fail to gather collateral information from other sources to determine the pertinent issues and the best approach that can be achieved through consensus; they fail to consider how additional information can inform the outcome.

Perhaps the most hotly debated issue from the position of the university counseling centers is the slippery slope of what should be shared and with whom and at what point the student body begins to lose confidence in the privacy afforded them within the frame of the doctor–patient relationship or the educator and student relationship. The Virginia Tech tragedy highlighted the perhaps extreme heights to which HIPAA and FERPA may have been taken. Had the communication between the faculty, students, counseling center, law enforcement, and administration been based on common-sense principles, perhaps Seung-Hui Cho would have received the scrutiny that he did not receive. Even though the symptoms of his unraveling thought processes were evident to all around him, there was no viable mechanism to connect the dots of his odd, bizarre, and fearsome behaviors and insist on intervention.

Within the hospital setting post-commitment, the physician who evaluated Seung-Hui focused on his mental status at that given moment. Had additional information been gathered to flesh out the picture of what was concerning to Seung-Hui's suitemates or others that eventually led to the hospitalization, perhaps the alarm bells would have rung in the psychiatrist's mind and his assessment of Seung-Hui might have been more comprehensive. Knowing the impending winter break and the lack of college supports, perhaps he would have involved Seung-Hui's parents. As a rationale for the brevity of his assessment, the psychiatrist cited HIPAA concerns for not obtaining collateral information, the lack of time available for each evaluation, and, finally, the paucity of resources around the area to make recommendations for ongoing and continued care.

Health histories are another matter for discussion. To what extent should practitioners take at face value denials of previous mental illness from the patient if there is reason to suspect earlier problems and if the patient has an incentive to hide the truth? The failure at St. Albans to obtain corroboration from other key sources (other doctors, parents, campus police, etc.) and seek out collateral information about Seung-Hui's mental health history led to underdiagnosis and a failure to recognize that his emotional state had been problematic for most of his life. Central to that problem were procedural rules that prevented sufficient time to conduct anything more than a relatively superficial health history analysis.

The Tech incident casts a bright light on the fallacies surrounding both HIPAA and FERPA. A summary of the actual guidelines for HIPAA and FERPA is outlined in Table 5.1.

In the case of Seung-Hui Cho, his strange behaviors should have invoked FERPA exceptions: As a dependent child, disclosure to his parents was permissible; disclosure to law enforcement was permissible because of safety issues; Virginia Tech administration could have been informed about the fact that one of their students had been committed to the hospital. (Within a commitment hearing, the name and fact of a

Table 5.1 Summary of HIPAA and FERPA

HIPAA

Exceptions for the release of information under HIPAA, which apply to all health care providers:

- If the patient asks for release of information that pertains to him or her
- When necessary for care and to allow communication between providers for treatment
- To the guardian of the incapacitated person
- When the person makes a threat to another person

FERPA

- Only applies to educational records and applies to all federally funded programs; does not apply to private institutions. Under FERPA the school cannot release records except by permission of parents (K–12) or students (>18 years old).
- Does not include personal observations which can be freely disclosed: if a faculty member observes aberrant behavior, they can freely discuss this with fellow faculty, the dean of students, etc.
- FERPA restricts any use or disclosure of medical records maintained by schools.
- FERPA *does not* apply to campus police records created and maintained for law enforcement purposes. (Following the incident at Virginia Tech, there has been a growing appreciation of the role of law enforcement on campus to keep its mission and role distinct from the educational mission of the university. This allows the campus police to act freely on information it gathers without being bound by FERPA and to communicate with the university personnel when dangerous situations evolve.)
- If law enforcement creates a record to be used in student disciplinary proceedings, FERPA applies to the records.

Exceptions to FERPA:

Records can be released to:

- Parent who claims an adult student as dependent
- Parent when the student is in a health or safety emergency
- Parent of a student under 21 if there is an alcohol or controlled-substance violation
- School officials and teachers (appropriate persons): records of disciplinary action taken against students for conduct that poses a significant risk to the safety or well-being of that student or school community (to protect the health or safety of that student or other persons)
- Law enforcement, mental health and medical services, courts, child- and family-serving agencies within the juvenile justice system

---

hearing are not confidential information.) Virginia Tech administration could also have been given a police department report (transportation and detention information is not confidential). Moreover, Cho's behaviors should have invoked HIPAA exceptions: Carillion Hospital could have shared information with Cook Counseling Center and the Community Services Board, the local mental health agency, to facilitate treatment.

This case illustrates the need to assemble accurate guidance for organizations and individuals with a stake in student behavior, as there has been the tendency to over-interpret the law. There has also been action to amend certain provisions in FERPA prompted by the Virginia Tech tragedy. On January 8, 2009, significant changes to the FERPA regulations went into effect. Rinehart-Thompson (2009) provides an overview of these changes.

The final FERPA regulation consists of three broad categories:

(1) *Amendments to school safety disclosures* (health and safety emergencies and disclosures to parents)
(2) *Improved access to education data* for research and accountability, and
(3) *Safeguarding privacy and education records*.

Receiving the greatest level of attention were the changes related to health and safety emergencies, which now allow greater flexibility in sharing information from a student's education record. According to Section 34 CFR 99.36, educational agencies and institutions are now permitted to disclose personally identifiable information, without consent, from education records to appropriate parties, including parents, whose knowledge of the information is necessary to protect the health and safety of the student or others. Institutions are allowed to share information with parents regarding the college student if a student is a dependent on the parents for federal income tax purposes and to all parents if an issue of health or safety emergency exists. This broader language gives higher institutions much more discretion to share information about a potential health or safety emergency and has significantly reduced the fear of being penalized for wrongful disclosure.

Reconciling FERPA and HIPAA

Information relating to a student's health, including a student health record, may be contained within a student's school record, prompting questions about the applicability of the HIPAA privacy rule to this information. However, student health information is generally not subject to HIPAA privacy rule requirements. The student's health information, if maintained by a school that receives Department of Education funds, will be subject to FERPA and will meet the definition of "education record" or "treatment record." Both education and treatment records are excluded from HIPAA coverage and are subject to FERPA. Of particular interest, if FERPA applies to the post-secondary institution, the student records maintained by health clinics that are operated by such an institution will qualify as either education or treatment records under FERPA, because the health clinic provides health care services on behalf of the institution and with regard to the individual's status as a student. HIPAA will not apply.

In contrast, students who are treated at university hospitals associated with the university are not subject to FERPA. In this situation, the hospital does not provide health care services to students either on behalf of the institution or with regard to the individual's status as a student. FERPA will not apply, and the HIPAA privacy rule will. Schools that do not receive Department of Education funds and do not meet the definition of a HIPAA-covered entity are not required to comply with requirements of either law. Once it is determined that a health record meets the requirements of FERPA, HIPAA, both laws, or neither law, a determination may be made regarding the sharing of information with relevant parties, particularly where the health and safety of individuals are at stake (Rinehart-Thompson, 2009).

Though the primary focus of a university is education and learning, both physical and mental health issues are part and parcel of student well-being. There are a large number of individuals with serious mental illness who attend college and are functional. Universities have variable degrees of sophistication in handling aberrant behavior in students and faculty. An understanding of the socioethnic demographics and the varied extracurricular needs of a student body, including those of physical and mental wellness, can be a starting point for the college administrator who is planning to make changes in policy.

In the wake of the Virginia Tech tragedy, mental illness, its consequences, and specifically the potential for violence have enthralled the American people. It is imperative that we maintain an awareness of the danger that this heightened focus on mental illness could have on admission to universities, if it dictates screening out those with mental illness. During the period of the Virginia Tech panel's investigation, communications were received from parents who had essentially been asked to take children home who had sought help from the counseling center at Virginia Tech for certain illnesses, namely depression and substance abuse. This information was not part of the panel report but came to the attention of panel members during the investigation. The events that led to these directives from the university had occurred prior to the tragedy, except for one instance of stalking of a female by a male peer, which was current and under investigation. These parents were irate and felt that the university had abandoned their children and was ostracizing them for having treatable mental health problems, depriving them of an educational opportunity. Although investigation of these reports was not part of the panel's work, the quantity and quality of the complaints gave the panel a sense of the unwritten and unpublicized nature of the culture within the university that may have contributed to the failures of the Cook Counseling Center.

The idea of using mental illness as a variable in admission considerations to universities did come up as a possible recommendation in the panel report. There were discussions about why we obtained information about physical illnesses and even immunization status but not mental illness as part of the admission process. Should the student be obligated to provide this information? Should the information be obtained and kept in a sealed envelope, only to be opened if concerns came up? Just as it would be unreasonable to expect an entire student body to have no physical ailments, similarly, it would be untenable to expect that no student on campus would have mental health issues. Although no particular decision came out of that line of inquiry in the panel's work, it does raise an awareness of how ubiquitous these problems are, and how potentially dangerous they can become if not addressed proactively.

Stigma, lack of communication, inadequate services, and misinterpretation of privacy laws are causes of the less-than-optimal function of our campus mental health systems. The assumption that we cannot prevent every negative outcome is correct. However, when we do observe warning signs they need to be taken seriously, even if the subsequent quest to uncover the information yields nothing. Ultimately, any university that will successfully grapple with and develop effective structures for handling mental health issues will have to address stigma, by allowing easy access to appropriate care without fear of reprisals, such as academic probation or discrimination based on mental illness.

For universities, development of individualized approaches to today's growing diverse student body is going to be a challenge. Screening out for mental illness is not a solution; given the high incidence of diagnosable and treatable mental disorders in the college-entering population, enormous talent would be forfeited. The solution is in the creation of rational policies to handle mental illnesses within the university that are based on a reasonable understanding of the magnitude and the characteristics of the problems in the mental health arena. A viable approach would be to adopt and promote "mental wellness" as an institutional value and an integral part of campus life, to reduce stigma and increase recognition of impairment. Coupled with adequate access to optimum services, this would reduce the overall morbidity from these disorders.

6

BEST PRACTICES AND RESOURCES
NATIONAL MODELS FOR COLLEGE STUDENT
MENTAL HEALTH

Adele L. Martel and Aradhana Bela Sood

Most colleges and universities have come to recognize that campus mental wellness is vital to achieving their academic missions and have made efforts to improve their mental health services. This involves creating a culture that espouses tolerance of differences, including recognition of mental illness as an eminently treatable entity; recognition and differentiation of adjustment stress from serious mental illnesses; identification of intervention approaches to the entire spectrum of emotional and behavioral disorders; and, most importantly, resource development, both within the university and off campus, that can support access for intervention. Because colleges and universities are varied in their size, geographic location, diversity, administrative structure, availability of resources, and crisis exposure, the process of developing a campus mental wellness plan will be unique to each institution. However, there are common principles that should guide each school as it builds and fortifies its mental health services.

This chapter begins with a brief review of the impact of mental health issues on the individual student and the campus community. We then describe principles and concepts to guide campus wellness planning, such as systems of care, ethical and legal considerations, prevention, and evidence-based practices. We present a strategic approach to altering campus culture and attitudes toward the mental health needs of students. These are followed by a closer look at program development in two areas that are key to campus wellness planning and the overall promotion of mental health on campus: (1) suicide prevention and (2) transition planning for students with already diagnosed mental illnesses.

IMPACT OF MENTAL HEALTH ISSUES
ON COLLEGE CAMPUSES

The prevalence and severity of mental health concerns on college campuses across the country have been documented in various studies and surveys and were described in some depth in the previous chapter. For the individual student, these mental health issues clearly have a negative impact on academic and social functioning. In the spring 2010 American College Health Association National College Health Assessment (ACHA-NCHA) II survey (ACHA, 2010a), 6 of the top 10 factors listed by students as affecting their individual academic performance were of a psychological/emotional nature (Figure 6.1). There are also data that associate psychiatric disorder with truncated educational attainment (Breslau, Lane, Sampson, & Kessler, 2008; Hunt, Eisenberg, & Kilbourne, 2010; Kessler, Foster, Saunders, & Stang, 1995; Lee et al., 2009), which in turn affects the individual's job choices and future earning potential. Distressed students impact the overall college experience of peers as well, particularly roommates and classmates. On a larger scale, a student suicide or homicide has repercussions through the entire college community with concerns of security and safety.

In their book, *College of the Overwhelmed*, Kadison and DiGeronimo (2004) make a poignant and convincing case for the development of strong mental health services by colleges and universities. They describe how individual students, the entire student body, and the institution itself benefit from the philosophical and fiscal commitment to providing such services. The discussion is approached from the view of a college's

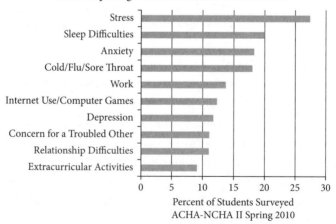

FIG 6.1 Data taken from the spring 2010 American College Health Association National College Health Assessment II, which surveyed 95,712 students at 139 schools. Impacting academic performance was defined as "received a lower grade on an exam, or an important project; received a lower grade in the course; received an incomplete or dropped the course; or experienced a significant disruption in thesis, dissertation, research, or practicum work."

academic mission, ethical and legal concerns, financial liabilities,and marketing inter-ests, as well as the institution's responsibility to society at large.

Former *Time* magazine editor and author Garrett Seaman comes to a similar con-clusion, that it is time colleges and universities renewed their commitment to responsi-bility for the personal safety and well-being of the student body, based on his intensive investigation into college life as detailed in his 2005 book, *Binge*. Drawing from two years spent interviewing students and living in the dorms at a dozen top-rated uni-versities, he brings to light the truth of today's college experience and the immense pressures—academic, social, and emotional—those students are experiencing. His book also reveals how the institutions themselves succeed or fail in preventing and mitigating the rising incidence of behavioral and mental health problems on campuses throughout North America.

CHANGING THE CAMPUS CULTURE

In planning campus systems of care for mental wellness, the overarching goal is to cre-ate a caring, connected community. All campus constituents—administrators, faculty, staff, mental health providers, students, and parents—need to be committed to and responsible for "a safe, caring, cooperative, and well-managed learning environment" (Cooper, 2008) within which the centrality of mental health to the academic success of the student is recognized. Collaboration and communication among all constituents are vital to the success of any campus-wide program.

The spate of recent school shootings serve to underscore the value of develop-ing programs that embrace a culture of openness about mental health programming. Counseling centers should be actively creating short-term and intermediate-term plans of change with an evolving vision for the future. These plans must involve insti-tutional leadership, or the role and work of counseling centers will remain marginal-ized within the university and changing the campus culture will not be achieved. One strategy is to seek an audience with key leaders who have the power to change policy and the capability to innovate, and who are receptive to the idea that holistic health of a student is vital to success within the university. Identifying champions within the campus leadership who can support programs that promote mental health on campus should be an ongoing effort.

Another strategy is to have a counseling center clinician or administrator rep-resented in the university leadership group to articulate the mental health needs of students and keep the issues of the counseling center on the radar of the university. Still another strategy is for campuses to consider forming case management or care teams, multidisciplinary coalitions of health care providers (primary care providers, psychologists, psychiatrists, disabilities specialists) as the "first circle" of intervention

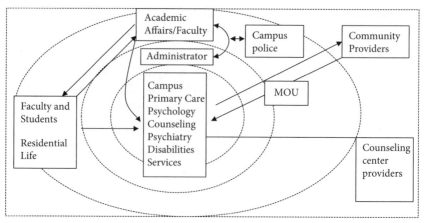

FIG 6.2 Circles of care within a campus. MOU, memorandum of understanding.

to monitor and support students at risk for various health problems (Figure 6.2). As part of this strategy, the "strength" of alliances with primary care needs to be gauged. If the relationship is minimal, then it requires strengthening by formalizing reporting structures. The next concentric circle would include administrators who can support the inner circle administratively and function as the liaison to the academic affairs/ faculty team. This structure would be linked to a cadre of providers within or outside the campus.

Moreover, the active promotion of a positive, engaged, and supportive campus culture has to occur simultaneously with the collaborative establishment of an enforceable campus code of conduct. This code of conduct, applicable to faculty, staff, and students alike, should specify communication pathways to the administration and a protocol for closure feedback to the individual reporting the concern or infraction to encourage adherence to the code of conduct (Sood, 2009a; see also Chapter 7 in this book). That is to say, all campus constituents should be educated around what is and what is not aberrant behavior. They should be comfortable discussing behaviors that concern them and know to whom to report the behavior and what to expect in return. For concerns about students, the Dean of Student Affairs generally handles such matters; for concerns about faculty, reports are typically made to the Dean of Faculty; for concerns about staff, reports are typically made to Human Resources (Figure 6.3). For students, the ensuing triage is usually conducted by university committees that determine whether the presenting problem is a disciplinary, academic, mental health, or law enforcement issue; similar proceedings could apply to faculty and staff. It is important that action is taken to resolve the issue. (Post–Virginia Tech, one of the lessons learned was the need to create a feedback loop to the concerned faculty, informing them that an action had been taken and that their continuing responsibility was to hold the student accountable to the code of conduct for the university.)

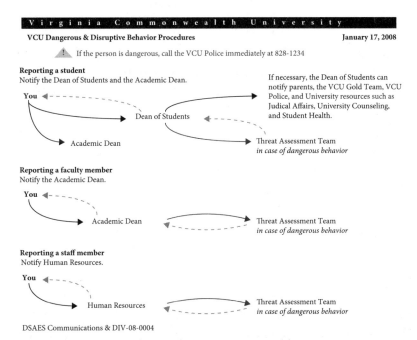

FIG 6.3 Looping communication between disparate systems: A model.
From Dangerous and disruptive behavior reporting framework (Division of Student Affairs & Enrollment Services, Virginia Commonwealth University, 2008)

KEY PRINCIPLES IN PROGRAM DEVELOPMENT

The establishment of a comprehensive campus mental health plan requires several steps (Davidson, Eells, Marchell & Silverman, 2008; Davidson, Hull, & Schaefer, 2008; Davidson, Moses, Silverman, & Spencer-Thomas, 2009; DiFulvio & Rutz, 2009). The institution must first identify problem areas and establish priorities. The Healthy Minds Study, described in Chapter 5, is a questionnaire/survey designed to provide such information to participating schools on mental health issues on their campuses (http://www.healthymindsstudy.net). Then, following a needs assessment, which includes an inventory of currently available resources, strategies are selected and programs are enhanced or developed. The programs or activities are then implemented. An evaluation is conducted at some designated time point to assess outcomes of the intervention(s) and for quality improvement. In addition to these concrete steps, the principles of community systems of care (Winters & Pumariega, 2007) should be adapted and utilized to inform the planning process (see Appendix, Table 1). Although they refer to the child and family unit, they can be modified to be used in the college setting, as they embrace principles that are client centered. Of particular importance to the college-aged population are the systems of care principles that emphasize the characteristics described next.

Developmentally Oriented

As discussed in Chapter 5, college-aged individuals face many significant developmental challenges, including separation-individuation, identity formation and solidification, and achievement of intimacy. Developmentally informed programming and treatment can help students navigate these developmental tasks. This concept includes being attuned to the nature of the college experience in the new millennium (Seaman, 2005), with its academic and career pressures and social pressures regarding body image, sex, sleeping habits, and use of alcohol and drugs. Mental health professionals working with college-aged students should be well-versed in human development and the organization of the university system.

Culturally Competent

The demographic changes in the college student population, with regard to all aspects of diversity (ethnicity, race, gender, age, disability status, religion, etc.), underscore the need for programming and services to be culture and diversity sensitive.

Evidence-Based

When available, programs and treatments shown to be effective with a college-aged population should take priority in the planning process, especially in the context of budgetary constraints. Evidence-based practices from other populations may be modified for use with the college-aged population as long as the nature of the college experience is taken into consideration (developmentally vulnerable population, built-in discontinuities in treatment with semester and summer breaks, the vicissitudes of the academic year with mid-terms and finals, complex privacy laws, etc.). Practices based on an empirically defined need, those which adhere to national and community standards, and those based on empirically derived models can also be prioritized.

Address Relevant Ethical Issues

Awareness and application of ethical principles to the development of a campus mental health wellness plan should guide policy development and program selection. The ethical issues of prime importance are beneficence, autonomy, and justice (Francis, 2003). *Beneficence* has to do with the principle of doing good and avoiding harm and respecting the dignity of clients. *Autonomy* has to do with the rights of self-determination and includes the concept of informed consent. *Justice* involves not only the fair distribution of services but also the sense of fair procedures.

Compliant with Legal Statutes

Knowledge and understanding of legal statutes such as FERPA and HIPAA and how these laws apply to the educational setting should also inform planning for campus mental wellness and policy development. Recommendations regarding the sharing of information under FERPA and HIPAA are reviewed in Chapter 5.

Incorporate a Public Health Approach

The field of public health has long recognized the importance of health promotion and prevention in controlling a health problem. In developing campus mental wellness plans, colleges, universities, and their counseling centers will need to include programs and activities that span the entire spectrum of prevention, treatment, and maintenance. The public heath approach is elaborated on later in this chapter.

Training of Mental Health Professionals

As a brief aside, these same principles and characteristics have implications for the training of mental health professionals working with the college-aged student population (Davar, 2010; Kay & Schwartz, 2010). In addition to knowledge of, and skills with, best practices in assessment, diagnosis, and treatment, it is necessary for these practitioners to understand the legal and ethical issues pertinent to this population. Attitudes that are developmentally informed and culturally sensitive are also essential. Training of psychologists and social workers has been ongoing in college and university counseling centers. Psychiatry residents can elect to rotate in university counseling centers. There are two fellowship programs in college student mental health for psychiatrists, one at Ohio State University and the other at the University of Chicago; Yale University does such training on a less formalized basis (T. Kramer, personal communication, 2010). Child and adolescent psychiatrists, by virtue of their unique training and collaborative natures, are well-suited to understanding and treating the diverse problems of the college student population.

In the following text we demonstrate the use of these protocols, models, and concepts in developing plans for suicide prevention on campus and college transition planning for students with already diagnosed mental illnesses.

SUICIDE

Suicide is a complex behavioral manifestation of multiple biological, psychological, social, and cultural risk factors. When a student commits suicide, family members, friends, the campus community, and often the community at large are significantly impacted. Suicide taps into many core professional, legal, and ethical issues, including questions about prevention and protection and the role of the university *in loco parentis*. The prevention of suicide in the college-age population is a major mental health concern on college and university campuses across the country.

Suicide is the third leading cause of death for 15- to 24-year-olds in the United States and the second leading cause of death among college-aged students. The Big Ten Suicide Study (Silverman, Meyer, Sloane, Raffel, & Pratt, 1997) found that the overall student suicide rate was 7.5 per 100,000 students on Midwestern university campuses. Based on the projection that approximately 20 million students (undergraduates, graduate students and first-year professional students) will be enrolled in degree-granting institutions in the United States between 2011 and 2013, the anticipated number of college student suicides per year is approximately 1,500.

Mood difficulties, suicidal ideation, and suicide attempts are even more common. A recent study (Drum, Brownson, Denmark, & Smith, 2009) found that 6% of undergraduates and 4% of graduate students had seriously considered suicide in the past 12 months. Recent data from the ACHA-NCHA II indicated that within the last 12 months 45.6% of students felt things were hopeless; 30.7% felt so depressed it was difficult to function; 6.2% of students seriously considered suicide; 5.3% intentionally cut, burned, bruised, or otherwise injured themselves; and 1.3% attempted suicide (ACHA, 2010a). The profile of students who actually sought counseling center services at 66 colleges and universities during the fall of 2008 included 10% with a history of non-suicidal self-injury, 14% who seriously considered suicide, and 3% with a prior suicide attempt (Center for the Study of Collegiate Mental Health, 2009).

Risk factors for suicide and attempted suicide have been widely recognized and published. They include previous suicide attempts, having a psychiatric diagnosis, feelings of hopelessness, interpersonal conflicts or loss (relational, social, work, financial), impulsive or aggressive tendencies, family violence including physical and sexual abuse, family history of suicide and mental disorders, medical problems (typically chronic), and easy access to lethal means. Though less well-studied, protective factors include easy access to care and support for help-seeking, effective clinical care for mental and physical disorders, adaptive problem-solving and conflict resolution skills, a sense of connectedness (family, peers, community), and cultural or religious beliefs that support self-preservation (Centers for Disease Control and Prevention [CDC], 1999). Information is available from various sources, including epidemiological survey data, descriptive studies, and evidence-based literature, which can help guide institutions of higher education in planning for campus-wide mental wellness programs and suicide prevention.

In the United States, over 90% of those who commit suicide at any age have at least one diagnosable psychiatric illness, most commonly a mood disorder, substance abuse disorder, and/or anxiety disorder (Jed Foundation, 2006). Specifically regarding college students, an analysis of data from the 1995 National College Health Risk Behavior Survey (Brener, Hassan, & Barrios, 1999) found a clear association between substance use and suicidal ideation and behavior among college students. Students who had considered suicide in the previous 12 months were significantly more likely to engage in use of tobacco, alcohol, marijuana, and/or cocaine. Furthermore, in the National Epidemiologic Survey on Alcohol and Related Conditions, 20% of college students, aged 18–24, met criteria for alcohol abuse or dependence; only 5% of these students sought help for alcohol problems in the year preceding the survey (Blanco et al., 2008). In the same study, over 10% of students met criteria for a mood disorder and over 12% for an anxiety disorder. This information tells us that a plan for suicide prevention on college campuses must include identification and treatment of students with psychiatric disorders and that a coherent policy regarding substance use and abuse on campus should be devised and implemented.

A recently published study examined the entire suicidal continuum, from passive suicidal thinking to multiple attempts, for over 26,000 undergraduate and graduate students at 70 U.S. colleges and universities (Drum et al., 2009). The results highlighted the impact of academic stress, relationship difficulties, and connectedness in the suicidal continuum. Two-thirds of those who disclosed suicidal ideation did so to a peer (romantic partner, roommate, or friend). Students who sought professional help were less likely to attempt suicide than those who did not seek help. This interesting and unique study has wide-ranging implications for prevention and intervention, including the role of peers and the importance of providing opportunities for students to connect with others.

Data on help-seeking and access to mental health care are also crucial to the development of comprehensive campus mental health programs. As mentioned previously, less than 25% of college students meeting criteria for a psychiatric disorder sought treatment, with the percentages varying across different disorders (Blanco et al., 2008). As part of a Web-based survey, Eisenberg, Golberstein, and Gollust (2007) looked at mental health service use by students with positive screens for anxiety and depression. Depending on the disorder, 37%–84% of students with positive screens did not receive treatment. Predictors of not receiving services included a lack of perceived need, being unaware of services and insurance coverage, skepticism about treatment effectiveness, low socioeconomic background, and being Asian or Pacific Islander. Other studies have found that culture of origin, male sex, living off campus, and fewer years in college were barriers to seeking services (Yoo & Skovholt, 2001; Yorgason, Linville, & Zitzman, 2008). These data show that education about the signs and symptoms of mental illness, marketing of available resources, and outreach to particular subpopulations is essential to a comprehensive campus mental wellness plan.

In 1996, the Air Force implemented "a community-wide suicide prevention program aimed at decreasing stigma, enhancing social networks, facilitating help-seeking through system level policy changes, and enhancing understanding of mental health" (Knox et al., 2003). The program was based on 11 initiatives, which included leadership involvement, community education and training, and an integrated delivery system. Trend analysis over a six-year period revealed a 33% risk reduction for completed suicide. Colleges and universities seeking to develop and/or rework their policies and procedures for working with suicidal students can apply aspects of this model to the campus system, as it highlights the importance of changing social norms, reducing stigma, and inclusion of all constituents. The program is listed in the Substance Abuse and Mental Health Services Administration's (SAMHSA's) National Registry of Evidence-Based Practices (http://www.sprc.org/featured_resources/bpr/standards.asp). This study suggests that a comprehensive, campus-wide plan for suicide prevention that is based on a public health approach could be successful, and that responding to traumatic events, including completed suicides, should be part of the plan.

TAKING A PREVENTIVE APPROACH

The public health classification system of disease prevention traditionally describes three types of prevention: primary, secondary, and tertiary prevention. It is generally considered that *primary prevention* is the prevention of a disease before it occurs and includes health promotion and activities to protect against the development of disease. *Secondary prevention* is the prevention of recurrences or exacerbations of a disease and often involves screening, early detection, and early intervention. *Tertiary prevention* is the reduction in the amount of disability associated with a particular disorder to achieve the highest level of function. In practice, the boundaries between primary, secondary, and tertiary prevention measures are not always clear. The Institute of Medicine (IOM) (1994) suggested an expansion of this scheme when planning and studying public health initiatives for mental health disorders. This scheme, pictured in Figure 6.4, includes (1) prevention, (2) treatment, and (3) maintenance. Prevention efforts are further defined as *universal* (targeted to an entire population group), *selective* (targeted to individuals or a subgroup of the population whose risk of developing a mental illness is higher than average), and *indicated* (targeted to high-risk individuals

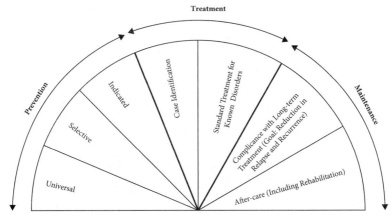

FIG 6.4 The mental health intervention spectrum for mental disorders (Institute of Medicine, 1994).

who have minimal but detectable signs, symptoms, or markers for a mental disorder). This last category is similar to early recognition and early intervention and the more classic secondary prevention.

According to the U.S. Department of Health and Human Services (1999), "treatment refers to the identification of individuals with mental disorders and the standard treatment for those disorders, which includes interventions to reduce the likelihood of future co-occurring disorders and maintenance incorporates what the public health field traditionally defines as some forms of secondary and all forms of tertiary prevention." In order to emphasize the importance and breadth of a public health approach to suicide prevention on college campuses, the best practices described next are labeled as primary, secondary, or tertiary prevention strategies.

BEST PRACTICES IN SUICIDE PREVENTION ON CAMPUS

A comprehensive approach to suicide prevention and mental health promotion on college and university campuses was proposed by the National Mental Health Association and the Jed Foundation (2002) subsequent to a roundtable discussion attended by experts from various fields. This plan has many features in common with the Air Force Program. Figure 6.5 (Davidson, Eells, et al., 2008) is a schematic of the key elements of this program, which targets both the general campus population and students at risk. This model uses a population-based, public health approach and incorporates many of the key system-of-care principles previously discussed. The rationale behind a public health approach was proven by the success of the Air Force Program and was addressed by Drum et al. (2009). The model has been elaborated on and updated by various organizations and authors (Davidson & Locke, 2010; Drum et al., 2009;

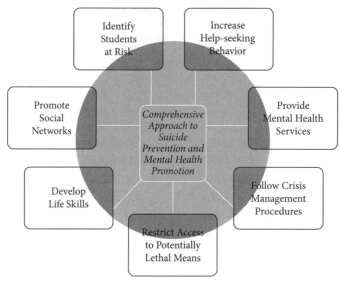

FIG 6.5 The Jed Foundation/Suicide Prevention Resource Center comprehensive approach to suicide prevention and mental health promotion (Davidson, Eells, et al., 2008).
Reprinted with permission from Reducing Risks for Mental Disorders: Frontiers for Prevention Intervention Research, 1994, by the National Academy of Sciences, Courtesy of the National Academies Press, Washington, DC.

Fassler, 2008; Grayson & Meilman, 2006; Jed Foundation, 2006; Jed Foundation and Suicide Prevention Resource Center, 2009; Kadison & DiGeronimo, 2004; Silverman, 2008; Stone & Archer, 1990; Suicide Prevention Resource Center [SPRC], 2004); their work is synthesized in the next sections. What follows is a list of the seven key areas for program development defined by this model, a brief description of the goal(s) to be addressed in each area, and some examples of programs and strategies used by institutions of higher education to address those goals. The Jed Foundation and SPRC (2009) note: "Campus planners are cautioned to ensure that adequate institutional capacity exists and that linkages to community services are in place before they create programs that will significantly increase the numbers of students seeking services."

Develop Life Skills (Primary Prevention)

The goals of life skills development are to "improve students' management of the rigors of college" and negative life events by equipping them with "tools to recognize and manage triggers and stressors" (Jed Foundation, 2006). This can include a variety of offerings ranging from sessions and campaigns on healthful habits, stress management, study skills, relaxation training, conflict resolution skills, time management skills, and advocacy campaigns (relationship violence, alcohol use, etc). Many institutions of higher education utilize Web-based services to provide these self-help guides.

Some schools have gone a step further. "Recognizing that many first-year college students are not fully prepared for the emotional upheaval they will experience" (Shatkin, 2010), the NYU Child Study Center and the Steinhardt School of Education developed a course entitled "Transition to College and Young Adulthood," which is taught every semester and is open to all undergraduate students at New York University. University 101 (The Student in the University) at the University of South Carolina and Quinnipiac 101 (The Individual in the Community) at Quinnipiac University are freshman-level courses designed to promote healthy academic and personal growth and a successful transition away from home to the campus community.

Promote Social Networks (Primary Prevention)

The goals of social network promotion are to "reduce student isolation and promote a feeling of belonging" and "develop smaller groups within the larger campus community" (Jed Foundation, 2006). In 2008, the Centers for Disease Control (CDC) described a five-year strategy to promote health and prevent suicide by "building and strengthening connectedness or social bonds within and among persons, families, and communities" (CDC, 2008a). This strategy is particularly relevant to college and university campus communities. In a recent article drawing on data from the Healthy Minds Study, Hefner and Eisenberg (2009) found that students with lower quality of perceived social support were more likely to have mental health difficulties. Many institutions of higher education have created living-learning environments, with a variety of goals in mind, one of which is to foster relationship building among students, staff, and faculty. Middlebury College in Vermont has a Commons System, Cornell University has a First-Year Experience, and Union College has a Minerva House System, to name a few examples, all of which are designed to reinforce a sense of campus community and caring. Certainly, the traditional religious, sports, and special interest groups serve this purpose as well. However, the special living-learning environments have the potential to impact more of the student body.

The National Study of Living-Learning Programs (NSLLP), a national, multi-campus study of living-learning programs, investigated how these programs influence various academic, social, and developmental outcomes for students. Karen Inkelas, Ph.D., at the University of Maryland–College Park, and Aaron Brower, Ph.D., at the University of Wisconsin–Madison, were the principal investigators. The Center for Student Studies, the organization responsible for conducting the Healthy Minds Study, was involved in developing the questionnaire for online administration. Findings from the first two national surveys completed in 2004 and 2007 are reviewed in various articles, including those by Inkelas, Soldner, Longerbeam, and Leonard (2008) and Brower and Inkelas (2010).

Identify Students at Risk (Secondary Prevention)

The goals are early identification of "high-risk and potentially high-risk students" (Jed Foundation, 2006), proper referral of those students, and partnering with those students to promote safety and wellness. Success in this area clearly relies on the existence of an appropriate and high-quality network of treatment providers and services to refer at-risk students. There are some evidence-based strategies that are applicable to these goals.

Web-Based Screening

Beginning in 2001, the American Foundation for Suicide Prevention (AFSP) developed an interactive, Web-based screening method to identify college students at risk for suicide and to encourage them to seek assessment and treatment. This outreach tool was piloted over a three-year period at Emory University in Atlanta and at the University of North Carolina at Chapel Hill. The pilot data (Haas et al., 2008) revealed that nearly 20% of the students found to be at moderate to high risk completed an in-person evaluation and almost 14% entered treatment. Seen as a promising tool for encouraging previously untreated at-risk college students to seek help, the use of this program has expanded to several other institutions of higher education. The ethical and legal ramifications of such a tool and the importance of having treatment resources available for the students identified in this fashion were carefully reviewed in the study.

Gatekeeper Training

Gatekeeper training has been viewed as an important suicide prevention strategy. Such training typically involves a review of suicide statistics, suicide warning signs, education about available mental health resources, strategies for engaging and supporting students at risk, and typical emotional reactions experienced by gatekeepers interacting with students in crisis. Possible gatekeepers on campus include, but are not limited to, residential life staff, faculty, campus security, medical/health center staff, and student leaders (Kognito Interactive, 2009). *Campus Connect*, developed by the Syracuse University Counseling Center; *Question, Persuade, Refer (QPR)*, developed by the QPR Institute, Inc.; the Army's *ACE Suicide Intervention (ACE-SI) Program*; and Kognito Interactive's *At-Risk for University and College Faculty Gatekeeper Training Simulation* are four such education and training programs listed in the Suicide Prevention Resource Center's Best Practices Registry for adherence to standards (http://www.sprc.org/bpr). Based on their findings, Drum et al. (2009) recommend that for gatekeeper training efforts to be more effective, there should be an enhanced focus on peers.

Students of Concern Teams

Many educational institutions have formed interdisciplinary teams "charged with detecting and monitoring students of concern and managing the flow of information regarding such students" (Dunkle, Silverstein, & Warner, 2008).

Alliance with Primary Care

Physical and mental health care coordination is gaining increasing momentum, as lack of communication between providers has been identified as a major interference in safe health care delivery. More specifically, collaboration between campus primary care providers and counseling center staff, linking mental health and physical health within co-located offices, and even combining records in one chart could be of significant assistance in improving early recognition and intervention of mental health problems (ACHA, 2010b). Students at risk do not always seek psychological help, but may present with somatic complaints like headaches, dizziness, and fatigue. Counseling centers, in conjunction with the medical clinic, can focus on highly prevalent psychiatric disorders (depression and anxiety) and require the use of simple screening instruments as part of general medical visits to campus health centers (Alschuler, Hoodin, & Byrd, 2009).

Case Example: Zoe

Zoe, a 22-year-old student, has come to the health clinic with complaints of palpitations and dizziness. This is her third visit to the clinic in three weeks. The clinic MD finds her in good physical health, except for gastritis. Although she does not directly reveal any tension or fear, the clinic MD is concerned about her pallor and inability to engage in conversation. On probing further, the MD is alarmed to hear that Zoe hates the university. She states she has no friends. The MD calls her colleague from the suite next door who serves as the UCC counselor. She sets up an appointment. Zoe states she is relieved to talk to someone. She has been worried about her parents, who she has just learned are on the verge of separating. Zoe was followed up by her counselor, whom she met with every week within the same office as that of the primary care MD.

As primary care is usually the portal through which students enter treatment, alignment between primary care clinicians and their colleagues in mental health will allow relatively quicker access to treatment and could also ease the stigma around seeking help for emotional problems.

A similar strategy involves the medical history forms completed by all incoming students. Most institutions of higher education contact incoming freshman before their arrival on campus with information on campus medical services and a questionnaire about their own health, including a mental health history. One purpose here is to normalize mental health issues for students by placing them in the overall context of general health (Voelker, 2003). The aim of this strategy would be to provide targeted outreach to those students who indicate risk factors for suicidal ideation or behaviors. For example, general medical clinic personnel could review any mental health history that was documented on the form, assess the status of the mental health condition, and make referrals, if necessary, as part of any medical visit.

Mandated Assessments

The Suicide Prevention Program at the University of Illinois evolved to a policy of requiring four sessions of mandated professional assessment for any student who threatened or attempted suicide. These sessions are meant to "foster the students' willingness and ability to maintain a reasonable concern for their own self welfare." This policy, which is clearly outlined in the student code of conduct (http://admin.illinois.edu/policy/code/), is supported by a suicide assessment team and allows for appeals. Mandated students who do not participate in the program are at risk of being withdrawn from the university. The university has documented an overall decline of 45% in student suicides during the 21 years the program has been in effect (Joffe, 2008). This program is not without controversy, however, as it touches on several professional ethical principles, particularly autonomy. Hernandez and Fister (2001) listed three concerns about mandated treatment. (1) Both counselors and administrators are put in awkward roles, the counselor as a quasi-disciplinarian and the administrator as a quasi-counselor. (2) It impacts the informed-consent nature of counseling with the inherent ability to withdraw voluntarily. (3) The counseling process can be slow at effecting behavioral change; disciplinary action may be more effective at motivating students to make behavioral changes quickly. In 2007, the Association for University and College Counseling Center Directors (AUCCCD) stated that it was opposed to ongoing mandated treatment yet recognized "the value of mandated assessment when it is precipitated by clear problematic behavior and violation of college and university conduct codes" (AUCCCD, 2007, para. 3).

Increase Help-Seeking Behaviors (Primary and Secondary Prevention)

The goal here is to increase the likelihood that a student who needs services will seek them out. Strategies include those which decrease stigma about mental illness and mental health treatment, those which emphasize the importance of seeking help when warning symptoms emerge, and those which remove obstacles to accessing treatment.

Campus-wide education about the signs and symptoms of mental disorders and suicide has been a widely used approach to destigmatize mental illness. These programs take a variety of forms, including pamphlets, e-blasts, mental health forums with easily recognized keynote speakers, counseling center staff participating in health fairs, and mental health screenings as part of national mental health awareness days. Counseling center staff at many institutions of higher education also teach classes, increasing their visibility. Specific outreach to those groups who are at higher risk for suicide and those groups who, for cultural reasons, tend not to seek mental health services is important. As mentioned in the previous section, asking for details about mental health history on the general medical forms of incoming students begins to set the tone for mental well-being as part of overall health.

Creating courses for undergraduates pertaining to mental health issues that are fun and debunk myths about mental illness could effectively reduce stigma. NYU has developed a minor in Child and Adolescent Mental Health Studies (CAMS) for undergraduates. One goal of this course of study is to improve understanding and awareness of childhood mental health issues and their ongoing impact on adolescents and adults (Addasi & Shatkin, 2008).

Student-driven mental health awareness groups can play a crucial role in decreasing stigma and encouraging help-seeking. Active Minds, Inc. (http://www.active-minds.org) and NAMI On Campus (National Alliance on Mental Illness) (http://www.nami.org) are two such organizations that promote mental health awareness, education, and advocacy.

Many organizations interested in promoting mental health awareness have made use of the Internet. For example, mtvU, MTV's college network, partnered with the Jed Foundation to produce the "Half of Us" campaign (http://www.halfofus.com). Interviews with students and high-profile artists help promote dialogue about mental illness, provide information, and encourage help-seeking.

Ulifeline, another Web-based service (http://www.ulifeline.com), is offered free to colleges and universities by the Jed Foundation. It is an anonymous, confidential, online resource center for college students to get information regarding mental health and suicide prevention, take a mental health screening tool, and link to their own campus counseling centers.

To eliminate financial barriers to help-seeking, nearly all counseling centers have dropped the practice of charging fees for personal counseling, down from 17.2% of those surveyed in 1996 to 6.1% in 2009 (Gallagher, 2009). In addition, most institutions of higher education require that all students have health insurance and advocate for policies with solid mental health benefits to remove access barriers.

Session limits are imposed by some counseling centers as a means to manage their resources. However, session limits may serve as a deterrent to seeking treatment.

Several students, personally known by the authors, have hesitated to use services, questioning whether their current level of distress warranted use of one of their six allowed sessions. Data from the National Survey of Counseling Center Directors (Gallagher, 2009) reveal that the average number of counseling sessions per client tends to be the same (approximately six), whether the student receives treatment at a counseling center with session limits or one without formally established limits. The practice of limiting the number of session appears to be waning. In 2009, 31% of counseling center directors reported the practice, in contrast to 47% in 2005 (Gallagher, 2005, 2009).

Increasing awareness of the mental health services available to students and providing clear information on how to access them, essentially marketing campus resources, are fundamental to increasing help-seeking behaviors (Golberstein, Eisenberg, & Gollust, 2008). There are many ways of conducting such marketing (Kadison and DiGeronimo, 2004), including handing out informational packets to students, using online messages, and providing free items labeled with important contact information (stress balls, pencils, water bottles, etc.). For continued effectiveness, this information should be offered several times during the academic year.

Parents, too, must be educated about the signs and symptoms of mental illness, the resources available, how to communicate with their children about mental health issues, and how to communicate their concerns to college and university personnel (Locke & Eichorn, 2008). Many schools have begun to partner with parents during campus orientation sessions for accepted students or even earlier with informational sessions during college campus tours. Many campuses have offices dedicated to parent relations or parent programming. Institutions of higher education are communicating with parents more regularly about campus happenings via the Internet, e-blasts, and websites. The University of Minnesota, for example, has an elaborate parent section on its website (http://www.parent.umn.edu). Parents can access online workshops and guides about mental illness, the problem of alcohol use on campus, and the mental health resources available on campus. Of particular note is the "Timely Issues" page, which highlights issues or events connected with the academic calendar that could be impacting their child's mood and functioning.

Provide Mental Health Services (Secondary and Tertiary Prevention)

The goal here is to provide and/or make available appropriate, timely, and high-quality mental health services. Addressing mental health issues on campus and reducing the morbidity and mortality associated with psychiatric disorders require a comprehensive and collaborative approach. Ideally, all levels of service—from assessment and triage (Rockland-Miller & Eells, 2006), outpatient care, intensive outpatient programs, partial-hospitalization programs, crisis intervention, to inpatient psychiatric units—should be accessible. Procedures for after-hours emergencies should be carefully defined. Various therapeutic modalities, including support groups, group therapy, and individual therapy (brief and long term), as well, high-caliber and collaborative psychiatric consultation and treatment should be available. While it may not be feasible for all of these services to be available on campus, it is essential that all campuses have qualified professional staff that can assess and triage those students seeking services. Importantly, university counseling centers need to know the limits of their assessment and treatment capacity and be prepared to refer students whose needs cannot be met on campus. This capacity to triage students with unique psychiatric needs to appropriate providers should be established through memorandums of understanding (MOUs) with off-campus providers such as community agencies, private providers, or academic psychiatry departments so that students do not have to wait through crises and develop complications. The pros and cons of parental notification, and the new amendments applied to FERPA/HIPAA, should be actively considered when off-campus providers are required or utilized. Lists of off-campus providers and their contact information should be regularly updated.

Many college counseling centers will not accept involuntary patients; this presents challenges when a student presents in crisis or has an altered mental status or irrational thought processes. Their ability to seek treatment may be limited. Universities must develop plans to address this dilemma by having alternate facilities and providers who will accept involuntary patients. These policies of exclusion and alternate strategies must be well known to area providers as they plan disposition and ensure adequate follow-up after the acute crisis is resolved. In the case of Virginia Tech, the on-call psychologist who took the call from Carillion Hospital indicated that Cook Counseling Center did not accept involuntary patients and had no alternatives to offer. Cho decided to go to the center voluntarily that afternoon, but he did not receive any follow-up.

Whether services are provided on campus, split between a campus provider and a local community provider, or split between a school provider and a provider in the student's home community (perhaps in another state), clinical care should be well coordinated. During care coordination or during the transfer of care, providers can use evidence-based, standardized, and routine patient safety protocols to communicate with each other. One such protocol is ISBAR, which many hospital personnel are taught to use during patient hand-offs between shifts or with a change in service (Rhode Island Hospital, 2010). It involves

Identifying yourself and the name of the patient
Determining the Situation

Providing pertinent **B**ackground information related to the patient

Assessment of the patient's current condition or situation, and a

Recommendation of what you would like to see done for the patient.

In the case of the transitioning college students with mental health issues, this communication should include what medications the patient takes (if any), when the last prescription was given and the number of pills prescribed, how care will be coordinated during semester breaks and summer vacation, and provider contact information. Please see the section on transitioning patients from high school to college in the latter part of this chapter for further information.

For schools that provide diagnostic services and psychotherapeutic interventions on campus, we recommend that psychiatric services be available on site as well. This practice promotes easy coordination of services. If this is not possible, transportation to off-campus psychiatric providers, simplified means of filling prescriptions, and regularly scheduled communication with the psychiatrist are important. Use of a diagnostic system, such as the *DSM-5* (American Psychiatric Association, 2013), can enhance care coordination. Despite their liabilities, such diagnostic systems aid discussion about individual patients and allow for symptom tracking and standardized treatment selection.

Today, the vast majority of psychiatric disorders can be treated effectively with evidence-based psychosocial and pharmacological approaches. Details for treating the various disorders will not be presented here. Practice parameters developed by the American Academy of Child and Adolescent Psychiatry (http://www.aacap.org) and practice guidelines developed by the American Psychiatric Association (http://www.psych.org) summarize the treatments for various disorders and the evidence supporting their effectiveness. These materials can be adapted for use with college-aged students, whose living and learning environments pose unique challenges for treatment providers (semester breaks, the ebb and flow of the academic year, prevalence of substance use and abuse).

Some clinicians and researchers have presented best practice guidelines specifically related to the college student population. Given the concern about stimulant abuse and recreational use on college campuses (DeSantis, Webb, & Naar, 2008; Garnier et al., 2010), students seeking an initial diagnosis of ADHD as young adults present diagnostic challenges to campus mental health professionals (DuPaul, Weyandt, O'Dell, & Varejao, 2009; Harrison & Rosenbaum, 2010). Also, those students already being treated for ADHD may need adjustments in the dosing and timing of their medications because class schedules and study schedules vary widely in college from those in high school. Nutt and colleagues, for the British Association for Psychopharmacology (2007), have published evidence-based guidelines for the management of ADHD in the college-aged population. Chan (2009), at the University of California in Irvine, and Thomas, at the University of Alabama (Caley & Thomas, 2009), among others, have addressed these challenges at their own universities by establishing protocols for assessment and treatment of ADHD on campus. There is an effort by the ACHA to produce guidelines for treating ADHD on college campuses.

Students with autistic spectrum disorders are likely to be particularly stressed by the pressures to achieve academically, develop new social relationships, and be more self-sufficient. Vanbergeijk, Klin, and Volkmar (2008), Volkmar and Wiesner (2009), and Wolf, Thierfeld, and Bork (2009) have identified some best practices for this subgroup; the reader is referred to those sources for details.

While campus programs to address substance use and abuse on campus are beyond the scope of this chapter, we would note that universities will have to address lax policies regarding alcohol consumption and how they impact the school or college culture and how alcohol infractions are dealt with. In addition, universities need to increase the level of awareness on campus of substance abuse as a serious psychiatric issue and not just a social nuisance. The Task Force of the National Advisory Council on Alcohol Abuse and Alcoholism (2002) has provided a concise guide to best practices in the development, implementation, and dissemination of a coherent policy regarding substance use and abuse on college campuses. DeJong Larimer, Wood, and Hartman (2009) have summarized research conducted on college drinking prevention and intervention since the Task Force Report.

One special circumstance that arises in the treatment of college students is students studying abroad for a semester or two. These students, many of whom are stable and in the maintenance phase of their treatment, present particular challenges. What therapeutic supports are available at institutions of higher education overseas? Are similar medications available? Are there physicians available who are specifically trained to monitor psychotropic medications? Does their health insurance cover treatment conducted overseas? We recommend that colleges and universities obtain and publicize information for their study abroad programs on the availability of mental health services and how to access them. Students themselves should consider such resources before choosing a particular study abroad program.

Follow Crisis Management Procedures (All Levels of Prevention)

The goal here is to respond effectively to the student in need and to help survivors deal with grief and confusion. Once a student has been identified as being in crisis, the institution's safety protocol should be implemented. The Jed Foundation and several co-sponsors (2006) prepared a very detailed framework for the elements that should be included in a campus safety protocol. In general, this protocol defines policies and procedures for assessment of the student in crisis, including who should be involved in decision-making and issues around voluntary and involuntary hospitalization and documentation of contact with the identified student. This safety protocol should also include an emergency contact notification protocol. Prior to a crisis event, students with serious mental illness may want to consider a psychiatric advance directive, to establish their treatment wishes and emergency notification list. Scheyett (2009) interviewed 40 students with serious mental illness from one large state university about advanced directives for mental health and found the respondents to be overall positive about the possible utility of such a document. Defined medical-leave policies for mental health reasons and a policy or process for re-entry to campus and the academic program complete the campus safety protocol. The Jed Foundation framework identifies the many layers of each aspect of the safety protocol, by asking key questions to help determine the best course of action. For example, a suicide attempt may justify notifying parents, but involvement of the parents in the aftercare plan may not be in the best interest of the student if the family is not supportive.

Support for those in the campus community impacted by a crisis and strategies to manage the media in the event of a campus suicide or crisis are two additional aspects of campus crisis management that are critical to address (Jed Foundation, 2006; Mental Health America, 2007; SPRC, 2004). Postvention efforts to assist those affected by the crisis include making students aware of the typical responses to a campus crisis and what supports are available. Stambaugh (2008), in the United States Fire Administration Report of the Northern Illinois University shooting, states that "the detailed after action analysis and report on the Virginia Tech incident...was mentioned by nearly every office or department...as having been a critical source of information for...recovery at the university and the related first responder organizations." Postvention guidelines for responsible reporting by the media can be found in a joint publication by the Centers for Disease Control and Prevention (CDC), National Institute of Mental Health (NIMH), Office of the Surgeon General, Substance Abuse and Mental Health Services Administration (SAMHSA), American Foundation for Suicide Prevention, American Association of Suicidology, and the Annenberg Public Policy Center (2001). Of prime importance is that all key stakeholders (students, parents, administrators, faculty, and staff) be educated about the safety protocols, including campus behavioral expectations, self-care expectations, and what events or situations will initiate the protocol.

Restrict Access to Potentially Lethal
Means (Primary Prevention)

Restricting "access to potentially lethal means" (Jed Foundation, 2006) is a commonly used prevention strategy. On college campuses, this includes policies against having firearms on campus, restricted access to potentially lethal chemicals, and restricted access to balconies, tall buildings, and windows. An alcohol and drug policy on campus, which restricts availability and deters use, also serves as a means of restriction. Additionally, safe prescribing practices and limiting quantities of certain medications may help prevent suicide by overdose.

In summary, the development of a comprehensive plan for campus suicide prevention is a complex process involving an assessment of campus values, fiscal commitment, and collaboration by all key constituents. Institutions of higher education do not, however, need to develop these plans from scratch but can draw from helpful guidelines developed by mental health advocacy groups and governmental agencies, practices implemented and used on other campuses, as well as the nascent evidence-based literature related specifically to college student mental health. As Silverman (2008) so aptly put it, "although we can't ever 'fix' the problem of suicide or stop all violent deaths from occurring on our campuses, we can at least demonstrate to our students and faculty and staff members some better ways of communicating and caring for one another by exhibiting appropriate attitudes, beliefs, values, and skills that can be applied throughout life. Suicide prevention is violence prevention, and compassionate and caring campus communities are crucial" (p. A52).

THE TRANSITION FROM HIGH SCHOOL TO COLLEGE

Case Example: John

A 19-year-old college freshman, John came to the counseling center in November of his first semester upon the recommendation of his home-based psychiatrist. John had a history of anxiety, depression, and insomnia in high school and had attended an intensive outpatient program during his senior year of high school. Before leaving for the college of his choice, which was located across the country from his home state, John had experienced a significant lowering of his mood, so his psychiatrist increased the dosage of his antidepressant. He also prescribed John sleeping medication and provided enough refills for his medications to last to Thanksgiving break. After one month of classes, as the academic work began to pile up, John found himself less able to concentrate; he was restless and fidgety; he was having more trouble falling asleep. He contacted his home psychiatrist, who suggested that he increase both of his medications. One month later, John again called his home psychiatrist. He described disabling anxiety; he had begun to drink on a daily basis to calm himself and to aid falling asleep and was struggling to complete assignments. He had received a warning from campus security for some disruptive behavior while drinking. At this time, his home psychiatrist suggested that he see someone on campus or in the nearby community. John became involved in therapy and had his medications managed on campus by counseling center staff. Over time, it became apparent that the increases in John's medication had paradoxically agitated him. Treatment services during semester breaks and summer vacation were coordinated with his home provider. Careful documentation of his mood and function over the next year resulted in the diagnosis of bipolar disorder. On the positive side, John had been taking his medications as prescribed and had reached out to his provider.

Had John and his provider proactively established a plan for him to receive follow-up treatment upon his arrival to campus, some of these difficulties could have been avoided. Also, it is not advisable to send an unstable patient off to college with a four-month supply of medication, as it provides a false sense of security that all is well.

Case Example: Amber

An 18 year-old college freshman diagnosed with bipolar disorder during her junior year of high school, Amber had been in twice-monthly therapy and was on a mood stabilizer and antidepressant prior to her arrival on campus. Her home psychiatrist had provided her with a treatment summary including a medication history (with the date of her last medication refill) and the results of some recent labwork. He indicated that he was concerned about a tremor that Amber had developed and wanted her monitored for worsening of the tremor. He also described themes that had been prominent in her individual therapy sessions and had suggestions for ongoing therapy and medication changes (if necessary). Amber began therapy and medication management on campus. She continued to see her home psychiatrist during all visits home. With Amber's permission, all providers communicated via voicemail or fax about her adjustment to college and the stability of her mood. Amber's college years were not easy. Medication side effects and symptom exacerbations brought on by sleep deprivation during midterms and finals compromised her academic performance and relationships. As she learned more about her illness and lifestyle strategies to help stabilize her mood, she became more successful academically and socially.

The importance of planned transitions for youth with chronic illnesses to adult health care was brought to national attention by the Surgeon General in the 1980s and has been designated by the Maternal and Child Health Bureau of the U.S. Health and Human Services as a core component of its Healthy People 2010 and Healthy People 2020 agendas (http://www.healthypeople.gov/2020/default.aspx). Though the original focus was on youth with chronic medical illnesses, a broader definition is now used: "those who have or are at risk for a chronic physical, developmental, behavioral, or emotional condition and who also require health and related services of a type or amount beyond that required by children generally" (McPherson et al., 1998). Many youth transitioning to college have chronic emotional and/or developmental disorders and require ongoing supportive, treatment, and preventative services.

The transition from high school to college for youth with pre-existing mental health issues presents particular challenges. Many of them take one or more psychotropic medications, are in therapy, and receive support services and accommodations at their high schools. Heading to college means separation not only from family and friends but also from these supports. With the excitement of being accepted to college and as part of their search for identity and autonomy, many of these same individuals may plan to halt all treatment and support services and garner a fresh start. During this significant and complex developmental transition, these students are at high risk for exacerbation of their symptoms, relapse, suicide, academic difficulties, and social difficulties. Disruptions in continuity of care and/or inadequate coordination of services can have devastating consequences.

With improvements in the diagnosis and treatment of mental health disorders during childhood and adolescence, such as mood and anxiety disorders, pervasive developmental disorders, learning disorders, and ADHD, many youth previously unable to attend college are heading to campus. This means that many of these youth have actually been in treatment with various mental health providers for several years before the college application process even begins. These providers, whether physicians, psychologists, social workers, or school counselors, have important roles to play in helping their patients transition to college. For the providers prescribing psychotropic medications (child and adolescent psychiatrists, general psychiatrists, primary care providers, advanced practice nurses) the process of transitioning patients is complex, time-consuming, frustrating, and fraught with legal and ethical concerns (Professional Risk Management Services, Inc. [PRMS], 2005). However, with thoughtful and proactive transition planning, these providers are positioned to help their college-bound patients transition into adulthood and become more independent in managing their mental health needs.

The evidence-based literature specifically addressing transition planning for students with mental health issues, such as depression and anxiety, from high school to college is scant. The codes of ethics of various mental health professions certainly guide the process. We can also draw from the literature on systems of care, educational transition planning, patient safety protocols, and anticipatory guidance to aid in developing best practices for mental health providers to use during the transition from high school to college of youth with pre-existing mental illness. Such practices need to emphasize independence and safety. Educational transition planning, as derived for implementing the Individuals with Disabilities Education Act (IDEA) transition mandates, emphasizes setting goals, identifying key members of the team, and establishing functional connections. Of particular importance in educational transition planning is involvement of the individual; self-determination is relevant to investment in the plan and the outcome (Hasazi, Furney, & Destefano, 1999).

Community systems of care principles (see Appendix, Table 1) emphasize that significant attention be paid to transitions between care teams making continuity of care, services from various components of the system, and service coordination priorities. System-of-care principles also promote clinician familiarity with the organization and function of the systems they are working with in order to advocate effectively for their patients and families.

A study on transitioning youth to adult community mental health services suggests that transitions be "planned, orderly and purposeful, taking into account both developmental needs and illness specific needs" (Singh et al., 2010). Furthermore, this study described optimal transitions as having information continuity and a period of parallel care (relational continuity). Tenets of anticipatory guidance are of particular usefulness, in that information and guidance help prepare patients and their families for expected changes and stresses during various developmental stages. The routine use of patient safety protocols focused on effective communication among all health care providers, especially during transfers of care, is particularly applicable here. Pediatric perspectives on transitioning youth with chronic medical illnesses to adult health care emphasize similar themes (McManus, Fox, O'Connor, Chapman & MacKinnon, 2008).

The implications of these concepts for students with pre-existing mental illness transitioning to college are as follows: (1) students should be intimately involved with setting short- and long-range treatment goals; (2) key stakeholders such as mental health providers, parents, high school planning staff, college administrators and counselors, and the students should work as a team; (3) knowledge of adolescent–young adult development should guide the process; (4) knowledge of the vicissitudes of college life, the resources available at the college and how to access them, and online resources should be shared among all; (5) transition planning should be proactive and take place over several months or even a couple of years; (6) current treatment providers should make contacts with new providers on behalf of their college-bound patients, preferably routinely, using a communication protocol such as ISBAR (described earlier in this chapter); and (7) significant effort should be made to have the transitioning youth talk with and even meet new providers prior to or at the start of the academic year.

With these principles in mind and with the overall goal of reducing the potential risks in the setting of an upcoming transition, the following model is proposed for use by mental health providers. Using a framework of "anticipatory guidance," in which physicians provide information and guidance to help prepare patients and their families for the expected changes and stresses associated with various developmental stages (Caplan, 1981; McInerney, Adam, Campbell, Kamat, & Kelleher, 2008), treatment providers can hold discussions regarding the transition to college. Beginning in 10th or 11th grade, targeted discussions about diagnosis, medications, obstacles to compliance with medications on college campuses, personal strengths and liabilities, and strategies for enhancing coping are held (Martel, 2010; Martel & Namerow, 2010). The practices suggested in this model are geared toward use by mental health providers who are helping launch their patients to college. Vanbergeijk, Klin, and Volkmar (2008), Kadison and DiGeronimo (2004), Shatkin (2010), Fassler (2008), and various advocacy groups, including the Jed Foundation (2009) and NAMI on Campus (National Alliance on Mental Illness [NAMI], 2010), have produced lists of recommendations for students, parents, institutions of higher education, and practitioners to promote a healthy and safe transition to college of young people with diagnosed mental illnesses. Some of their suggestions have been adapted for this model geared to mental health practitioners. In addition, the authors have participated in a College Student Mental Health Special Interest Study Group held at the Annual Meeting of the American Academy of Child and Adolescent Psychiatry, at which the nuances and complexities of transition planning were discussed and practices shared.

CAMPUS LIFE is a helpful mnemonic that can focus the purpose, process, and content of the discussions.

C—Collaboration and Communication. The college-bound patient and provider discuss short- and long-term treatment goals and needs, including what a transfer plan might look like. This includes talking about whose input would be valuable in formulating a transition plan. The "transition team" might include high school counselors, parents, primary care providers, a staff member from the college disabilities office and/or counseling center, and the receiving providers. The student/patient needs to sign releases for team members to communicate with each other. Establishing treatment goals would mean discussing what aspects of a long-standing therapeutic relationship have been particularly helpful, when and how a patient might taper medications, what services are needed, and the frequency of visits. The National Alliance on Mental Illness (NAMI) has a practical and frank set of recommendations for students with mental illness who are applying to college; patients should be provided a copy of those recommendations to discuss and review (http://www.nami.org). The Transition Year, a joint project of the Jed Foundation and the American Psychiatric Foundation, emphasizes emotional health in the transition to college and is a valuable online resource for students as well as parents (http://www.transitionyear.org).

A—Anticipate. The obstacles to treatment compliance should be openly discussed. This includes predicting that student/patients who are excited about this new life stage and who feel that their mental health issues reside in their home town or high school may wish to start anew and remake themselves by stopping medication, therapy, educational support services, or a combination of these upon arrival to campus. Such students will feel strong and stable during less intense periods during the academic year and may be tempted to halt treatment. Worries about confidentiality and worries about stigma should be addressed proactively. Students with serious mental illness may even want to consider an advance directive for mental health, in the event that they decompensate and are no longer capable of competently stating their treatment preferences and needs (Scheyett, 2009). Students should be encouraged to disclose their health histories, and for those who have received educational support services through a 504 Plan or an individualized educational plan (IEP), to self-identify with disabilities services at their colleges.

M—Manage. Around the middle of high school, patients should begin, with parental support, to manage routine aspects of their treatment, such as scheduling and recording appointments, ordering refills of medications, using a pill box to help keep track of medications, and using an insurance card. Transitioning students should also manage their future treatment by making phone calls to new providers and perhaps even scheduling an appointment before college classes begin. They should learn how prescriptions can be filled on or near campus and how to arrange transportation to off-campus providers.

P—Psychoeducation. Frank discussions should be held about diagnosis, prognosis, signs and symptoms of relapse, and stressors that have historically resulted in symptom exacerbations for the individual. The student should be able to list diagnoses, past treatment history, and current medication(s). The patient and provider can prepare a portable medical summary (Shah, 2010), focused on mental health.

U—Utilize. The student should be encouraged to utilize the full range of resources available on or near campus. Patients can print off materials from campus counseling center websites and review them together with their provider. If the home provider has a computer in the office, perusing the college's website together may be a useful strategy. Look for campus wellness programs, student-driven mental health support groups, crisis management services, academic support programs, and psychoeducational materials. The provider should take time in the office for the student to store the phone numbers of all providers, old and new, on his or her cell phone.

S—Sleep. Discuss sleep hygiene. Review the student's current sleep patterns. Review the possible impact of disrupted sleep on mood disorders. Review obstacles to getting a good night's sleep on campus. Review the surveys in which college students typically rank sleep difficulties as the second most common factor impacting their academic performance (ACHA, 2010a).

L—Lifestyle. Campus life can be overwhelming for some individuals. The availability of alcohol and drugs, the prevalence of sexual activity, and the lack of parental control over use of video games are part of campus life. For those students who are overstimulated by the latter activities, alternative ways to structure and fill their time should be explored. Signs of excessive involvement with these activities and their impact on physical and mental wellness and self-esteem should be discussed.

I—Independence. Building independence in daily activities and self-advocacy skills does not magically begin when one walks onto campus. It is important for students to attend their high school educational planning meetings to understand the content and process of those meetings and to build self-advocacy skills. Practicing activities of daily living such as setting an alarm to wake up in the morning, doing laundry, managing a bank account, paying bills, and keeping a calendar prior to leaving for college can also diminish stress and promote self-confidence.

F—Family. The process of separating from family can produce tension, conflict, and regression. Discussing how to say good-bye to family members and how to stay connected with them in a healthy fashion can help keep intact this major source of support for college-bound patients.

E—Evaluate and Embrace. Encourage the student to evaluate and embrace all aspects of him- or herself, including strengths and liabilities in academic and interpersonal realms, gender, sexuality, ethnicity, religiosity, personal values, personal goals, and having a mental illness.

A parallel series of discussions should be held with parents. Recognizing college students as young adults in transition, counselors need to partner with parents in ways that promote separation and independence and maintain confidentiality, but use parents and families as resources for assessing and promoting a student's mental health (Girard, 2010). Parents of college-bound students must learn and practice healthy ways of communicating with their emerging adult children about their mental well-being. During the college application process, parents should openly discuss with their children who have been diagnosed and treated for a mental health issue the importance of looking at the spectrum of mental health services available at various schools as well as the size, location, diversity, academic programs, and social offerings (Jed Foundation, 2007). Once their child is accepted and makes a college selection, parents should encourage their college-bound students to fully disclose their health histories, including mental health concerns, and to seek accommodations or other support services, if eligible. Teaching college-aged children about health insurance and how to fill prescriptions may sound trivial, but this is important for self-efficacy. Parents should be encouraged to become familiar with college counseling center websites. Letting go of college-aged children is difficult for most parents, but when the child has struggled with mental illness the process can be more difficult and unsettling. Most college and university websites offer general yet practical suggestions for parents to help deal with the letting-go process.

From the perspective of the institutions of higher education, the attitudes and initiatives previously described for promoting campus mental wellness and preventing campus suicide are applicable to this particularly vulnerable cohort of students. In addition, early in the college application process, during campus informational tours, schools can raise the topic of mental wellness and services available on campus. This tactic may help desensitize students to discussions with their parents and current treatment providers about taking into account their mental health issues when selecting a college. Similarly, these issues can be raised again during orientation activities for new students and their parents. The creation and sharing of developmentally appropriate, well-integrated, and confidential ways of reaching out to incoming students who document a mental health history on pre-admission health forms also makes practical sense.

One such strategy is being used at MIT. In addition to asking about mental health history on pre-admission health forms, MIT (and likely other institutions of higher education as well) specifically asks incoming students if they are "interested in obtaining more information about mental health services at MIT" and if they "would like a referral to a mental health clinician at MIT" (http://www.mit.edu). In a personal communication from 2010, K. Girard, M.D., former Associate Chief of Mental Health Services at MIT, stated that

support staff in the mental health department send information to anyone who indicates an interest, and one of the triage clinicians contacts those who want to make an appointment. The chief of the mental health service contacts all of the students who report having a mental health history to help facilitate an early connection with the service. He accomplishes this in the form of a welcome letter and indicates that he routinely reviews the medical screening information for all of the incoming students and routinely contacts students who report a mental health history to tell them more about the service and to invite them in for an appointment.

This process can best be illustrated by looking at the transition to college of two patients who attended high school in the same town, graduating two years apart from each other.

Case Example: Andrew

Andrew is a 17-year-old Caucasian male who was hospitalized early in 10th grade and diagnosed with psychotic depression. He has a family history of bipolar disorder and ADHD. He had been in split treatment, seeing a social worker for weekly therapy and a child and adolescent psychiatrist for medications, and was doing well. During the spring of his high school junior year, in conjunction with his treatment providers and parents, Andrew decided he wanted to attempt a medication taper and to decrease the frequency of his therapy visits. Andrew had been stabilized on two medications and an atypical antipsychotic medication. He managed, over a period of a few months, to taper and discontinue one of the antidepressants and to tolerate a 50% decrease in the dose of the antipsychotic. Additional medication changes resulted in return of mood symptoms.

Since his departure for college was now only six months away, Andrew recognized and accepted that he would head to college on medication, but on a simplified regimen. His coping skills had become more developed and he managed well with fewer therapy sessions. Sessions had begun to include more anticipatory guidance, including a frank discussion of the family history of bipolar disorder, Andrew's risks for that disorder, signs and symptoms to watch for, and the importance of sleep hygiene and avoiding excessive substance use. Andrew chose a school near a large city, approximately 2.5 hours from home.

With the help and encouragement of his providers, he connected with a therapist in the city and with an Advanced Practice RN (APRN) on campus prior to the start of classes. All four providers communicated by phone during the transition to college. One topic discussed with Andrew and among the providers was Andrew's family history of bipolar disorder and what that might mean during this developmental transition. Interestingly, the campus APRN was specifically designated as a transition provider at that school; she made sure that new students had follow-up and medications until the campus psychiatrist could be seen. Andrew stayed in touch with his previous providers on school breaks.

The transition process went fairly smoothly; there were a few episodes of mild to moderate decompensation during college, but these were managed in a swift and coordinated fashion. Andrew is a college graduate and still takes medication.

Case Example: Karen

A 17-year-old Caucasian female, Karen was diagnosed with social phobia and major depression in 10th grade. She had a family history of anxiety disorders and alcohol dependence. She was in treatment with a psychiatrist for both therapy and medication management. As the end of her junior year approached, she was on one medication and had successfully been using skills learned through cognitive-behavioral therapy; therapy visits were on a monthly basis. With proactive discussion about the transition to college, which was 15 months away, Karen, her provider, and parents decided on a trial of medication taper and discontinuation. During the taper, Karen's psychiatrist requested that she return for weekly and then twice-monthly visits for monitoring and support and further development of coping skills. Despite best efforts, it was necessary for Karen to stay on the full dose of her medication. This process was repeated at Karen's request after she had been accepted early decision to the school of her choice, eight months prior to matriculation.

Again, Karen had a recurrence of her symptoms and went back on her full dose of medication. The psychiatrist and Karen processed that she would likely have a better transition to college if she remained on medication. Karen took over dispensing her own medication, with minimal supervision from parents, as practice for when she went off to college. Discussions were held about the challenges she might face at school, having been an only child, not having dated in high school, and having a family history of alcoholism.

Throughout the process, Karen was adamant about wanting to go to a college quite a distance from home and in a more rural setting. The college she selected required a half-day plane ride in order to visit home and it was located in a small, rural community. There were limited services on campus and in the nearby community. The internist at the college health center agreed to prescribe medication. The college referred her to a therapist during orientation week who was located a half-hour taxi ride from campus. The home psychiatrist and new therapist spoke by phone about Karen's treatment history. The internist preferred to get information via fax to include in the student's medical record and only called if he had any questions about the written record. Karen met the internist one time for a refill and did not find him helpful. She found that the taxi ride to and from the therapist was a burden, with planning, travel, and session time taking up to three hours of her day. She stopped her medication and therapy on her own six weeks into the semester without informing anyone and without follow-up. (There was no system in place at the campus medical clinic for following up with students who missed appointments.) Her roommate had expressed some concern to her about her increasing isolation.

When she returned home for Thanksgiving break, it was apparent to her family that she was depressed again. She returned to her former psychiatrist and agreed to be more compliant with her medications, but she had already declined so far in her academic functioning that she failed two first-semester classes. Karen eventually moved back home, took a semester off, and graduated from another college.

There has been no formal data collection to assess the impact of a model such as CAMPUS LIFE. Clinical feedback suggests that proactive, developmentally based transition planning, when performed in a routine and evidence-based manner, can be an effective strategy for promoting success, supporting autonomy, and avoiding psychiatric crises in the context of a major life transition. For various reasons, some students/patients may be resistant to this type of intervention. Others may have well-structured transition plans fall through at the last minute. Still others may find that the college of their choice was not a good fit and return home. Those working with college-aged students should anticipate resistance, expect some failures, remain flexible in treatment planning, and encourage healthy decision-making in regard to mental well-being.

Now more than ever, students entering institutions of higher education offer both challenges and opportunities for administrators to create an environment of learning that takes into account their physical and mental health. Campus administration and faculty can play a significant part in launching students into a lifelong trajectory of healthy ways of dealing with transitions, stress, and crises through policies informed by best practices that are evidence-based and data-informed and adhere to national standards.

The massacre on the Virginia Tech campus and the spate of violence on other campuses and in public places has generated enough interest and awareness to embrace the challenge posed by the heterogeneity of the student body in colleges and the unique challenges of transition that this phase of life brings. It is not a surprise that after Virginia Tech, colleges have developed excellent response systems to deal with sentinel events through improved alerting and communication systems, better dissemination of information, and timely law enforcement and medical response systems. However, the complexity of violence and the resulting difficulty in predicting it has made the a priori recognition and prevention of these events difficult. Utilizing knowledge of the human mind, psychiatric illnesses, and the predisposing events that lead up to crises that include violence, practitioners have developed promising and evidence-based models that are being increasingly incorporated and used on college campuses. The efficacy of evidence-based models of care will be enhanced in a college culture that encourages all three levels of prevention in health care. It is imperative that we evaluate and gauge the effectiveness of these models in reducing the baseline occurrence of catastrophic events and in the improvement of overall mental and physical health on our campuses. As scholars evaluate what works and what does not, the widespread dissemination of the models of evidence-based and best practices into colleges (and schools) should be a high priority from a public health perspective.

7

PREDICTING VIOLENCE IN PUBLIC PLACES

Cheryl S. Al-Mateen, Sala S. Webb, and Aradhana Bela Sood

1966: Charles Whitman, a 25-year-old student at the University of Texas at Austin, experienced headaches. He met with a campus psychiatrist in March and told him about a growing sense of rage, as well as about thoughts of shooting people with a rifle from the tower at the university. After one session, he was told to return in one week for follow-up. He did not. A former marine, Charles had a recent history of amphetamine use, was upset about his parents' recent separation, and had been court-martialed in the marines. In the early hours of August 1, he killed his mother and wife; later that day he went to the university tower and shot and killed 16 people, wounding 32. Autopsy revealed a glioblastoma in the brain, which may have contributed to the homicides. (Langman, 2009; Megargee, 2009; Texas Governor's Fact Finding Committee, 1966)

1997: Michael, a 14-year-old ninth grader in a Southern town, was frequently teased as a "dweeb" or "faggot" and was regularly bullied. He was labeled "gay" in the school paper. He had mentioned the idea of bringing guns to school to peers. He was also known to be a bit of a comedian. He told some students to stay away from the school lobby during the following week. No one told an adult. He stole a semi-automatic weapon from a neighbor and took it to school, shooting eight times into a group of students who had gathered for prayer in the school lobby. He killed three and wounded five. (Langman, 2009)

2009: Frank, a 15-year-old male, was a ninth-grade student in a public high school in an affluent neighborhood in a Southern town. His family had moved to the area when he was in the seventh grade. He always made A's and B's, was on the junior varsity football team, and attended various school events. He counted some of the most popular teenagers in his grade as his friends on Facebook, including varsity football players and cheerleaders. A few months after school started, he noted that he was not included in invitations to some events and began to ask why. On his Facebook page, he began to identify certain peers as being on his list of "special friends." Some students perceived this as creating a "hit list" and confronted this on his Facebook wall; others notified school administration, bringing printouts from Facebook to the principal's office. Frank's parents were contacted and he was referred to his community mental health center for emergency evaluation. He was immediately hospitalized for psychiatric assessment and treatment.

Violence in public places is usually planned, and those plans are often told to others before the event. As a society, we have learned how to interpret the information that may be revealed before a school shooting, although it is difficult to identify one common predisposing factor that leads to a violent act. The examples given above show a progression in our ability to recognize the potential for danger presented by some students in our schools and universities. In the earlier incidents we find that students did not tell anyone about a potential threat. We have progressed to a time in which students recognize the appropriateness of reporting danger instead and the priority of maintaining a safe environment.

Youth violence has been designated a public health concern by the U.S. Surgeon General, and "no community, whether affluent or poor, urban, suburban, or rural is immune from its devastating effects" (U.S. Surgeon General, 2001). Violent acts that occur on school property are referred to as school violence. Henry (2000) has defined school violence as "the exercise of power over others in school-related settings, by some individual, agency, or social process, that denies those subject to it their humanity to make a difference, either by reducing them from what they are or by limiting them from becoming what they might be" (p. 21). Such violence includes "physical aggression...psychological traumas, sexual abuse and numerous other 'boundary' violations" (McLaughlin & Miller, 2008, p. 431). The school is often a venue and context where students develop a sense of their identity and, as such, it can become the setting within which both positive and negative events in a student's life are played out.

How can youth violence be prevented? Generally speaking, mental health professionals have been more effective at retrospective reconstructions of the elements involved in a violent act than in accurately foretelling when one will occur. Prevention often rests, in this context, upon students' peers reporting worrisome behavior to the authorities. However, in the case of Virginia Tech, despite worrisome signs of an unraveling mind, accessible through information provided by the English Department faculty and his fellow students, both the professionals at the Cook Counseling Center and the administrators at Virginia Tech seemed to have lost the opportunity to predict that Seung-Hui Cho could be a threat. While precise prediction is still not possible in a general sense, the methods and tools available to help identify those factors associated with heightened risk for an individual to engage in violent acts have evolved over the past three decades. Students have learned to recognize warning signs and report them. In the past, students would focus on the negative social repercussions of "tattling" on their peers; today, many realize that reporting ensures safety.

This chapter will take the reader through the evolution of the field of public violence prevention: beginning with some pertinent definitions, elucidating the components and influences involved that create the "perfect storm" for a violent occurrence, highlighting some methods of assessing the level of threat, and, finally, suggesting points of intervention to reduce potential negative outcomes, with particular reference to universities. Each of these topics could comprise a book in itself; as such, this may be considered a brief review, with references to definitive works. We will review literature relating specifically to rampage type shootings, as they create a considerable challenge for administrators. We will use case examples from the known events as well as from clinical practice.

On the surface, public acts of violence often lack an obvious rationale and thus preventive measures may appear virtually impossible to implement. However, knowledge of antecedents of mass violence, characteristics of the perpetrator, and recognition of warning signs can assist policy-makers and school leaders in developing coherent procedures and action steps that have the potential to prevent or reduce these tragic occurrences.

AGGRESSION AND VIOLENCE

Aggression, in some form, is usually present when a violent act transpires. It is a universal construct, seen in the animal kingdom and sanctioned in various forms throughout the history of human society. Aggression (Megargee, 2009) is an overt verbal or physical behavior that can harm people and other living creatures by causing them distress, damage, pain, or injury, or by damaging their property or reputation with the intent to harm. On the other end of the spectrum, violence is severe physical aggression that is likely to cause serious damage or injury. Delizonna, Alan, and Steiner (2006) conclude that violence comes from a combination of "psychological variables, external events, risk factors, and contextual dynamics" (p. 618). A biopsychosociocultural perspective, as discussed below, is helpful to acknowledge the impact of environmental circumstances, or the context, that leads up to the violence (Muschert, 2008).

The factors that contribute to aggression progressing to overt violence are many, including inherent characteristics of the aggressor and the aggressor's external milieu. The environment heavily influences an individual's decision-making process.

INTERNAL FACTORS
Biological and Physiological Factors

From the time that the fetus is conceived in the intrauterine environment, biological factors are at work: genes passed down from parents to their offspring can carry traits for certain conditions or diseases. If the fetal brain is exposed to any insults that may result from injuries or exposure to toxins, these can impact development of the brain. Certain diseases and disorders of the central nervous system such as epilepsy or brain tumors can also interfere with fetal brain function. Likewise, dysfunctional hormonal (e.g., steroids, thyroid) and neurotransmitter (e.g., glutamate, serotonin) systems can influence behavior (Hart, 1995). Other forms of physical illnesses and their chronicity with associated pain or disability can account for permanent changes in personality (Megargee, 2009). Perinatal exposure to abuse can have lasting effects on neuroplasticity and optimum neurotransmitter development. All of these early influences can sensitize the brain to extremely low levels of arousal. Catastrophic emotional reactions to minor stimuli in later life may be a result of these historical factors.

James is a 9-year-old male who was born full-term with prenatal exposure to cocaine, alcohol, and nicotine. His parents had a difficult relationship, and his father physically abused his mother throughout the pregnancy. Because his parents separated and divorced by the time he was 15 months old, James lived with his maternal grandparents while his mother was in drug rehabilitation. James' grandparents found him to be extremely impulsive and hyperactive, and had difficulty keeping him in daycare because he was so disruptive to his peers and teachers. James responded with aggression to unpredictable events, and started seeing a therapist at age four. His first hospitalization was at age six, and he has been admitted two or three times yearly since that time. His family now receives services from the community mental health center, including integrated wraparound services that include therapies at school and an in-home therapist that comes almost daily to both home and school. He has received different psychotropic medications with minimal effect. After a consultation with community mental health and school resources, he was referred for residential treatment.

Psychological Factors

Among other skills, innate cognitive ability allows an individual to appraise his or her environment in a realistic fashion. Borum (1996) states that the risk of violence increases for those with lower intelligence and mild mental retardation. This can be understood in terms of the misperception of any given situation and the misreading of cues, with resulting inappropriately exaggerated reactions with aggression being one of them. Logical analysis and debriefing with the individual does not have lasting effect, as the behavior makes good sense to the individual at the particular moment it occurred. Personality attributes such as being over-controlling and narcissistic, having a hypertrophied sense of injustice, and believing in an external locus of control have been associated with violence (Loza & Dhaliwal, 2005). In addition, the presence of psychopathic traits (which includes the combination of impulsivity, callousness, and a lack of remorse) raise the chances of violent behaviors (Hart, 1995).

Psychiatric Factors

Loza and Dhaliwal (2005) found that the psychiatric conditions with the strongest positive predictors for future violence were paranoid psychoses, active delusions (particularly those persecutory in nature), and personality disorders (maladaptive and seemingly persistent patterns of behavior that hinge on chaotic and disruptive interpersonal relationships or lack thereof). In Seung-Hui Cho's case, although anxiety and selective mutism were childhood characteristics, the probability of a developing delusional disorder while he was at Virginia Tech (proposed in Chapter 4) could explain the switch to violence. Ho, Thompson, and Darjee (2009) determined that it was not simply the presence of any one condition, but the *combination* of schizophrenia/schizoaffective disorder with substance and alcohol abuse and personality disorder that was particularly potent in the emergence of serious violence.

Substance Abuse

Multiple studies have revealed that substance and alcohol abuse or misuse is significantly correlated with violence (Norko & Baranoski, 2005). The impact of substances is greater than that of mental illness and amplifies when the two are combined, especially when the individual is nonadherent to treatment medications.

Motivations

These are synonymous with the driving forces behind the act of violence and are unique to the individual. A person can become violent in an effort to respond to an aversive event or provocation; to defend territory; to attain a personal, religious or political goal; or as part of a job description (professional sports, law enforcement, and military) (Megargee, 2009).

Inhibitions

Based on the model that there is some form of decision-making or intentionality involved prior to a violent act, it stands to reason that inhibitory influences occupy a role. At the basic level, these may be moral in nature, that is, the belief that being violent is bad. A person can prevent him- or herself from being violent by considering that possible punitive consequences may follow, or that the plan being attempted may not succeed (Megargee, 2009).

EXTERNAL FACTORS

Cultural Factors

If one lives in a society or subculture that promotes aggression and violence, it is easier to engage in these behaviors (Hayes & Lee, 2005). As evidenced in riots and warzones, the immediate climate of a location can also promote hostility as acceptable in the moment (Megargee, 2009).

Situational Factors

When someone is attacked or threatened, the innate need to retaliate and defend oneself often facilitates violence (Megargee, 2009).

Models and Reinforcers

Persons who have suffered abuse at the hands of caregivers are at heightened risk of becoming abusers themselves, thus perpetuating a cycle of brutality (McCloskey & Bailey, 2000). Berkowitz (1970) first described the phenomenon now known as the *contagion effect*, in which there is an increase in violence following highly publicized aggressive crimes.

Group Pressures

In order to be identified with a chosen assemblage of peers, an individual may engage in violent acts to seek the group's approval. Examples of this are seen in gang initiations, fraternity hazing, group bullying, and extremist political and religious organizations, as well as in various cults (Megargee, 2009).

STATIC VARIABLES

Static variables are the historical components of an individual's profile that are fixed, yet have proven utility in predicting long-term risk for violence. Examples include the following:

1. Male gender
2. Witnessing violence
3. Early age of onset of violent behavior
4. Greater number of past violent transgressions
5. History of childhood pyromania or cruelty to animals

6. Exposure to harsh, erratic, or neglectful parenting (Loza & Dhaliwal, 2005; Norko & Baranoski, 2005)

DYNAMIC VARIABLES

These factors are amenable to change and as such are potential treatment targets or points of intervention to reduce the risk of future violence (Loza & Dhaliwal, 2005). Examples include the various environmental and social constructs, such as:

(1) Poor ties to the community
(2) Limited educational and vocational resources
(3) Easy access to weapons or potential victims

Dynamic variables also encompass psychological elements, such as:

(1) Negative beliefs
(2) Poor coping skills
(3) Acute psychiatric illness
(4) Substance use (Scott & Resnick, 2009)

On the other side of risk factors are protective factors. Just as risk factors do not necessarily cause an individual child or young person to become violent, protective factors do not guarantee that an individual child or young person will not become violent. They reduce the probability that groups of young people facing a risk factor or factors will become involved in violence. These protective factors can reside (1) in the individual (intolerant attitude toward deviance, a high IQ, perceived sanctions for transgressions, being female), (2) family (warm, supportive relationship of parent with the child, parents' positive evaluation of the child's peer group, adequate parental monitoring), (3) peer group (friends engaging in conventional behavior), (4) school (strong commitment to school) and/or the community (low-crime neighborhood, organized community) (U.S. Surgeon General, 2001).

DEFINING SCHOOL VIOLENCE

Various types of violence—physical or verbal assault, theft, sexual assault, rape, homicide, and suicide—can take place on school property or during transportation to or from school (Murakami, Rappaport, & Penn, 2006). Incidents may involve other types of crime, such as robbery or vandalism, and may target victims (Henry, 2009). However, targeted school violence is defined as "any incident of violence where a current student or recent former student attacked someone at his or her school with lethal means and where the student attacker purposefully chose his or her school as the location of the attack" (Vossekuil, Fein, Reddy, Borum, & Modzeleski, 2002). These forms of violence occur on a continuum and have cumulative escalation of negativity based on perceived interrelational and interactional problems between the perpetrator and the victim. Violence may be literal (physical) or symbolic (emotional). It may be perpetrated by the student toward another student, toward a teacher, or by groups of students toward an individual or group of students (i.e., high school cliques and hierarchy of power based on social position within the group).

The pyramid of social standing in middle and high school is complex. Students may feel isolated and feel identified by others as losers, placing them at higher risk of being bullied either physically or socially. Students in particular sports or extracurricular activities may receive more recognition for their accomplishments, leaving other students feeling overlooked despite significant achievements (Newman, Fox, Roth, Mehta, & Harding, 2004). Violence may also be perpetrated by a teacher or administrator toward a student through individual or institutionalized interactions (Henry, 2009).

J.D., a 13-year-old resident of Texas, was given a school assignment to write a "scary" story about Halloween. He wrote a story that included someone shooting up a school. (Frost, 2001; Martin, 2001)

Michael, aged 14, stole one pistol, two shotguns, two semi-automatic rifles, and several hundred rounds of ammunition. He showed them to his peers over the weekend, then brought them to school, hoping they would think he was cool. (Kimmel & Mahler, 2003)

Rampage School Shooting

A "rampage school shooting" is aimed at the school as an institution (Fox & Harding, 2005) and has four main characteristics:

(1) The location of the incident is a "public stage," either on the school property or at a school-related function.
(2) The shooters must be current or former students of the school
(3) There must be multiple victims (fatal or nonfatal) or at least multiple targets.
(4) While some victims may be targeted specifically because they have wronged the shooter, there are typically others who are chosen only for their symbolic significance or are shot at random (Harding, Fox, & Mehta, 2002).

Cornell and Sheras (2006) note that homicides by students are actually very rare occurrences. Given that there were 103 such events from the 1992-3 through the 2003-4 academic years, the average occurrence is 8.58 homicides per year. As there were 119,000 schools in the United States at that time, it can be concluded that a school may expect a student-perpetrated homicide once every 13,870 years. It is useful to consider that typically, school-related homicides are single-victim incidents, in areas designated as urban or large towns (Centers for Disease Control and Prevention [CDC], 2008b). Typically, less than 1% of homicides in youth aged 5–18 are associated with schools (CDC, 2008b). Student fights, bullying, theft, and other forms of crime are more common.

In 2007-8, over 55.7 million students were enrolled in schools in the United States. During that academic year, there were 43 school-associated violent deaths and 1.5 million victims of nonfatal crimes (Dinkes, Kemp, & Baum, 2009). From 1999 to 2006, most school-associated homicides included gunshot wounds (65%), stabbing or cutting (27%), and beating (12%) (CDC, 2009). Similarly, homicides on college campuses are a rare event. Between 2001 and 2005, 51 of the 76 homicides reported on college campuses in the United States were of students, which is about 10 per year. Most of these did not involve rampage shootings (Fox & Savage, 2009).

While much less frequent than other forms of school violence, the rampage school shooting provokes a great deal of fear at the school where it has occurred, in the immediate community, as well as in the nation (Vossekuil et al., 2002). Although the first rampage school shooting took place in 1966, there has been an explosion in the literature on school shootings since a cluster of these occurred in the United States in the late 1990s (Brown, Osterman, & Barnes, 2009; Callahan 2008; CDC 2008b; DeJong, Epstein, & Hart, 2003; Delizonna et al., 2006; Fox & Harding, 2005; Harding et al., 2002; Kaiser, 2005; Kimmel & Mahler, 2003; Langman, 2009; Larkin, 2009; Leary, Kowalski, Smith, & Phillips, 2003; Muschert, 2008). Larkin (2009) identifies the Columbine school massacre as a watershed event in rampage shootings; there have been copycat or memorializing attempts with a rapid connection made to Columbine since April 1999. Further, schools have increased security measures and instituted "zero tolerance" policies toward any behavior that has even a hint of violence. Despite the high-profile nature of Columbine, the policy of zero tolerance for any perceived threat has been unfortunately less than visionary, as its primary focus has been on safety without any mandates to consider rehabilitation. The immediate expulsion of a student without a parallel process of exploring possible causal mental health issues misses an opportunity for intervention for often highly treatable situations (Skiba et al., 2006). In the wake of Virginia Tech and similar tragedies across several universities, students now have a heightened awareness of the social responsibility to report aberrant behavior or suspicious comments that may suggest violent leanings to school authorities. In the past they might have ignored the comments or behaviors out of fear of being labeled a "tattler" or a "snitch."

Significantly, there have been at least 11 international rampage school shootings since Columbine, with six students making direct reference to the April 1999 event (Larkin, 2009) (see Appendix). Interestingly, besides students, faculty, administration, or staff can also be perpetrators in a school shooting (Muschert, 2008).

CHARACTERISTICS OF PERPETRATORS OF SCHOOL VIOLENCE

Internal Factors

Despite numerous attempts to draw a clear profile of the rampage school shooter, none exists (Kimmel & Mahler, 2003; Klein, 2006; Larkin, 2009; Leary et al., 2003; Vossekuil et al., 2002). Individual factors that increase the likelihood of committing rampage school violence include being a white male, having a history of teasing by peers as someone who is less than masculine, having a sense of alienation, and experiencing romantic rejection by a female peer (Kimmel & Mahler, 2003; Klein, 2006). Larkin (2009) notes, however, that three college campus rampage shootings were by minority students, while only two post-Columbine secondary school shootings were by students of color. Perpetrators have also often been found to have a strong interest in firearms or bombs or to have a fascination with death or Satanism. Many have difficulties with impulse control or have sadistic tendencies, depression, or suicidality (Leary et al., 2003, Vossekuil et al., 2002). Seaton (2007) as well as Schiele and Stewart (2001) note the heightened level of isolation and invisibility experienced by the rural white male student who becomes violent in this manner. They also point out the relationship between perceived masculinity and aggression and the lack of expected privilege that may contribute to rampage shootings. "Privilege is an advantage...people enjoy from their similarity to the norms operating in a particular situation. The more similar a person is to the valued norms, the more privilege or advantage the person enjoys" (Parsons, 2001, p. 322). Privilege is inherited, not earned, and has been associated with male gender as well as white race (McIntosh, 1986). In some of these situations, we see white males reacting to a perceived loss of this privilege.

In his analysis of 10 rampage school shootings, Langman (2009) divides school shooters into three types: psychopathic, psychotic, and traumatized. He describes the psychopathic shooters as having "narcissism, callousness, immorality and other features," and difficulty with anger management. He notes that the psychotic perpetrators have a history of some form of mental illness, including symptoms of depression, hallucinations, paranoia, and severe social impairment; he describes them as having schizophrenia-spectrum disorders. Traumatized shooters have a significant life history of emotional, physical, and/or sexual abuse. The dynamic operative in the repeatedly traumatized individual who is transformed from being a victim to a perpetrator is the externalization of the internalized angst, distress, and bitterness produced by years of being bullied and abused. The last two groups of perpetrators, the psychotic and the traumatized youth, experience conditions that could be addressed proactively to prevent future violence. Samples of these typologies are reviewed in the following case histories.

Andrew G., aged 11, grew up in a family that hunted regularly. He drew a picture of two guns when given a school assignment to draw something that was representative of his family. He was known to behave relatively well with his parents and in school. On very few occasions, however, he did get into trouble at school. After one incident, his grandfather yelled at the teacher, not at Andrew. In another incident, a teacher corrected Andrew's behavior and his parents pulled him out of that classroom. Away from school, Andrew was often threatening and aggressive to other children. He was cruel to cats, starving them or slitting their throats. One day, Andrew and his friend deliberately missed the school bus, and took guns from his and his grandfather's house. After lunch, he pulled the fire alarm, waited for everyone to leave the building, and then began to shoot with his friend. They killed four girls and a teacher and injured nine students. (Langman, 2009)

Andrew W., age 14, left a suicide note in his room when he went to his eighth-grade dinner dance. He took his father's pistol from the house. He alluded to having a gun to his friends while at the dance. Although they were worried he might kill himself, they did not inform any adults, but tried to watch him themselves. He began shooting randomly and killed one teacher, wounding two students and another teacher. He was stopped by an adult. He stated, "I died four years ago. I've already been dead and I've come back. It doesn't matter anymore. None of this is real." (DeJong et al., 2003, Langman, 2009)

Evan, age 16, was living in a foster home. His father had just been released from a 10-year prison sentence for a rampage shooting at a newspaper office that refused to print a letter he wrote to a government official. Evan's girlfriend had broken up with him and his CD player had been confiscated at school. Starting at the age of seven, Evan and his brothers were intermittently removed from their mother's custody and placed in foster care related to their mother's alcoholism and neglect. In addition, their father and at least two of their mother's boyfriends had been violent toward her. While in foster care, they would run to their principal's house and would be returned to foster homes as many as 10 times. Evan began attempting suicide at age 10. He was physically and sexually abused by at least one older boy. At age 16, he decided to take a weapon to school and showed it to his peers. They encouraged him to establish a hit list and kill several others; one peer taught him how to use a shotgun. One student brought a camera to school to capture the events. None of the peers told their parents about Evan bringing a gun to school. Evan shot and killed a student and the principal. He held the gun under his chin to kill himself, but was unable to do so. (Langman, 2009)

Andrew G. would be considered "psychopathic" in the Langman typology. Andrew W. would be an example of "psychotic" and Evan would be an example of a traumatized rampage shooter.

In their review, Levin and Madfis (2009) list five stages of a rampage killing:

(1) Chronic strain
(2) Uncontrolled strain
(3) Acute strain
(4) Planning
(5) The massacre

They identify a basic level of chronic strain as a precursor of rampages in the family, workplace, and schools. Perpetrators who kill family members typically have long-term family conflicts and financial problems. Those who commit workplace shootings have had long-term stress at work and generally feel as if they failed at work because they have not achieved the professional advancement they expected.

Similarly, students may have experienced stress at home as well as at school. They have generally felt chronic rejection by their peers. Once an individual experiences this chronic strain, it is compounded by a lack of supportive relationships. Such individuals feel isolated or may be part of a marginalized or "fringe" social group. There is typically an additional, acute strain, which for adults may entail job, financial, housing, or relationship loss. In the instance of a school shooter, this loss may be a humiliation such as a romantic rejection, a decrease in academic standing, or expulsion from a group of peers.

For college shooters, academic failure is more likely an acute event than social failure. The college environment is conducive to living independently and the sense of community and social networks present in high school have not developed fully in the freshman year. The lack of familial and peer relationships, the unfamiliar environment, and the day-to-day challenges of transitioning to adulthood in the face of stress lead to a perfect storm that can transform into depression, substance use, rage, and resentment. The idea of the mass killing is seen as the only way to regain one's masculinity or to be accepted or respected by those who have ignored the perpetrator for far too long. Once the decision is made to commit a massacre, the event must be planned. This may take days to weeks, or months to a year or more.

External Factors

Henry (2009) notes that there is a range of precipitants for school shootings that include various forms of violence, such as "physical, psychological and symbolic" violence. Various macro- and micro-conditions have been considered as potential risk factors, including whether or not the school allowed corporal punishment. Arcus (2002) found that shootings were more likely to occur in states that permitted corporal punishment in schools. These states are identified by Brown et al. (2009) as having a "culture of honor." In these states, there is a long-term culture in which "insults and threats to reputation, self, home, or family are taken quite seriously and are often met with violence" (Cohen, 1998, p. 408) as opposed to some other method. Emotionality and open communication may be less valued than stoicism in these localities. In these states, students are more likely to bring weapons to school, and school shootings are more common (Brown et al., 2009).

Numerous authors have attempted to identify specific characteristics that led to shootings in the past (Arcus, 2002; Brown et al., 2009; Cohen, 1998; DeJong et al., 2003; Delizonna et al., 2006; Fox & Harding, 2005; Harding et al., 2002; Henry, 2009; Johnson & Fisher, 2003; Kaiser, 2005; Kimmel & Mahler 2003; Langman, 2009; Larkin, 2009; Leary et al., 2003; Levin & Madfis, 2009; Muschert, 2008; Newman et al., 2004; Schiele & Stewart, 2001; Seaton, 2007). Newman et al. (2004) describe that while many individuals working within a school may be aware of warning signs evident in a student's behavior, the organization of schools prevents the sharing of such information so as not to unnecessarily prejudice other teachers in the same school against the student. Information is filtered among administration, teachers, and guidance counselors. As rampage shooters do not typically cause numerous problems throughout the school community, details of their behavior generally have not been made known to all adults involved. Further, there may be a misinterpretation of a child's behavior.

There may also be a "loss of information" that occurs when teachers, schools, and communities do not have systems in place to pass on information regarding problematic behaviors to the subsequent school. Andrew G., described earlier, generally presented well to teachers, but he was quite different with his peers and was often aggressive. Fox and Harding (2005) reviewed two rampage school shootings in which information was available for months or years before the events that could have identified the high-risk status of the three shooters involved. Indeed, Seung-Hui Cho's case underscores the importance of loss of information in this shooting: no one at Virginia Tech put all the facts together, which might have brought him the much-needed mental health assistance and perhaps prevented the massacre. Kaiser (2005) notes that schools with class sizes of over 150 are at a higher risk for violence and antisocial behaviors. There is also concern that the reaction of and coverage by the media elevates these disastrous events into spectacles, perhaps serving as motivation for future shooters (Frymer, 2009).

An additional factor that may contribute to school shootings is the lack of resources in schools. While academic achievement is the priority, there is some recognition that school is an ideal place for the nurturance of social and emotional development of children as well. There may not be time or personnel for these additional agendas. Guidance counselors may be assigned numerous responsibilities by school administration, and maintaining emotional health of the students may be at or near the bottom of the list.

THE PREDICTION OF VIOLENCE AND THREAT ASSESSMENT

In recent years, the research on risk assessment has progressed from the less effective "prediction of future dangerousness" approach to the "violence risk assessment" (Cornell & Sheras, 2006). This new approach involves not only an appreciation for the base rates for commission of violence but also an understanding of the individual as a person and the potential for contributing (as noted in the previous section) to violence or protective or buffering factors (noted in the section Dynamic Variables). Because a rampage school shooting is a rare event, it is difficult to accurately identify potential cases without the misidentification of false positives as well (Mulvey & Cauffman, 2001). Newer models of risk assessment with management of this risk are both more appropriate and effective than attempts to predict whether a specific individual will become violent (Mulvey & Cauffman, 2001). Langman (2009) notes that the process of threat assessment is focused on students who *may* pose a danger to the school, whether or not the student has actually made a threat.

Threat assessment was initially developed by the Secret Service to manage events and intervene when a public official was threatened (Vossekuil et al., 2002). It can be used in any situation in which someone poses a threat; a specific direct threat is not required (Borum, 2000; Cornell & Sheras, 2006). The FBI recommended a four-pronged approach to assess the level of threat presented by a student (Critical Incident Response Group, 2000). This entails a multidisciplinary team, which assesses the following:

(1) The personality of the student (including behavior characteristics and personality traits)
(2) Family dynamics
(3) School dynamics and the student's role in those dynamics
(4) Social dynamics (of the community at large)

The team then ultimately concludes whether there is a low, medium, or high level of threat to the victim and public safety.

The Virginia model for student threat assessment (Figure 7.1) was specifically created for assessing the seriousness of a threat by a student in an educational situation. It also involves multidisciplinary teams of (school) personnel, adding others if needed. The group follows a decision tree to determine if the threat is transient or substantive. Substantive threats are further identified as serious or very serious. The transient threat may result in disciplinary action, mediation, and/or counseling. The serious threat requires precautions to protect the community, appropriate interventions, disciplinary action, and the possible involvement of law enforcement. The very serious threat requires a safety evaluation in addition to a mandatory mental health evaluation and those steps taken for a serious threat (Cornell & Sheras, 2006).

With the designation of "very serious," the individual will likely be placed in some form of restrictive environment. If there is no overt evidence of psychiatric or severe psychological impairment, the individual is taken into the custody of law enforcement; otherwise, hospitalization in a psychiatric facility, often against the student's will, is pursued. Significant substantiating data supporting the decision to take custody are required before limiting an individual's human rights. This takes into account the dilemma of weighing the need for public safety against the rights of the individual. A society can better tolerate false positives (individuals who are not future violent offenders but may receive more restrictive interventions) than false negatives (those who commit violent acts but evade restriction) (Megargee, 2009). Once a clear threat to harm an identifiable target has been expressed by a student in the presence of a mental health professional, the professional is ethically and legally bound to pursue some form of restrictive intervention, as previously described (Pabian, Welfel, & Beebe, 2009).

At times the threshold for sufficient dangerousness to necessitate hospitalization is not crossed, yet the individual may still need treatment because of significant occupational or social dysfunction. As insight may be diminished in the throes of the acute phase of illness, seeking voluntary treatment is often a challenge. In January 1999, Kendra Webdale was pushed in front of a New York subway train by Andrew Goldstein, a young man with a history of psychiatric illness and related hospitalizations. Recognizing the danger posed by individuals who by virtue of a history of mental illness do not voluntarily seek treatment and inferentially have a hard time living safely in their communities, Governor George Pataki of New York signed Kendra's Law (Chapter 408 of the Laws of 1999), creating a statutory framework for court-ordered assisted outpatient treatment (AOT). Commitment to mandated AOT has been suggested as a way of providing intervention in a least restrictive setting, recognizing the danger that "no treatment" poses.

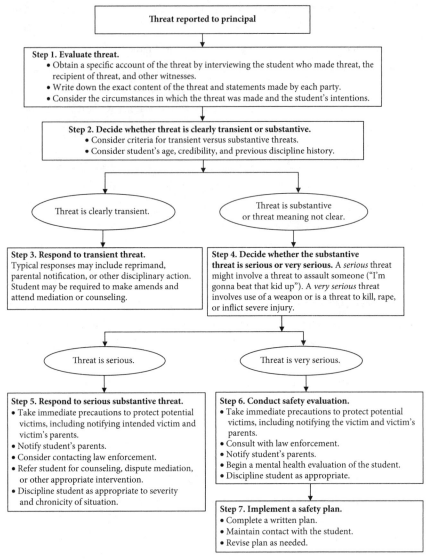

FIG 7.1 Virginia model of student threat assessment.

Reprinted with permission by Dewey Cornell and by Cambium Learning Group-Sopris Learning (Cornell & Sheras, 2006, p. 16).

Follow-up studies after this law was passed in New York have shown that in the few years of implementation, 77% fewer people had to be psychiatrically hospitalized (New York State Office of Mental Health, 2005) and arrests, homelessness, victimizations, and acts of violence dropped significantly (Hiday, Swartz, Swanson, Borum, & Wagner, 2002). All these interventions are humane ways of approaching illnesses so that those who suffer do not by default end up in the criminal justice system. The dilemma after an AOT is issued, however, is that it's not clear what checks and balances are available for the courts, providers, and family if the individual is noncompliant with the court order. In fact, Seung-Hui Cho had been ordered to outpatient treatment, a directive that no one followed up on, including Seung-Hui.

Scott and Resnick (2009) emphasize that all threats should be taken seriously and any associated details fully elucidated. Vossekuil et al. (2002) recommend training for school and law enforcement personnel in the gathering of information and appropriate interventions if there is concern about a school attack. In many circumstances, mental health professionals are consulted. The stated reason for mental health referral is typically for the clinician to determine whether someone is an immediate threat to the safety of others.

Mental health evaluators must identify any possible grudge lists, investigate any fantasies the potential perpetrator may have about violence, and assess the individual's risk for suicide, as violent suicide attempts increase the likelihood of future violence toward others. Acute psychiatric illness increases this risk, particularly active psychotic symptoms (Norko & Baranoski, 2005). Likewise, when the potential victim is readily identifiable and accessible, and the would-be perpetrator has devised a plan of how to procure weapons and carry out the threat, the level of alarm should heighten (Shaw, 2000). Long-term risk is established primarily through background and historical data. Information on demographics, childhood experiences, and previous patterns of behavior are included in this computation (Norko & Baranoski, 2005). Once an individual has been assessed regarding potential to commit a violent offense, the next step is to effectively convey findings to those involved and other stakeholders.

Jackson and Guyton (2008) have outlined a three-tiered approach to effective communication in regard to violence risk assessment. (1) The mental health professional determines whether the individual in question poses a high, moderate, or low risk and whether this is imminent or longer term. (2) Specific factors derived from the individual's static and dynamic variables that place him or her at risk are examined. (3) Lastly, interventions are proposed that could potentially reduce the likelihood of the individual acting violently.

Methods of Assessment

Mental health professionals conduct formal assessments of individuals suspected to be at risk for perpetrating violent events. They may use a wide range of instruments, ranging from an unstructured clinical interview, to measures that formally assess static and dynamic variables, to structured interviews that promote standardization. Some common examples of these are listed in Table 7.1.

Table 7.1 Methods of Violence Assessment

Category	Example	Comments
Unstructured clinical assessments	Clinical interview	This refers to the traditional style of conversational interview; it is heavily weighted on the acumen and subjectivity of the clinician.
Rationally derived assessments	Level of Service Inventory- Revised (LSI-R)	These are clinical scales that assess rationally (as opposed to empirically) derived static and dynamic variables with the goal of informing treatment interventions.
Actuarially derived assessments	Violence Risk Appraisal Guide (VRAG)	This form of assessment is derived from analyzing statistical data points that are associated with violence. It does not explain causation and only takes into account more static and historical variables, rather than more dynamic and psychological elements.
Self-reports	Self Appraisal Questionnaire (SAQ)	As the name implies, the individual being evaluated completes this questionnaire, which is then scored and interpreted.
Structured professional judgment	Historical/Clinical/ Risk Management-20 (HCR-20)	Its foundation is the traditional clinical interview, but provides specific guidelines to facilitate consistency and standardization of the process.

PREVENTION

With so many factors and catalysts to consider, there is no fool-proof way to forecast with absolute certainty when and if an individual will commit a violent act. The focus, then, is on *prevention* rather than *prediction*. Based on the components of aggression delineated earlier in this chapter and the numerous dynamic variables that lend themselves to change, it is likely that there are many points along a given individual's path that are ripe for intervention to reduce the risk of that individual becoming violent.

Prevention of a violent school shooting is two-dimensional. It involves recognizing and making interventions directed toward (1) a potential perpetrator of a shooting (individual factors), and (2) a situation which is ripe for such an event. These risk factors are described next.

Reducing Influence of Individual Factors

While there is no profile of the rampage school shooter, as discussed earlier, there are risk factors. As these risk factors are varied, so are the means to address them, and their presence indicates areas of potential intervention within the school system. The potential shooter, such as "Frank," described in the introduction, ideally should be identified early enough that he is not perceived as a threat to his entire school. If his problems are not recognized in a timely manner he may require placement in another setting, promoting more marginalization. This increased marginalization heightens his risk and may worsen his prognosis.

The identification of individual characteristics includes psychosocial as well as biological factors. Any treatable medical condition identified should be readily addressed. This includes the balancing of dysregulated hormones or antiepileptic medications for seizures. Likewise, psychiatric illness may require treatment through psychotropic medications, various psychotherapies, and hospitalization, if warranted. Appropriate individual and/or group therapy sessions may prove beneficial in ameliorating negative psychological influences. Individuals with substance abuse, dependence, or misuse concerns should be referred to validated substance abuse treatment programs. Bell and Fink (2000) identify the teaching of empathy as an important component in reducing the risk of violence. They cite prevention measures involving the institution of child-rearing practices designed to ensure bonding, attachment, and mastery as their primary method.

Risk factors, which may also be identified as early warning signs, are factors that various personnel in the school may be aware of (Table 7.2). These develop over time. The school may refer the child for intervention for any and all of these. Imminent warning signs are more acute indicators that a child may become violent in the future. Coupled with threats of violence, these signs should trigger an immediate response, including a threat assessment, if it has not been completed already.

All students with risk factors or warning signs will not become violent (Dwyer, Oher, & Warger, 1998). Personal resilience and protective factors (Al-Mateen, 2002) reduce the likelihood of negative effects of other risk factors. Examples of these are early bonding with parents, the presence of a consistent, caring adult, using available school and faith-based supports, and having a strong sense of personal control over one's own outcome (Anthony & Cohler, 1987; Gabarino, Dubrow, & Kostelny, 1992). The recognition and enhancement of these protective factors is essential in the prevention of violence. Therefore, they must be clearly identified by school personnel in the threat assessment.

Table 7.2 Risk Factors for Violence

Early Warning Signs	Imminent Warning Signs
Social withdrawal	Serious physical fighting with peers or family members
Excessive feelings of isolation and being alone	
Excessive feelings of rejection	Severe destruction of property
Being a victim of violence	Severe rage for seemingly minor reasons
Feelings of being picked on and persecuted	Detailed threats of lethal violence
Low school interest and poor academic performance	Possession and/or use of firearms and other weapons
Expression of violence in writings and drawings	Other self-injurious behaviors or threats of suicide
Uncontrolled anger	Has presented a detailed plan to harm or kill others
Patterns of impulsive and chronic hitting, intimidating, and bullying behaviors	Is carrying a weapon, particularly a firearm, and has threatened to use it
History of discipline problems	
History of violent and aggressive behavior	
Drug and alcohol use	
Affiliation with gangs	
Intolerance for differences and prejudicial attitudes	
Inappropriate access to, possession of, and use of firearms	
Serious threats of violence	

Reducing Influence of External Factors

The immediate environments are the family, the neighborhood, and the school. The first need is to ensure safety in these environments. This may be achieved through hospitalization if the child is an imminent risk to others. It could also mean removing a child from dangerous parents or encouraging an adult to leave an abusive partner. A family may consider leaving a particular neighborhood if there is rampant community violence or war. Similarly, a recovering addict may need to move or stay away from the surroundings associated with former drug use. However, changing location may not always be feasible. Neighborhoods can be made safer by promoting the proper use and storage of weapons, enforcing curfews for adolescents, and facilitating constructive activities for youth to do after school hours and on weekends (Bell & Fink, 2000; Bell, Flay, & Paikoff, 2002; Mihalic & Elliott, 1997). Mentoring (Tierney, Grossman, & Resch, 1995), along with providing opportunities for community service and the development of leadership skills, are additional ways to introduce positive modeling and enhance self-esteem (Bell & Fink, 2000; Schwartz, 1996).

Recognizing the presence of risk factors (both internal and external) and providing treatment for them as early as possible is the ideal (Dwyer et al., 1998; Veltkamp & Lawson, 2008). This includes having systems in place that identify school-based resources for children at risk. This is a difficult process. The first hurdle that must be overcome is teaching the various school personnel about violence prevention (Callahan, 2008). The prevention of (as well as response to) an event such as a school shooting requires a multidisciplinary team, including health care providers, educators, social services, lawmakers, and community leaders, to address the needs of the child or adolescent, the school, and the community (Callahan, 2008; Delizonna et al., 2006).

A systematic review (Hahn et al. & Task Force on Community Preventive Services, 2007) conducted for the CDC's *Guide to Community Services (Community Guide)* found that institution of universal school-based programs decreases rates of violence among school-age children and youth. All school program intervention strategies (informational, cognitive/affective, and social-skills building) were associated with a reduction in violent behavior. Over all grades combined, the median effect was a 15% relative reduction in violent behavior, with *greatest effect seen at the pre-K/K level* (32.4% reduction). Program effects were consistent across grade levels and school environments (socioeconomic status, crime rates). A 2007 updated meta-analysis by Wilson and Lipsey that used roughly the same framework, definitions, and methods of the CDC *Community Guide* and assessed similar outcomes had similar findings: School-based programs for the prevention of violence are effective. Different treatment modalities (behavioral, cognitive, social skills) produced largely similar effects. Effects were larger for programs involving students at higher risk for aggressive behavior. These data support institutions taking a focused approach that emphasizes prosocial behaviors in children and adolescents and explicitly educating them about violence prevention very early on in their schooling.

The establishment of a safe school environment requires the work of numerous members of the school and its surrounding community: students, parents, teachers, guidance counselors, school nurses, psychologists, and administrators. School board members, community leaders, law enforcement, and even legislators are vital to this important process. Identification of risk factors or warning signs should generate an alert to needed school or community authorities (Strawhacker, 2002). It is imperative that open communication about violence increase in school settings—this involves the recognition of risk factors by staff, coping with potential risk factors, and stopping violent behaviors.

A positive school environment (Haynes, Emmons, & Woodruff, 1998) is an important preventive factor. In such an environment, students and teachers feel comfortable enough to share their concerns about troubled students with appropriate personnel. In the ideal environment, there is motivation to provide support and help (Mulvey & Cauffman, 2001). Newman and colleagues (2004) observed that an increase in mental health and counseling personnel as well as resource officers in the school would be helpful to increase communication and security in the schools. This will increase the number of adults who can connect with students, which in itself is a protective factor. Student safety, as well as the students' perception that they are in a safe environment, is a requirement. Newman et al. also recommend occasional programs to remind peers what to look for and how to report their concerns. Langman (2009) states that this would include teaching students "the difference between snitching…which is done to get someone in trouble, and reporting, which is done to keep people safe." Because many potential school shooters confide their intentions to one or more peers, a school culture that encourages adolescents to share their concerns about potential violence is also valuable.

Schools and colleges can create supportive atmospheres by promoting collegial and friendly attitudes, teaching about conflict resolution, educating about stress management, and providing each individual with the knowledge and tools needed to accomplish assigned goals. Administrators in these settings should remain cognizant of individuals who seem to be struggling in performance, socially isolated, or displaying other signs of concern. These persons should be referred to mental health or other appropriate agencies if the concern cannot be adequately addressed internally. Newman et al. (2004) note that transparency of academic, counseling, and disciplinary records should be maintained across the boundaries of grade levels as well as between different schools in the same district in order to decrease structural secrecy. Further, they suggest the use of a variety of teachers, noting that young male teachers provide an additional positive model of male adulthood that may be helpful. They add that increased recognition of the achievements of students in all activities increases cohesiveness between students and the community.

Levin and Madfis (2009) recommend the use of long-term prevention techniques, noting that time is of the essence once an event is in process. Because school shootings themselves typically last less than 15 minutes, a protocol must be in place so that resource officers, emergency plans, and other such measures can be activated quickly. Long-term strategies should include measures that will reduce chronic stress, by identifying risk factors that predispose individuals to violence and seeking help for those individuals. Institutions that place a high premium on (a) developing supports and interventions for such individuals, (b) articulating a zero tolerance policy for peer-on-peer crime, and (c) pursue a combined safety and rehabilitation model to address student misconduct will reduce the likelihood of morbidity and mortality from youth violence. These interventions increase the level and perception of safety in the school environment.

COLLEGE CAMPUS ENVIRONMENTS

Issues relating to college mental health were explored in Chapters 4 and 5. The concept of student-centeredness is paramount in establishing a supportive campus environment, particularly for graduate-level students (Fox & Savage, 2009). Because college students are not under the same scrutiny as students on a school grounds, aberrant behavior may go unnoticed or often ignored by peers and faculty. Universities should develop a clear student code of conduct for faculty, staff, and students and train students, staff, and faculty about acceptable behavior. Aberrant behavior should be recognized early and handled before it becomes a crisis. A robust and quick response mechanism to initiate a threat assessment should be available. There should be a clear reporting protocol for faculty and for resident advisors in dormitories regarding aberrant student behavior that involves notification of the dean of students or dean for academic affairs, and a feedback loop to faculty relaying what action has been taken (see Figure 6.3 in Chapter 6, on Virginia Commonwealth University policies).

As faculty and resident advisors are not trained mental health experts, their orientation should involve education about the meaning of disruptive behavior. Faculty may not report aberrant behavior for many reasons—they may think that the problems will spontaneously resolve; they may fear that problems will be perceived as a reflection of professional inadequacies or that they will receive inadequate administrative support; they may fear harming the student academically; or they may fear physical reprisal or the threat of litigation. Reviewing known situations from other schools with faculty may help them more easily recognize potentially dangerous scenarios in their classrooms.

Common disruptive behaviors in class include grandstanding, sleeping in class, prolonged chattering, excessive tardiness, leaving early, poor personal hygiene, overt inattentiveness, eating, wearing a pager or beepers, using cell phones, passing notes, text messaging, and disputing faculty expertise and authority (Amanda, 1999). Students may be disruptive because they are unaware of standards for behavioral conduct in higher education. They may be experiencing a difficult transition to college (i.e., still exhibiting "high school" behaviors). They may be stressed out, angry, or have mental health concerns. They may have cultural values, norms, and behaviors that are appropriate in their own cultural environment but clash with a classroom setting.

Proactive approaches for faculty include creating a classroom with a climate of respect, sense of community, and connection, with utilization of peer-to-peer reinforcement of support. Empathic listening and faculty-to-faculty consultation in cases of concern about a student can reduce the chances of missing inappropriate behavior that may be a harbinger of future trouble. Faculty should set clear expectations for behavior, communicate clearly and consistently, and confront inappropriate behavior immediately and assertively. A proportional and graduated response to disruptive behavior, with threats taken seriously and reported to the appropriate dean, should be made explicit to faculty.

Lamb (1992) has provided a blueprint of this graduated response to disruptive behavior: respond, don't react; meet with the student privately initially and ascertain if the student is aware that his or her behavior is disruptive. Faculty should attempt to identify feelings behind disruptive behavior, discuss consequences of continued disruptive behavior, and involve the student in addressing the problem and finding solutions. Faculty should also explore environmental strategies, such as changing seating within the classroom, identifying resources to assist the student, and consulting with other faculty. Documentation of behavior should describe the behavior, its time and date, and what actions were taken. The behavior of disruptive students makes teaching and learning difficult for others in the class, but these students may be distressed, experiencing emotional and psychological problems that interfere with their ability to learn and behave appropriately in class.

Distress signals include depression, which may present as poor concentration, loss of interest, withdrawal, agitation—the student may appear anxious, can't sit still—disorientation in which the student seems "out of it," bizarre behavior, expressed suicidal thoughts or threats, abuse of alcohol or drugs, and coming to class intoxicated. Assisting the distressed student may include talking with the student privately, showing concern, suggesting that he or she receive help for this distress, and providing the student with referral information for the campus counseling center. Information regarding the aberrant behavior should go to the dean, with the expectation that the disruptive behavior or distress will be resolved. Appropriate mental health treatment should be available within the university; if it is not, prompt referrals to providers in the community must be made available.

Bullying

Although rampage school shootings are rare, violence in schools is not. Bullying is the most common form of violence in society (National Association of School Psychologists, 2002) and occurs daily on school grounds. Children and adolescents who are fearful and want to protect themselves may carry weapons to school (Veltkamp & Lawson, 2008). The prevalence of bullying is not clear, but estimates for the percentage of students who have either been perpetrators or victims of bullying range between 15% and 30% (Card & Hodges, 2008; Meyer-Adams & Conner, 2008; National Association of School Psychologists, 2002).

Bullies and their victims may have academic difficulties, underdeveloped social skills, and emotional issues (Veltkamp & Lawson, 2008). The parents of aggressive children may have a history of being uninvolved or may be quite authoritarian, using harsh physical discipline (Veltkamp & Lawson, 2008). The parents of victims may be intrusive and overprotective, contributing to social-skills difficulties their children may exhibit. This situation can result in an insecure attachment, placing the child in a position of continually striving for the parents' approval, and it may make them more susceptible to victimization (Veltkamp & Lawson, 2008).

The presence of bullying is often the precursor to the rampage school shooter. It is important for school personnel to recognize who is being bullied in the school and to effectively shut it down. Bullies often have supportive peers; this dynamic can elevate to a gang or hate group, although such escalation is not required (Veltkamp & Lawson, 2008).

Bullies themselves are likely to feel alienated from their schools in some manner. A school environment that has high standards for respect and social interactions, such as holding everyone accountable for negative interactions, is less likely to have problems with violence or aggression (Veltkamp & Lawson, 2008). To facilitate the creation of such an environment disapproval of and intervention in bullying behaviors are required (National Association of School Psychologists, 2002) by school administration. Interestingly, only 4% of educators actually intervene in aggression seen at school. While this may be due to various reasons, the fact that bullies are often not checked leads to escalation of such behavior (Veltkamp & Lawson, 2008). Records of visits to the school health office may document violence-related injuries during and contiguous with school hours; this may be an indication of bullying (Brener & Krug, 1997; Strawhacker, 2002). Anti-bullying and conflict resolution programs improve the environment for all students and must be clearly supported.

Johnson and Fisher (2003) reported a study of teachers in a semi-rural area focusing on how to decrease school violence. While recognizing the multifactorial nature of episodes of violence in schools, there was clear recognition of the need for early intervention, parental supervision, and education of the effects of domestic and community violence for children and their parents. Respondents in the survey noted their fearfulness of violence from students as well as their parents. The conclusion of the study was that both school and pediatric practice nurses can provide needed education about media violence, parenting, and anger management. The need for timely mental health referrals was emphasized.

The following internal and external risk factors have been identified as contributing to bullying:

- Low school achievement
- Witnessing violence
  - Community violence
  - Domestic Violence

- Physical abuse
- Sexual Abuse
- Neglect
- Poor social skills
- Verbal learning disabilities
- Poor parenting skills
- Low engagement in school

There are numerous interventions that address these factors; such interventions are not discussed here. However, a comprehensive site from which to begin for preventing bullying is the "Stop Bullying" site from the U.S. Department of Health and Human Services: http://www.stopbullying.gov. Without addressing the causes of bullying it cannot be stopped (Beaty & Alexeyev, 2008; Card & Hodges, 2008; Dwyer, Oher, & Warger, 1998; National Association of School Psychologists, 2002; Veltkamp & Lawson, 2008). Bullying should be addressed as a school-wide measure, as merely identifying individual bullies may not be fully effective (Newman et al., 2004).

LESSONS LEARNED

From this review of the literature regarding the prevention of school violence and rampage shootings, we can gather clear lessons for parents, schools, and the community at large (Dwyer et al., 1998; Langman, 2009; Nation et al., 2003; Vossekuil et al., 2002; Williams, 2006).

Parents

- Parents with reasons to suspect that their child may act out violently should not prioritize privacy for their children above safety concerns.
- Parents should not lie to protect a child (about access to weapons or family history of mental illness).
- Parents should pay attention to a school's concerns about their child.
- Eliminating easy access to guns within the home for children and adolescents is important.
- Parents must follow through with schools if their child is being bullied. A zero tolerance policy for bullying should be adopted.
- Parents who are concerned about their child's behavior should seek expert evaluation.

Schools and Colleges

- Incidents of targeted violence at school are rarely sudden and impulsive. The attacker often reveals some aspect of his plan to others before the attack, though he does not threaten targets directly.
- There is no profile of the school shooter—A combination of early and imminent warning signs is the most appropriate indicator to identify the need for a threat assessment.
- Colleges and schools must recognize and embrace their responsibility to the holistic well-being of the student body; they must encourage a culture that recognizes that despite multiple competing needs, mental health is central to the academic success of a student.
- The most effective plans to prevent school violence are comprehensive and should involve a variety of methods to train a team of school and community personnel. They should focus on a positive school environment that is culturally appropriate for the school population.
- Colleges should revise polices relating to disturbed students both for mental health issues and for judicial infringements.
- It is important to follow through with due process policy, no matter who is involved.
- Assume threats are serious until proven otherwise.
- Punishment is not prevention (zero tolerance policies in schools that provide punishment or engage physical security measures are not effective without a threat assessment and/or treatment).
- Appropriate mental health treatment should be available within the university. If it is not, referral should be available to outside providers in the community.

Community

- The best prevention involves a team.
- Eliminating easy access to guns at the community level for children and adolescents is important.
- Any person can stop a potential school shooting by making a report about concerning behaviors. Most events that have been prevented were stopped by someone who was not affiliated with law enforcement.
- Effective communication about concerns regarding children and adolescents to the family, school, or community is an important means of prevention.

The prevention of violence in public places is a complicated process that will involve the use of multiple disciplines and areas of expertise. However, open communication and collaboration between all those who work with children and adolescents are the hallmarks of an effective prevention program.

PART THREE

THE MENTAL HEALTH CARE SYSTEM IN THE UNITED STATES

8

MENTAL HEALTH SERVICES IN THE UNITED STATES
PROBLEMS AND PROMISING APPROACHES

Aradhana Bela Sood and Robert Cohen

Failure to obtain appropriate mental health services by those who need them may have dire consequences for individuals, families, and communities. Numerous examples of individuals with psychiatric problems not receiving good treatment have been cited earlier in this book, foremost among them Seung-Hui Cho. Such inadequacies may be due to specific situational problems, such as a therapist having insufficient knowledge about an individual's condition or a family member not recognizing that a loved one's behavior was symptomatic of a serious mental health disorder. In many instances, however, poor treatment stems from fundamental deficiencies in our mental health service systems themselves. These systemic problems are not limited to one sector and, in fact, are prevalent at local, state, and national levels.

In this chapter we will examine the mental health services system in the United States. Although much of our focus will be on the system at a national level, we will also examine how mental health services are organized and delivered at the state and local levels. Our assessment is primarily oriented toward the overall mental health system, though we occasionally look at specific subsystems, especially services for children and adolescents. As a first step, we will look at frameworks for understanding the strengths and limitations, successes and failures of health systems. We will then provide a brief history of how mental health services have evolved in this country and describe the current status and shortcomings of our mental health system. Lastly, we will highlight some examples of effective approaches that might be considered in efforts to improve extant services and develop responsive, comprehensive systems of care. In Chapter 9, we explore how other countries address the mental health needs of their citizens and, where possible, compare how the United States responds in relation to other nations. Chapter 10 will offer specific recommendations for improving our current mental health system.

FRAMEWORKS FOR ASSESSING
MENTAL HEALTH SERVICES

In a report for the World Health Organization (WHO), Tandon, Murray, Lauer, and Evans (2000) examined the performance of 191 countries in terms of achieving three major health system goals. The first goal was improvement in the health of the population (both in terms of levels attained and distribution). For mental health, this pertains to (1) best attainable average level of mental wellness, for example, rates of depression; (2) equity in accessing treatments for conditions that are amenable to intervention, for example, adequate number of practitioners who can provide cognitive-behavior therapy for depression; and (3) there being little difference between individuals in the population (best off and worst off) resulting from inequity of access to care (person A can use the services of the provider as easily as person B or C or D).

The second goal was responsiveness of the health system to the legitimate expectations of the population. They defined *responsiveness* as the non–health improving dimensions of the interactions of the population with the health care system. In terms of mental health this would mean that provider behavior reflects respect for people by according them dignity and confidentiality, and that the provider collaborates with patients and clients to develop their own plans of care. The provider must make every effort to ensure that patients' and clients' orientations to the delivery of health services remain positive and are based on the respect they have been accorded. This attitude helps in developing mutual trust, encourages future preventive help-seeking behavior, and improves compliance with cost-effective, low-level treatment plans, among other factors.

The third goal used in the study was fairness in financing and financial risk protection. The aim was to ensure that poor households not pay a higher share of their discretionary expenditure on health than that of richer households.

The framework used in the Tandon study underscores the importance of considering not only the overall level of health or mental health care technology and resources available but also how a nation deploys its services and resources. The extent to which the system is equitable and responsive to consumer expectations and needs will significantly impact the health outcomes for that country's population. Thus, while the United States far outspends other industrialized nations on health care, its outcomes as measured against the parameters mentioned here are poor. The study found that the United States ranked 37 out of 191 countries for overall health system performance. Given that there is a direct correlation between health expenditures and health outcomes (Tandon et al., 2000), the poor performance of the United States indicates that the problem is not just in financing (as we outspend other nations) but in the way we approach health care delivery and eventually deliver care.

Over the last two decades, citizens of the United States have not gotten healthier. The focus of health care has been to move from crisis to crisis on an individual and a national level. When in crisis mode, policies that help steer people toward wellness are not a priority; the focus becomes how to move out of illness. Prevention efforts such as fully funded early intervention for toddlers, parenting programs, and home health visits for women identified in obstetrician's offices as having a high risk for mental health problems are examples of programs that may improve population health but will take political sway and visionary thinking, as none of these programs produce immediate visible results in quality of life.

In the United States, we largely separate mental health from other aspects of health. In contrast, many other countries have deliberately integrated mental health into primary health care (World Health Organization [WHO], 2008). A fundamental principle for reducing stigma around mental illness and improving general well-being, as well as increasing health-seeking behavior among those with mental illness, is to link mental health to physical health, legislate parity for coverage, and promote preventive care. Even today with parity laws for mental health coverage, there are recurrent attempts by third-party payors and some government officials to interpret these statutes in various ways that result in the whittling down of coverage. Aside from parity in coverage and reimbursement, mandating that a fixed amount of each dollar spent on health care must go toward primary prevention would be an excellent step toward improving the population health of this country and reversing the poor return on investment.

Over the past 30 years, increased attention, energy, and resources have been devoted to mental health reform in the United States, but no state can claim to have anything approaching an ideal system of care. In 2009, the National Alliance on Mental Illness (NAMI), a grassroots organization dedicated to improving the lives of individuals and families affected by mental illness, issued its second report card grading mental health systems state by state (NAMI, 2009). In some manner, this is similar to the WHO report. The survey measured the performance of states in the following domains:

(1) Health promotion and management. This measure included workforce development, mental health coverage for the insured and uninsured, data on health disparity, psychiatric beds, ER wait times, treatment methods, wellness promotion, and mortality reductions plans. *The average grade for all states was a D.*

(2) Financing and core treatment and recovery services. This measure included quality and number of care professionals, treatment, transportation, state and Medicaid support for community treatment, case management, and family self-care education and opportunities. *The average grade for all states on financing and services was a C.*

(3) Consumer and family empowerment. This measure included consumer and family monitoring teams, inclusion of families in committees that develop policies, education of families regarding their illness, involvement of peers, and involvement of providers in policy development. *The average grade for all states was a D.*

(4) Community integration and social inclusion. This measure included housing, jail diversion for the mentally ill, Medicaid support after incarceration, police crisis intervention teams, and mental health courts. *The average grade for all states was a D.*

Overall, the nation earned a grade of D for its mental health system, the same as in 2006, when the first report card was issued. In 2009, no state received a grade of A, and only six states—Connecticut, Maine, Maryland, Massachusetts, New York, and Oklahoma—received a B. Unfortunately, even these highly ranked states fail to provide adequate services and supports. Within each state there is considerable variation, with some areas of the state providing excellent care while other areas offer less optimal care. Eighteen states received a grade of C, 21 got a D, and 6 received a score of F.

These and other studies provide objective data that can potentially be used by states to inform small- to moderate- to large-scale changes to policy that could improve health care delivery. These data can also be used at a federal level to monitor progress and hold states accountable for mental health service planning and implementation, especially in relation to expenditure of federal funds.

A BRIEF HISTORY

Over the past 50 years, the philosophy of and programmatic approaches to serving individuals with mental health problems have undergone significant change in the United States. The advent of deinstitutionalization in the 1950s and the movement to providing community-based services in the 1960s began a transformation that is still in progress. During the first part of this period most of the significant changes involved shifts in the location in which individuals were served and the introduction of new treatment technologies, such as psychotropic medications and psychosocial rehabilitation programs.

In the 1970s and 1980s, there was growing awareness of the importance of providing adequate support and services in order to sustain individuals with mental health challenges in the community. In addition to addressing basic needs such as food, shelter, and transportation, consumers, practitioners, and policy-makers also recognized that it was essential to provide opportunities for social, educational, vocational, recreational, and spiritual experiences. Proponents of community-based care emphasized that it was not enough to provide the discrete experiences for each of these components; these resources and opportunities had to be offered in a holistic and integrated fashion. Mental health reformers such as Richard Lamb (1984) pointed out that the state institutions, which had come into disfavor, had nonetheless provided a comprehensive and integrated milieu that addressed all of the critical life domains through its program of asylum. Although it is widely recognized that these institutions also produced many detrimental outcomes, the concept of providing a comprehensive system of service in the community can be traced to the asylum model.

As the movement to establish community-based care evolved, advocates and planners became more sophisticated, not only about programmatic aspects but also in regard to political challenges, such as addressing community resistance to individuals with mental health challenges residing in their neighborhoods and funding obstacles. The expansion of community-based programs also raised questions about who was going to be responsible for paying for these services. Clarifying the governance and fiscal responsibilities at federal, state, and local levels continues to be contentious.

Through the years, there has been growing consensus on what constitutes the core components of an effective mental health system. These include a specific, verifiable set of diagnoses, availability and appropriate administration of evidence-based clinical treatment approaches, and a comprehensive mental health policy that addresses advocacy, promotion, prevention, treatment, and rehabilitation (WHO, 2005). With the evolving sophistication in diagnosis, recognition of risk factors, and identification of effective treatment algorithms, the need for organized mechanisms for funding and delivering care through a sufficient work force, appropriately trained to provide this type of care, has become apparent. There also has been recognition that it is not sufficient to simply provide specific modalities of care. As noted earlier, it is also important to take into account the multiple dimensions of functioning for each individual—for example, social, vocational, spiritual—as well as the various environmental domains with which a person interacts—for example, family, school, neighborhood.

This recognition has given rise to the development of a comprehensive and coordinated approach to serving individuals with severe mental health challenges. This approach refers to (1) a range of services on a continuum from least restrictive—for example, family and community-based settings—to most restrictive—for example, hospital based—and (2) an infrastructure that facilitates seamless transfer of the person being served between the various components of the continuum of care (Remschmidt & Belfer, 2005). In the latter part of the 20th century, proponents for both child and adult mental health articulated and established comprehensive visions and models of care, based on research evidence and practical experience.

In the following pages we describe several variations of this comprehensive, holistic approach. Although different terms are used to identify these models of care, such as, *systems of care*, and *community support system*, they all share the same core philosophy: guiding principles and infrastructure components. (These principles are referenced in Chapter 6.)

The System of Care Approach

During the early 1980s, Stroul and Friedman (1986) developed a comprehensive care model for children and adolescents with serious emotional behavioral problems. This model, eventually known as system of care, emphasizes involving the family, using the strengths of the child and family, and ensuring that services are provided in a culturally sensitive and competent manner. This model also acknowledges that child and adolescent services are more complex than services for adults, because of the number of service systems involved; all children are served within the education system and many are also involved in social service and juvenile justice systems.

Burns and Hoagwood (2002) describe a system of care approach as "a comprehensive spectrum of mental health and other services and supports organized into a coordinated network to meet the diverse and changing needs of children and adolescents with severe emotional disorders and their families" (p. 19). The three major elements of a system of care are as follows:

(1) Activities of the system are guided by the needs and preferences of the child and family, which are responded to using a strengths-based approach.
(2) Services are based and managed within a multi-agency collaborative environment that has a strong community base.
(3) All services, participating agencies, and programs are sensitive to the cultural context and characteristics of the child, family, and community (Burns & Hoagwood, 2002).

The Comprehensive Model of Care Approach

Prior to the establishment of a system of care for children and adolescents with mental health challenges, there were similar efforts to ensure that individuals with psychiatric disabilities received holistic, community-based services and support. In the area of adult services, the comprehensive model of care was initially labeled the community support system (CSS) (Mueser, Bond, Drake, & Resnick, 1998; Turner & TenHoor, 1978). This service model is based on principles of serving people in the least restrictive settings combined with the importance of addressing all of an individual's core needs in a compassionate, comprehensive, and integrated fashion. Thus the CSS model addressed housing, social, vocational, recreational, health, and psychiatric needs through a unified program of care.

In the 1980s this community support model was further refined through the work of Stein and Test (1980) and became known as the Assertive Community Treatment (ACT) program. ACT represented an evolved version of the earlier community support models, incorporating applied research evidence to frame a prescribed program methodology and staffing model that provides a comprehensive array of essential community-based services provided by a highly trained multidisciplinary team. ACT has become widely accepted as the model of choice for persons with serious and persistent mental health challenges. The ACT program is usually implemented through a community-based team, often affiliated with a local community mental health center. The team typically consists of a physician, psychiatric nurse, and social worker. This team carries a small caseload of individuals with serious and persistent mental illness and is responsible for ensuring that they receive the services and supports necessary to enable them to function optimally in the community.

In contrast to traditional psychiatric care, the ACT team members visit individuals they serve at the consumer's place of residence or other sites in the community. When an individual experiences a crisis the team works to stabilize the individual in the community. If the individual is admitted to a psychiatric inpatient unit the ACT team continues to follow the individual during his or her stay and works with hospital staff to achieve a successful discharge. Research indicates that this intervention model significantly increases individuals' ability to remain within the community and reduces hospitalization, as well as enhances their levels of functioning (Bond, Drake, Mueser, & Latimer, 2001; Dixon, 2000).

Unfortunately, because of the high cost of maintaining the intensive follow-up and follow-through that this model requires, it is often rationed and available only to a minority of consumers. Many mental health professionals and advocates believe that secondary and tertiary prevention of morbidity associated with these illnesses would offset the upfront cost of such a program in the long run. However, these potential benefits have never had a significant impact on health care policy, which is frequently focused on short-term rather than long-term gain.

CURRENT STATUS OF OUR MENTAL HEALTH SYSTEM

As the system of care model has evolved, supporters of this approach have acknowledged and addressed many of the contextual forces that inhibit our ability to provide services and support in a comprehensive and coordinated fashion. For instance, behavioral health services for children and adolescents are provided by multiple child-serving agencies including mental health, juvenile justice, social services, education, and health. Given the narrow and often rigid eligibility criteria under which these agencies operate, it is often difficult for families to access services and especially challenging for them to work with more than one agency in situations where their child has multiple needs. Because of this silo mentality within child-serving agencies, families are often forced to deal with agency and jurisdictional boundaries that are daunting and frustrating.

For example, a child who has been deemed eligible for special education and also requires psychotherapeutic intervention, medication, and treatment for a chronic health problem will need to coordinate efforts with schools, mental health clinics, and health care providers. Because personnel in these agencies often do not communicate well with each other, families are forced to expend additional effort to reconcile discrepancies and coordinate activities involving these entities. In some cases, funding and decision-making take place beyond the local community, at the state level. This adds additional complexity to an already fragmented system. Recognizing this impediment, designers of systems of care have attempted to blend or braid funding streams to be more consumer-friendly.

Intergovernmental conflict is another source of considerable confusion and frustration. Disagreement about who is responsible for providing and paying for services often diverts the attention of policy-makers and providers away from their intended focus—children and families in need of mental health services.

Paying for health care remains a major challenge for many Americans, young and old. The funding of health care in the United States is primarily through public and private plans of insurance. Tracing the history of health care financing shows that insurance was provided as a benefit of employment dating back to World War II. Until the 1960s, fee for service was the predominant method of paying for health care. As health care costs spiraled, Medicaid came into existence, and in a parallel fashion, managed care organizations (MCOs) sprang up as a viable alternative to the existing models of indemnity/fee for service. These managed care entities developed with the expressed purpose of curtailing spending by creating competition between health care providers. The appeal of MCOs was not only their power to negotiate aggressively for reductions in provider reimbursement but their pledge to plough money saved by cost containment back into prevention and population health. The recently enacted federal health care reform legislation (Patient Protection and Affordable Care Act, 2010) may offer increased coverage and benefits for individuals seeking mental health services. However, the actual impact the act will have is not yet clear.

Even with these changes, reimbursement for mental health services has continued to be treated as a low priority in health care and, in many instances, over time, managed care policies have resulted in even less funding for individuals seeking mental health treatment. The consequences of delinking mental health from physical health in our health care system are reflected in the greatly divided manner in which these services are delivered in the United States. Mental health "carve-outs" in managed care policies that produce inequity in reimbursement, and the lack of parity in coverage of physical versus mental illness both contribute to the inherent stigma around mental illness. This affects access to care for the consumer, as well as the consumer's view of his or her own mental wellness.

The Paul Wellstone Mental Health and Addiction Equity Act of 2008 mandates that group health plans provide mental health and substance-related disorder benefits that are at least equivalent to benefits offered for medical and surgical procedures. The legislation renews and expands provisions of the Mental Health Parity Act of 1996. The law requires financial equity for annual and lifetime mental health benefits, compels parity in treatment limits, and expands all equity provisions to addiction services. Prior to 2008, insurance companies used loopholes and, though providing financial equity, they often worked around the law by applying unequal copayments or setting limits on the number of days spent in inpatient or outpatient treatment facilities (General Accountability Office, 2000). Even now, whether the recent parity legislation will be implemented in both letter and spirit remains to be seen. Generally, the act requires parity of mental health benefits with medical and surgical benefits with respect to the application of aggregate lifetime and annual dollar limits under a group health plan. However, the law provides that employers retain discretion regarding the extent and scope of mental health benefits offered to workers and their families, including cost sharing, limits on numbers of visits or days of coverage, and requirements relating to medical necessity.

Many Americans have no health insurance at all, which greatly impacts their access to mental health services. The annual Census Bureau estimates released in 2010 showed that 50.7 million people, or 16.7% of the U.S. population, were without health insurance during 2009—a 5.2% increase from 2002 (DeNavas-Walt, Proctor, & Smith, 2010). In the United States, those who are uninsured or underinsured can lose their entire life savings if they have to pay out of pocket for a single hospitalization, which can be far worse for physical illness than mental illness.

Other factors such as income inequality (not just poverty) within the United States make it difficult to achieve good health (Kaplan, Pamuk, Lynch, Cohen, & Balfour, 1996). Income inequality has been linked to the highest mortality and morbidity rates (Kennedy, Kawachi, & Prothrow-Stith, 1996), as the ability to purchase high-cost services is within the grasp of only a relatively small proportion of the population. Reiman (1990, p. 75) refers to the lack of daily necessities, complicated by a lack of access to medical, dental, and mental health care, as being responsible for serious illness in the poor. Of particular note was the finding that adults living below the poverty level were more than four times as likely to report serious psychological distress as adults in families with an income at least twice the poverty level (7.2% compared with 1.6%, age-adjusted). The impact of major depression and other treatable mental illnesses on the economy, society, and family is enormous.

Although the United States has the most technologically sophisticated response system for emergency procedures and critical care, there are other critical areas of the health care system in which we do not excel. In contrast to the progress we have made in tertiary care, we have not given sufficient attention to dealing with disorders and disabilities earlier in the cycle. This lack of focus on preventive care is especially wor-risome, because these approaches often do not require sophisticated, expensive tech-nology. Examples of preventive approaches not being used effectively and efficiently are seen in the physical health care arena, in which costly tertiary interventions such as cardiac bypass surgery are fully covered but education regarding healthy eating, or cardiovascular fitness programs are minimally covered. In the mental health arena, education of family members regarding the risk imposed by high expressions of nega-tive emotions by family on the worsening of schizophrenia, and providing optional paid time off from work and availability of therapy after traumatic experiences are examples of interventions that could reduce psychiatric morbidity.

While Seung-Hui Cho was in middle and high school, his parents consistently fol-lowed through with recommendations for ongoing therapy. For a period of four years, this low-cost intervention probably forestalled hospitalization and possibly even the deadly outcome that he alluded to in his essay after the Columbine massacre. Despite Cho's introversion, could the Virginia Tech massacre a few years later have been averted if he had been made to follow through with the outpatient commitment orders by the judge at the Carillion hearing? Such care would be considered secondary prevention (prevention of morbidity secondary to illness).

Although much progress has been made in developing community-based services during the past several decades, there are few fully developed systems of care, and the quality of services is often uneven among localities within a state, as well as between states. The strongest examples of good systems of care are found at the local level. Some states have developed good conceptual frameworks and are providing a reason-able level of community service and support. Unfortunately, no states offer uniformly excellent systems of care. In the following sections, we provide examples of promising service systems at the state and local levels.

PROMISING APPROACHES

In principle, experts agree that plans that are driven by the needs of the consumer of health services, that reward multi agency collaboration, and that discourage a silo approach can achieve functionality that translates into economically feasible and clinically optimum health outcomes.

We must preface this discussion with the qualifier that the United States suffers from inequity in distribution of evidence-based programs (EBPs), or best practice programs, because of the heterogeneity of the delivery structure and the payor system, priorities set by local governments that may not include incorporation of EBPs, and the expense incurred in the importation and dissemination of EBPs. There is no federal or state mandate to braid or blend delivery structures within private, academic, and public institutions so that the consumer can seamlessly move from one system to another without duplication of records and costly services. Similarly, there is no mandate for a centralized sharing of patient information electronically to prevent duplication of services and laboratory workups or to enhance in quality and speed the communication between providers.

State Level

Several states with smaller populations have made noteworthy efforts to provide comprehensive systems of care for individuals with severe mental health challenges. Vermont and Alaska were early pioneers in the development of holistic, community-based services for children and adolescents. Ohio has earned a reputation for promoting the use of evidence-based services. Michael Hogan, the Commissioner of Mental Health Services in Ohio in the early 2000s, established a system of regional university-based centers to provide assistance to localities in developing and implementing evidence-based practices. State funds were allocated to establish professorships in five medical schools for the purpose of working collaboratively with local communities. In Cleveland at the Case Western University, more than a dozen psychiatry faculty provided direct clinical care and supervised residents in the community. They also hosted a statewide conference in community psychiatry. The partnership investment also produced specialty programs in forensic psychiatry, enhancement of services for co-occurring mental illness and mental retardation, and integrated treatment of dual substance abuse and mental illness. Training in rural psychiatry was offered to residents at Wright State University College of Medicine, and a diversion program for persons with mental illness involved in the criminal justice system was established at Northeast Ohio University. An additional benefit was a boost in recruitment of trainees remaining in the state after graduation. More than 50% of residents at Northeastern Ohio University College of Medicine and the Medical College of Ohio who received community mental health training chose jobs in the public mental health system (Svendsen et al., 2005).

Ohio also enacted legislation directed at redistributing financial resources from state hospitals to community support services for persons with severe mental disabilities

(SMD). The state conducted yearly service utilization assessments for a sample of 4,000 adults with SMD for five years to assess the impact of this redistribution. The analysis of service patterns showed a decrease in the number of individuals receiving little more than medication checkups as well as an increase in persons receiving combinations of at least two community services (Roth, Lauber, Crane-Ross, & Clark, 1997). As a result of the state's "pump-priming" investments of funds to community care, more than 80% of the local mental health boards chose to participate in the new funding formula, which allowed localities to create new community services (Hogan, 1992).

In 1992 the Commonwealth of Virginia passed legislation establishing the Comprehensive Service Act (CSA) for At Risk Youth and Families (Virginia Acts of Assembly, Chapter 880, Section 2.1-745). The passage of this ambitious legislative initiative followed an 18-month planning process involving 145 stakeholders representing consumers, providers, advocates, and policy-makers interested in improving services for young people facing serious emotional behavioral challenges. The legislation was unique in the sense that it not only provided a comprehensive and coordinated community-based service model but also addressed funding, organizational structure, governance, training, and other issues that impact quality of care. While the CSA appeared to address most of the concerns raised by advocates of child mental health reform, it has fallen short of achieving its lofty goals. There are several possible reasons for this act not being fully actualized.

First, the act called for integration of program services, funding, and governance. Many of these changes required agencies to give up long-standing authority, particularly in areas of funding, and to engage in more collaborative approaches to funding. In some areas of the state, there was considerable resistance to shifting away from traditional practices as this was perceived as being equal to giving up autonomy and funds.

Second, the Commonwealth of Virginia has a long history of strong governance at both the state and local levels. The initial CSA legislation contained language requiring collaboration among child-serving agencies, including education, social service, mental health, juvenile justice, and health. Many localities objected to having uniform requirements imposed on all localities. As a result, the governor loosened language about uniform requirements for collaboration in order to obtain support from local legislators. This modification weakened statutory authority to hold child-serving agencies accountable for working collaboratively on behalf of children and families.

Third, in Virginia the governorship is limited to one four-year term. Given the tendency of new administrations to establish their own programmatic agendas, it was difficult to sustain support for this complex and challenging visionary approach with succeeding administrations.

This example of Virginia's CSA initiative illustrates how political maneuvering can dilute the intent of technically sound and progressive solutions provided to state agencies. Future efforts to develop comprehensive statewide systems might learn from the Virginia experience. Among the most important lessons are the need for leadership at the local and state levels to acknowledge the importance of child mental health and to take an active role in bringing together the child-serving agencies and other key stakeholders in order to develop a collaborative and comprehensive response to the needs and strengths of at-risk youth and their families. With strong "buy-in" from the family and provider and agency groups interested in young people, it will be possible to mitigate the organizational and political forces that have constrained development of a responsive system of care for at-risk youth, by establishing mental health service delivery structures and processes based on the core principles of individualized, family-centered, community-based care contained in the initial CSA legislation.

The Substance Abuse and Mental Health Services Administration (SAMHSA) established the Children's Mental Health Initiative (CMHI) to encourage localities and states to establish comprehensive systems of care. Since its inception in 1993, SAMHSA has awarded 173 grants totaling more than 1.63 billion dollars to help communities to develop and implement systems of care for children and adolescents with behavioral health challenges (Bruns, Sather, Pullmann, & Stumbaugh, 2011). Until 2011, the primary focus of these grants had been to establish local programs. In 2011 the grant program was redirected toward enhancing state-level infrastructure. Although many states have made strides in establishing statewide systems of care, Virginia's CSA still provides the most comprehensive blueprint for transformation.

City and County Level

Perhaps the best example of a comprehensive system of care approach developed to meet the needs of children and adolescents with mental health issues is Wraparound Milwaukee, which was established in 1994, with a six-year grant from the Center for Mental Health Services (Milwaukee County Behavioral Health Division, 2009). Employing system of care principles, described earlier in this chapter, to guide service development, administration, financing, governance, and evaluation of this comprehensive effort, the program has grown from an initial budget of $2.5 million annually to its current budget of more than $33 million per year. By systematically organizing and managing a network of more than 200 community-based providers, Wraparound Milwaukee, which is administered by Milwaukee County's Behavioral Health Division, was able to provide comprehensive, coordinated, cost-effective, individualized services to 1,236 children and youth and their families in 2008.

One of the critical reasons for Wraparound Milwaukee's success has been the ability of its leaders to have a shared vision to respond to the needs and strengths of the child within the context of the child's environment. Building on this commonly held belief, which considers the whole child as well as the role of the family, neighborhood, school, and other forces that affect the child, the leadership of Wraparound Milwaukee designed a comprehensive system of care for children with serious mental health concerns who required the services of two or more child-serving systems and were at risk of being placed in an out-of-home setting such as residential treatment, juvenile corrections, or a psychiatric hospital. Initially designed for youth who were under a delinquency order or who were determined by the court to be in need of protection or service, Wraparound Milwaukee has since expanded to serve children before they become involved in the court system.

Recognizing that actualizing this ambitious vision requires a strong infrastructure, the developers of Wraparound created an organizational structure that addressed funding, responsive service delivery and management, and quality care. Wraparound Milwaukee combines multiple federal, state, and local funding streams to create a flexible pool to pay for services and supports tailored to the identified needs of the child. Services are available from a network of providers who have met the agency's qualified provider criteria and whose performance is continually monitored by the Wraparound Quality Assurance Committee. Priority is given to offering evidence-based services through a planning and management process that involves the family in their child's care as well as broader system change efforts. Managing a network of eight coordination agencies and more than 200 providers, Wraparound is able to provide a wide range of community-based services, including mobile urgent treatment, short-term crisis beds, professional foster parent services, and wraparound services. In all of its work, Wraparound Milwaukee places a high premium on ensuring that all efforts are responsive to child and family needs and are provided in a seamless manner, to avoid confusion, fragmentation, and duplication.

The results produced by Wraparound Milwaukee are striking. Youth enrolled for one year or more improved significantly in their functioning at home, school, and community after leaving the program. Recidivism rates for participants continued to decline three years after completion of the program, and the number of young people placed in residential treatment declined by 50% in one year (Hansen, Litzelman, Marsh, & Milspaw, 2004). The average monthly cost of serving a child in Wraparound in 2008 was $3,800 compared to more than $8,000 for residential treatment facilities. From the youths' and families' perspectives, Wraparound Milwaukee appears to be doing a good job. In their most recent participant survey, in which respondents rated their satisfaction with the program on a scale from 1 to 5, with 5 being the highest rating, the average satisfaction score for youth was 4.24; for adults completing the survey it was 4.07 (Milwaukee County Behavioral Health Division, 2009).

While Wraparound has been the recipient of numerous local, state, and federal awards and accolades, perhaps the most impressive recognition it has received is the

2009 Innovations in American Government Award. Wraparound was selected by the Harvard Kennedy School of Government as a recipient of this prestigious award for the novelty, significance, effectiveness, and transferability of its program. Wraparound Milwaukee was one of six programs chosen from a pool of 700 applicants nationwide.

Community Level

A growing number of interventions and programs have undergone rigorous empirical evaluation and have proven to be effective in producing positive outcomes for young people and adults (Bartels et al., 2002; Dixon et al., 2001; National Research Council and Institute of Medicine, 2009; Yannacci & Rivard, 2006). In spite of this rapid proliferation of best practices, few of these interventions have gained wide acceptance or been replicated in a significant number of localities. Some of this slow expansion is due to the lengthy and intricate process required to "translate" treatment approaches that have been validated under ideal conditions into programs that are suitable for real-world situations. This entails recognizing that typical practice settings usually have fewer resources than are available in research settings. Interventions also have to be adapted to accommodate the unique characteristics of consumer groups, that is, age, culture, etc. (Burns & Hoagwood, 2002). In other instances, administrators and practitioners simply do not have the knowledge required to develop and implement these evidence-based approaches, and would benefit from the availability of "toolkits" to guide them through the process of applying these practices to their local setting (Torrey et al., 2001).

There are many examples of local initiatives for serving adults and children. Some of these are spearheaded by a single organization or agency, while others grow out of genuine collaborative efforts. Unfortunately, these exemplary programs are not typically incorporated into the formal structure of local government, making it difficult to sustain these efforts over time. Likewise, state governments have not often supported replication of model programs throughout the state. Although this reticence is often attributed to the need to recognize unique differences among localities, the reluctance to replicate these programs is really due to a lack of political will to ensure uniform excellence in service throughout the state, as evidenced in the CSA program cited earlier, in which Virginia failed to fully transform the visionary enabling legislation into an effective statewide system of care for at-risk youth and their families (Cohen & Cohen, 2000).

Early Intervention and Prevention

Most of the examples of comprehensive efforts to address mental health needs in this chapter are designed to serve individuals with serious and persistent mental health challenges. It is widely recognized that while tertiary care systems are needed, ultimately early prevention and early intervention efforts will have the greatest impact on promoting positive mental health. While everyone agrees at a philosophical level that prevention is important, there has been an ongoing debate about the desirability and feasibility of investing resources on early intervention and prevention efforts. Some of this reluctance derives from a fear that the limited resources currently devoted to mental health care, tertiary in nature, will be further reduced if prevention becomes a priority. The impact of early intervention and prevention is not seen for decades but is embedded in concepts of improving population health. Other objections focus on lack of clarity about what constitutes effective prevention and what population is most critical to target.

The quest for establishing evidence-based intervention programs has been challenging. Often programs that have empirical evidence supporting their efficacy have been limited in scope and cannot be generalized. Limitations include the scope of the population (e.g. age, gender, socioeconomic status), the setting in which the intervention has been applied (controlled laboratory conditions versus community treatment program), and duration of follow-up to determine if positive results are sustained. For example, suicide prevention hotlines have been shown to be helpful to at-risk school- and college-age youth who have used this source of support. However, the population at risk that can be positively impacted by such interventions is hard to identify and target, as students contemplating suicide do not often publically disclose their intentions. In contrast, postnatal home visits by nurses, which have a target population that is easier to identify, have been shown to be effective in reducing neglect and improving long-term functioning (Olds, 2006).

Confusion about prevention stems, in part, from the larger debate about whether the source of mental health problems is primarily environmental or biological. Current thinking views individuals as differentially predisposed to psychiatric disorder, based on genetic and biological attributes, but the extent to which these conditions are actually manifested is influenced by the specific experiences of that individual. In fact, the literature indicates that high genetic risk and early abusive experiences can be counterbalanced by warm nurturing parenting along with predictability and stability of the environment. This conceptual paradigm of prevention has led to the development of a range of interventions that modify or ameliorate individual, family, neighborhood, school, and other community-level environments, to enhance resilience or provide additional support for individuals. These prevention programs are typically divided into two categories: universal approaches that are directed toward all individuals, and targeted approaches designed for individuals who have identifiable risk factors and thus may be more vulnerable to environmental forces. What follows are examples of several prevention programs that have been empirically validated.

The High Scope Perry Preschool Project is one of the best know examples of an early childhood program able to demonstrate the long-term, positive impact of early education on at-risk children. In the early 1960s, a group of three- and four-year-old children from a high-risk, impoverished community in Michigan were randomly assigned to either a high-quality preschool program or a comparison group in which no preschool program was offered. In a follow-up evaluation nearly 40 years later, adults who had participated in the preschool program had significantly higher earnings, held jobs longer, were more likely to have graduated from high school, and had committed fewer crimes than adults from the comparison group (Schweinhart et al., 2005).

The Nurse Home Visitation Program, developed by David Olds, has been cited by the President's New Freedom Commission on Mental Health as a model program for "intervening early for preventing mental health problems." The program includes periodic home visits from paraprofessionals and nurses during pregnancy and the first two years of the child's life. Findings from 15-year follow-up research show that home visit participants had 58% fewer doctor and hospital visits, a 48% reduction in child abuse and neglect, 69% fewer convictions of children through age 15, and an 83% increase in workforce participation by low-income, unmarried mothers by the time their child reached four years of age, compared to groups that did not receive home visitation. This program has subsequently been adapted and replicated. By 2005, the nurse visitation program was being implemented in 20 states, serving 20,000 families (Olds, 2006).

Programs such as the Clarke Cognitive-Behavioral Prevention Intervention program, which aims to prevent depression, target specific disorders. Using a 15-session group that focuses on helping individuals cope with stress, researchers found in a 15-month follow-up that at-risk youth completing this program had significantly fewer major depressive episodes than a similar cohort who received usual care (Garber et al., 2009). Other preventive programs have shown promising results in preventing substance abuse, anxiety, and eating disorders (National Research Council and Institute of Medicine, 2009).

A wide range of approaches have been employed to prevent or reduce aggressive and violent behavior. Some programs work with individual children to teach self-control and problem-solving skills. The Promoting Alternative Thinking Strategies (PATHS) program was conducted in 18 special education classrooms in which students were assigned to an intervention or control group. PATH students had fewer externalizing and internalizing problems and a greater decrease in depression during a three-year follow-up than control group participants (Kam, Greenberg, & Kusche, 2004).

Other efforts have focused on changing classroom structure. An example of this approach is the Good Behavior Game (GBG), which encourages elementary school children to remain on task in the classroom in order to receive rewards. The theory behind this approach is that reducing early aggressive behavior will modify the developmental trajectory associated with aggression and other problems in later life. Controlled studies of this approach have shown that participants in GBG not only demonstrated reduced levels of disruptive behaviors in school, but individuals who had exhibited aggressiveness earlier subsequently exhibited lower levels of aggressive behavior (Murthén et al., 2002) and less use of alcohol and illicit drugs. Boys who exhibited aggressive behavior in school who participated in GBG had fewer suicide attempts and were less likely to receive a diagnosis of antisocial personality when they were young adults (Wilcox et al., 2008).

Given the importance of the family and school in promoting positive development, some preventive programs have focused on strengthening parents' and teachers' abilities to reduce risk factors and enhance protective factors for children. The Incredible Years program combines parent, teacher, and social skills development in helping children with conduct disorders as well as those showing early risk indicators. The program encourages positive interaction and communication and emphasizes the value of praise and reward as well as time-out. Dinosaur puppets are used to teach social skills. This program has been used with children as young as two or three years of age. In an evaluation of children from low-income families in Head Start and first grade, students participating in the program were rated as being more socially competent, having greater ability to self-regulate, and displaying fewer conduct problems (Webster-Stratton, Reid, & Stoolmiller, 2008).

The broader community plays a significant role in reducing risk and promoting resilience. Designing preventive interventions for an entire community is even more complex than addressing individuals, families, or schools. There are many examples of multilevel efforts to support or mobilize communities on behalf of at-risk individuals. These include policing strategies, community mobilization, and voucher programs for public housing residents. Because most of these efforts employ multiple strategies to address the various subsystems within the community, it is difficult to ascertain the specific factors that influenced change. For instance, the Boston Gun Project (BGP), a well-publicized community effort to reduce youth violence is often credited with a dramatic reduction in youth homicides, gang activities, and the number of gun assaults in that city (Piehl, Kennedy, & Braga, 2000). A systematic review of this project concluded that there were many other potentially influential events and forces occurring at the same time which may have had an impact on these indicators and that it would be difficult to identify the precise role the BGP played in reducing violence (Wellford, Pepper, & Petrie, 2005).

Research indicates that community mobilizations targeted at reducing substance abuse have also produced promising results, but at this time there is not enough evidence to support the effectiveness of this approach on reducing violence and related outcomes (Doll, Bonzo, Mercy, & Sleet, 2007).

CONCLUSION

In spite of all of the progress in research, and improvement in treatment and service delivery during the past several decades, availability and accessibility of appropriate mental health services lag considerably behind the well-documented need. Some of these shortcomings can be attributed to the complexity of mental health disorders and the relative early stage of scientific development in this field. There are, however, other contextual factors, such as the continuing stigma, prejudice, and misconception associated with mental illness that hamper public support and make individuals who may need help reluctant to come forward for fear of how they will be perceived. Funding mechanisms structured to promote inequity of reimbursement, and lack of parity in coverage of mental health also increase stigma and impede access to care. A lack of policy to mandate communication between provider and consumer through rapid access or technology, and the complexity of interrelated but unlinked systems which have no incentive for interagency cooperation all lead to a system that, despite pockets of excellence, is overall weak and failing. Lack of public understanding and support also contributes to the hesitancy of executive and legislative bodies at all levels to take decisive action to address mental health issues.

Fifty years ago, people were hesitant to utter the word *cancer*, instead referring to this dreaded disease as "the big C." It was not until public misconceptions associated with cancer were dispelled and replaced with more objective information that significant progress began to occur. In recent decades, funding for research and treatment expanded exponentially, leading to many advances in the diagnosis, prevention, and treatment of cancer. On the community level, fund-raising for cancer has become commonplace. The Susan G. Komen foundation and its pink color has become emblematic of the breast cancer prevention and research movement and is recognizable anywhere. It is difficult to imagine parallel progress in mental health until more objective perceptions of this subject pervade all levels of society.

Given the existing societal impediments it is not surprising that few effective models exist for providing comprehensive, compassionate, and appropriate mental health prevention and care. Even in Europe, where there is greater public acceptance and more equitable and accessible funding for mental health, it is difficult to identify countries that provide optimal services. However, states or agencies that are willing to import EBPs should be funded to do so; such efforts are a high-yield investment. In addition to developing and implementing interventions that work, investigators that use promising models of intervention should be generously funded to assess whether the interventions they are using actually work; if not, there should be encouragement and funding to develop treatments that do. Pay-for-performance programs are gaining ground in approximately 30 health plans covering 30 million people (Endsley, Kirkegaard, Baker, & Murcko, 2004).

There are many excellent examples of interventions and programs that have been shown to be effective in preventing and treating mental health challenges. By using scientifically credible research approaches, the developers of the interventions cited in this chapter as well as others have been able to demonstrate that many programs are able to achieve their desired outcomes. Many of these approaches have been widely replicated. One indicator of progress in this field is the number of randomized controlled trials that have been conducted. Within the scientific community these trials represent the gold standard for demonstrating efficacy of an intervention or program. For example, in the early 1980s, there were fewer than five published randomized controlled trials that addressed the prevention of emotional and behavioral disorders in young people. By 2000 there were 25 published trials, and in 2007 more than 40 randomized clinical trials in this field were published (National Research Council and Institute of Medicine, 2009).

There are also noteworthy examples of evidence-interventions for adults with severe mental health challenges. Assertive Community Treatment (ACT), originally developed in Madison, Wisconsin, provides a multidisciplinary outreach strategy for assisting persons with chronic mental illness to cope with community living (Stein & Santos, 1998). Controlled research during the past 40 years has demonstrated the effectiveness of ACT in reducing hospital recidivism and improving psychosocial functioning for adults with schizophrenia and other chronic mental disorders (Marshall & Lockwood, 2000; Rice, 2011). Although recent studies have found that ACT does not produce positive results for all individuals with severe mental health challenges, there is still strong evidence that this model of care is effective and cost-efficient (Bustillo, Lauriello, Horan, & Keith, 2001; Rice, 2011).

In the past 20 years randomized controlled trials have provided support for the effectiveness of other psychosocial interventions. Programs that teach families to understand the importance of reducing the level of expressed communication between family members and individuals with schizophrenia have had a positive impact on reducing relapse and adjustment (Hogarty et al., 1986; McFarlane, Dushay, Stastny, Deakins, & Link, 1996). There is also evidence that strategies like supported employment programs that place and train persons with chronic mental illness in real-work settings enable these individuals to achieve and maintain competitive employment and earn more money than similar individuals in a comparison group (Cook et al., 2005).

Broader replication of effective strategies, interventions, and service models, as well as development and evaluation of new approaches for preventing and treating mental health disorders, is needed. Some of these efforts require the development of new technologies. Given the considerable differences that exist among localities and states in regard to demographic, cultural, social, political, geographic, and economic factors, it is also important that we focus on how to adapt evidence-based approaches to the unique conditions of each site. There is some tension between proponents who believe in the importance of ensuring that replication of evidence-based approaches maintains fidelity to the original model and those who stress the importance of taking into account local conditions. If we are to be effective in achieving wide dissemination of best practices, it is incumbent on us to reconcile the demands of scientific rigor with real-world practicality. Eventually, overall mental health will be measured by the degree of dissemination and implementation of best practice models that improve functioning, the ability of people suffering from mental illness to access effective care, and, finally, the equity and parity in the financing of mental health care.

9

GLOBAL PERSPECTIVES ON MENTAL HEALTH CARE

Robert Cohen and Aradhana Bela Sood

In the previous chapter we cited the report of the World Health Organization on the elements that should be a part of a well-functioning health delivery system (Tandon et al., 2000). As noted, in its study of 191 countries, the WHO assessed the quality of the nations' health care systems, including mental health, on the following dimensions: (1) overall general health of the population; (2) fairness in financing, which includes the distribution of the health system's financial burden within the population; and (3) responsiveness of the system. This last dimension is measured by patient satisfaction and how well the system behaves in response to the needs of consumers in providing them dignity, confidentiality, autonomy to make decisions about their own health, and choice of provider. In addition, the WHO also studied access to care, health inequalities or disparities, and how well people of varying economic backgrounds felt they were being served by the health system.

The WHO correlated these variables with the level of sophistication in care and the degree of distribution of these important elements in the population to yield measures of equity of care and quality of care. As mentioned previously, the United States ranked 37th among all countries, with 17% of its GDP spent on health care, while the United Kingdom was 18th, with 6% of its GDP going to health care. Thirty-three other countries were ahead of the United States on 1,000 different parameters; France, Italy, and San Marino topped the list, and Sierra Leone came in last. Singapore was 6th, Norway was 11th, and the Middle Eastern country of Oman was 8th (WHO, 2005).

The WHO concluded that virtually all countries underutilize the resources available to them with resulting deaths and disabilities that are preventable. Fortunately, bringing about changes by reallocating resources is not unachievable and can produce results in a short period of time. As an example, Oman was not performing well on many parameters, including infant mortality, but major government investments produced significant improvements over a period of five years.

Another important factor in a well-functioning system is fairness in financing, which refers to the distribution of the cost of health care purchased: Are those with the least income paying the same as those with the highest income? In Colombia, South America, low-income people pay less for health care than do people with high incomes, $1 versus $7.60. This equity in cost earned it a high rank in the WHO study.

The WHO stressed the importance of two other factors: (1) workforce inputs and balance within the workforce, that is, the right number of nurses per doctor, and (2) extending insurance coverage to the entire population. The literature suggests that the prepayment for health care in the form of insurance, taxes, or social security reduces the cost of health care in the long run. Most industrialized countries have only 25% of health care being delivered via private entities, in comparison to 56% within the United States.

Although the WHO report does not break down the specific areas of health care into mental and physical, it seems logical to assume that the rankings for physical health reflect those for mental health. The WHO offers the following definition of mental health: "the state of well-being in which the individual realizes his or her abilities, can cope with the normal stresses of life, can work productively and fruitfully, and is able to make a contribution to his or her community" (Herrman, Saxena, & Moodie, 2005, p. 2).

Based on this broad definition, many countries are addressing the issue of mental health in a comprehensive and holistic manner, acknowledging the importance of addressing all aspects of an individual's functioning, including the strong interdependence of mental and physical health. (Nonetheless, it is important to note that the preponderance of resources in developing and Third World countries goes toward control of infection and acute illnesses, with mental health lagging far behind in priorities.) Progressive social policies in some industrialized nations such as Sweden, France, the United Kingdom, Norway, Denmark, and Germany, which have liberal paid maternity leave policies ranging from 18 to 32 weeks, clearly suggest recognition of the importance of good maternal physical and mental health for the well-being of an infant. Such social policies have a long-term impact on the well-being of the family.

It is noteworthy that the WHO decided to discontinue report cards on the status of health care in countries of the world after publishing its 2000 report (WHO, 2000), citing the enormous complexity and difficulty of the task. Nevertheless, this report gives nations of the world a strong platform from which to examine health delivery systems, including those focused on mental health.

In this chapter we review how various nations successfully approach the issue of ensuring positive mental health for their citizens. Wherever it appears appropriate we glean approaches and lessons that may be useful in improving the mental health system in the United States.

WIDE DISPARITIES EXIST AMONG NATIONS

Several conclusions emerge from a review of the limited literature on mental health services throughout the world. First, as might be expected, there is considerable variation in the scope and nature of mental health services. Some of these differences can be attributed to cultural perspectives that shape how a country defines and deals with mental health issues. While it is possible to identify prevalent national views and trends, there are often discrepant perspectives even within a particular country. For example, in the United States, most mental health professionals view the onset of mental illness as a complex interaction of predisposing and precipitating factors, and view the biopsychosocial approach as a useful conceptual model for understanding and treating these disorders (Pies, 1994). There is not a clear consensus on this issue, however. Many professionals view mental illness as primarily a biological phenomenon, while a segment of the population still considers all aberrant behavior to be a manifestation of immorality (Stier & Hinshaw, 2007).

The mind–body schism is reflected in the decades of disparity between the approach to delivering care and the funding of coverage of mental and physical health issues. In Asian cultures, emotional stress presents in physical ways, such as stomachaches, headaches, pseudoseizures, or myalgias, and seeking help for physical symptoms is a culturally accepted way of seeking help for stresses that cannot be publicly acknowledged. Systems of care delivery within those countries value biological origins as explanations of these presentations, and intervention is often provided within the physical medicine venue rather than within traditional psychiatry. General practitioners provide the bulk of interventions in China, which has undergone radical changes in political structure during the past several decades; parallel shifts have occurred in conceptualizing mental health problems and treatment. (Hong, Yamakazi, Banaag, & Yasong, 2004). Although there has been some movement toward co-locating behavioral health services in primary health care settings in the United States, we would benefit from further integration of behavioral and physical care service provision.

In China during the first part of the 20th century, Western medicine began to supplement traditional Eastern approaches to health and illness. While development of mental health services was largely dormant between 1930 and 1949 because of the war with Japan, during the Cultural Revolution, from 1950 to 1980, there was a growth in mental health services, with primary reliance on use of medication in both inpatient and outpatient settings. In the past 30 years there has been considerable reform in approaches to mental health within China (Hong et al., 2004).

On the continent of Africa, formal systems of care are beginning to emerge, but informal approaches such as those provided by folk and indigenous healers still play a significant role in dealing with mental health problems (Robertson, Mandlhate, Seif El Din, & Seck, 2004).

A second conclusion that can be readily drawn from the literature on international mental health is that the prevalence and impact of mental health disorders is significant but has not yet been sufficiently acknowledged by government authorities. For example, the WHO calculates the "burden of disease" in terms of disability-adjusted life years (DALY). According to the WHO DALY calculations, neuropsychiatric conditions account for more than 25% of the total burden of disease worldwide (Remschmidt & Belfer, 2005). In its report, "Caring for Children and Adolescents and Mental Disorders" (WHO, 2003), the WHO states that, worldwide, nearly 20% of children and adolescents suffer from a mental health disorder that has a disabling impact. These data are consistent with epidemiological findings of prevalence rates for mental disorders for children and adolescents in the United States (National Research Council and Institute of Medicine, 2009). Developing countries are frequently mired in constructing policies to manage acute physical illnesses and infectious diseases and do not have the manpower, resources, or national policy to meet the challenges of mental disorders. In the United States, however, the health care burden comes from chronic illnesses like cancer, cardiovascular disease, accidents, and mental illness.

Finally, there appears to be a large disparity in the degree to which countries acknowledge the importance of mental health and support work in this area. Sadly, no single country has achieved a level of development that represents exemplary mental health care. One measure of commitment is the amount of money budgeted for mental health as a proportion of the total health budget. In a report on 101 countries, covering a population of more than 1 billion people, 20% of countries spend less than 1% of their total health care budget on mental health services. In Africa and Southeast Asia, more than half of countries spend less than 1% of their health budget on mental health. In contrast, more than 60% of countries in Europe spend more than 5% of their health budget on mental health care, with at least six countries in Europe and the Americas allocating 10% or more of their health budget to mental health. The United States spends 6% of its health budget on mental health care (WHO, 2005).

Significant variation also exists in how mental health care is financed for people with different income levels. Specifically, out-of-pocket payment is the most prevalent form of financing in low-income countries in areas such as northern Africa and Southeast Asia, while Europe relies almost exclusively on tax-based and social insurance. Analysis of financing methods by income reveals that low-income groups are expected to pay a significantly greater proportion of their incomes for mental health care through out-of-pocket payment. For this group, self-pay (uninsured and paying out of pocket) is the most common method of financing for 3% of the population and the second most common method of financing for 35%. In comparison, out-of-pocket payment (insured but choosing to bypass insurance) is seldom used by persons at higher middle- and high-income levels, as tax-based and social insurance provide funding for mental health care for 90% of the population.

Another indicator of disparity among nations is the number of psychiatric services and professionals available. Countries classified as low income have a median number of 2.4 psychiatric beds per 10,000 people as compared to higher middle- and high-income countries, which have approximately 7.5 beds per 10,000. The United States has 7.7 psychiatric beds per 10,000 people, which is slightly less than the average for Europe—8 beds per 10,000 people (WHO, 2005). The same relationship of having fewer resources in poorer countries exists for the availability of mental health professionals. The United States has 13.7 psychiatrists per 100,000 in comparison to the African region, which has .04 psychiatrists per 100,000, and Southeast Asia, which has .2 psychiatrists per every 100,000 people (WHO, 2005).

Work force issues have impacted the delivery of health care even in the United States, where the availability of child psychiatrists (7,000) has never kept pace with the projected need for child psychiatrists (30,000) (Thomas & Holzer, 2006). In the United States and some other countries, the mental health needs of an individual are not considered to be primary care needs. This has contributed to a lack of funding for training people in the field of mental health.

APPROACHES TO MENTAL HEALTH AROUND THE WORLD

The way in which mental health disorders are manifested, the magnitude and nature of risk and protective factors, and the most appropriate ways to provide care vary from culture to culture. In Sub-Saharan, Africa, where 70% of all people with AIDS live, more than 13 million children under 15 years of age have lost mothers to HIV/AIDS since the epidemic began. As a result of the AIDS epidemic and multiple armed conflicts, 95% of all the worlds' orphans now live in Africa (Robertson et al., 2004). The loss and trauma experienced by young people living in these countries certainly pose extraordinary risks for their mental health and overall development.

While there are excellent examples of specific programs that address mental health issues at a local or regional level, it is generally acknowledged that, including the United States, no country has a comprehensive system of care for individuals with mental disorders (Belfer, 2004). Overall, the strongest systems of care in mental health are located in the United States and Europe, with considerable variation among the states in the United States and countries within Europe. In assessing the level of development of mental health services, it is useful to distinguish between the following aspects of systems of care: (1) the clinical and programmatic philosophies and paradigms used to educate staff and families on how to understand and treat mental health disorders, and (2) the structure and organization of service provided to patients (Rydelius, 2004).

While the development of the system of care paradigm and efforts to develop comprehensive service approaches originated in the United States, in some ways, European countries have made greater progress. Two factors that have influenced the rate of progression are (1) the relation to and integration of mental health services with primary care and (2) strong government funding of mental health services. Countries such as Austria, Finland, Germany, and Sweden have a long tradition of close collaboration between child psychiatry and pediatrics (Rydelius, 2004). In addition to typical consultation-liaison work, good collaboration has resulted in the development of special programs for pregnant mothers, newborn children with obstetrical/neonatal complications, abused children, and children with serious physical health diseases. Child and adolescent psychiatrists routinely provide services within pediatric clinics, and in those instances where cooperation between psychiatry and pediatrics is not strong, "social pediatrics" and "behavioral pediatrics" programs have been developed within some pediatric settings.

EFFECTIVE MENTAL HEALTH CARE
APPROACHES WORLDWIDE
Service Models

While the term *system of care* is relatively new, some of the principles embodied in this model have been incorporated in the care of persons with mental disorders for a long time. Perhaps the most noteworthy historical example of an authentic community-based care system for persons with serious mental disorders is found in Geel, Belgium. Beginning in the mid-13th century, persons with mental illness were brought to this small municipality in the northeast Belgium province of Antwerp to receive help. Initially, the cure consisted of a religious ritual designed to rid them of the evil spirits that supposedly possessed them. Over time, treatment evolved from a church-sponsored intervention to a system of psychiatric care, managed by the Belgian state, beginning in the mid-19th century. Persons from all sections of the country were sent to Geel for treatment. What made the Geel experience unique was that although almost all of the people served were severely disabled and exhibited symptoms of psychosis, they were not placed in an institution. Instead, they lived with local host families while they received treatment. This system of placing persons with mental illness in the homes of local residents resembles today's family foster care program (Roosens, 1979).

Although living conditions have improved considerably for the Geel patients since the 1850s, when they were often placed in irons or chained to walls, the basic concept of integrating persons with severe mental illness into the community has remained constant. Because patients consistently showed improvement, the number of patients sent to Geel continued to increase. At the turn of the 20th century there were approximately 2,000 patients participating in the Geel family care experience. The program peaked in 1938, when there were 3,700 participants. Today, Geel, with an overall population of 35,000 people, has approximately 500 patients with chronic mental illness living with families and participating in typical activities within the community.

Interestingly, research conducted on the Geel program found that these families did not see their participation as an act of charity. Rather, they viewed this work as a business, motivated primarily by the economic benefits it provides to the host families. Nonetheless, this unique family care program enables many individuals with severe disabilities to lead relatively normal lives within the mainstream community (Goldstein & Godemont, 2005; Roosens, 1979).

In the 19th century, many countries established institutions for persons with aberrant behavior. These institutions, initially referred to as asylums for lunatics or insane persons, eventually evolved into state-operated psychiatric hospitals. As attitudes and treatment approaches for persons with mental illness changed in the middle of the 20th century these facilities became unpopular. While there is much to criticize about how these institutions segregated individuals with mental illness from the mainstream community as well as the abuses that occurred within many of these cloistered facilities, it is worth noting that asylums and state-operated psychiatric hospitals performed some of the same functions as modern systems of care, albeit in much more restrictive settings. For instance, state hospitals addressed all the needs of the individual, including physical, medical, social, and spiritual, under a single administrative and physical structure. Critics of deinstitutionalization often point to the lack of attention to a holistic approach in the early days of transition from state hospital to community setting (Lamb, 1984).

Many countries in Europe have been progressive in their approach to mental health care. One of the strengths of the European Union is its systematic effort to monitor the health status of its citizens. Through assessments, such as the Survey of Health, Aging and Retirement in Europe (SHARE), the Health Behavior in School-age Children (HBSC), and the EU Labor Force Survey (LFS), the EU tracks the status and changes of different age groups in member states on a variety of indicators related to mental health. Given the importance of epidemiological data in formulating policy and practice, this comprehensive and systematic approach to measuring and monitoring a mental health status is worth consideration by policy-makers in the United States.

Scotland has adopted a national program that brings together policy, strategy, programs, research and evaluation, capacity building, and indicator development in an integrated approach, to promote and improve mental health and well-being of the entire population, prevent mental health problems and suicide, and support the improvement of quality of life, social inclusion, and health of people with mental health issues (Robison, 2009).

The Labour Force Service Centres (LAFOS) have been established in Finland to provide employment and social and health services for disadvantaged adults in an integrated fashion, at a common site. This one-stop approach has proven to be very effective (McCollam, O'Sullivan, Mukkala, Stengard, & Rowe, 2008).

In Germany, a systematic evaluation of inpatient versus home treatment of children and adolescents with psychiatric disorders found favorable results for home treatment. Germans have also introduced a systematic method for conducting routine quality assurance and evaluation of therapy, using telephone interviews (Mattejat, Hirsch, & Remschmidt, 2003).

The United States could benefit from adopting some of the constructive strategies employed by European countries. At the macro-level we need to place more emphasis on collecting and using data on the behavioral health status of our citizens, including outcomes associated with significant policy and program changes. Germany's use of systematic evaluation and quality assurance processes would be beneficial at local and program levels in the United States. In response to the desire to move care from restricted to community settings, there has been a proliferation of new community-based programs, such as group homes and in-home services. Unfortunately, efforts to ensure that these programs are appropriate and provide high-quality services have lagged behind the development of these new initiatives. If systematic monitoring efforts were in place, policy-makers and administrators would be able to identify problems in a timely manner and pursue corrective action strategies. If the United States adopted the routine, comprehensive data-gathering efforts employed in Europe we would be in a better position to improve services and hold providers accountable.

Funding

Perhaps the most significant difference between the European and American mental health service programs is the method of funding. In the United States, strong emphasis on managed care during the past two decades has taken a negative toll on support for mental health services. During the recent economic downturn, funding reductions have been made at state and local levels. At best, funding for mental health services in the United States is provided by a patchwork of government programs and private insurance companies that reimburse providers for specific services. It became evident during the discussions on health care reform that millions of individuals do not have any health insurance coverage. Given the lack of parity between physical and behavioral health insurance coverage, many individuals lack sufficient resources to pay for the care they need for their mental health issues. What is the effect of such policies, where a bulk of health care is privatized and a large population lives at or under the poverty line? With no insurance, the poor pay a disproportionately large portion of their income for health care needs and are often driven into debt, which impacts their overall well-being. The health care safety net is thus an important concept for policy-makers to grasp. Mental health delinked from physical health is often not on the radar of policy-makers and is further marginalized when resources are allocated.

In contrast, in European countries such as Sweden and Germany, which have compulsory health insurance, funding challenges are less complex. Moreover, it is clear that cheaper and more universal coverage than is provided in the United States is a characteristic of the British National Health Service (NHS). However, as we have seen in recent years, general economic conditions have had a significant impact on the availability of resources even in countries with universal coverage or publicly funded health care (Schleimer, 2002). While it is unrealistic to expect that we can buffer the mental health service system from the effects of a severe economic downturn, if we were able to create more rational funding policies and better integrate behavioral health with physical health care systems, it would be possible to realize some cost savings and perhaps make these services less vulnerable to large funding reductions that are often driven as much by political expediency as by cost–benefit analysis.

Integrating Mental Health with Primary Care

A report by the WHO and the World Organization of Family Doctors (Wonca) provides a compelling rationale for integrating mental health services into primary health care as the most viable method for enhancing availability of treatment and ensuring that people get the mental health care they need (WHO and World Organization of Family Doctors [Wonca], 2008). The report describes numerous efforts to achieve integration of primary care and mental health. Interestingly, many of the examples come from low- and middle-income countries where strong formal mental health systems do not exist. There are several examples of best practice in relation to integrating mental health into primary care.

In the Patagonia region of Argentina, primary care physicians are responsible for the diagnosis, treatment, and rehabilitation of individuals who have serious mental disorders. Outpatient treatment is provided in these communities, and psychiatrists and other mental health specialists are available to review and advise in complex situations. Complementary clinical care is provided at a community-based rehabilitation center which also serves as a training site for general medicine residents and practicing primary care physicians. This program has increased access for those in need of mental health services and lowered costs, while at the same time allowing people with mental disorders to continue to live in their home communities.

In Belize, psychiatric nurse practitioners play a critical role in delivery of service and preparation of primary care personnel to work with individuals with mental health disorders. The nurse practitioners make home visits to patients and work with primary care staff to improve their knowledge base and skills. Through these efforts, admissions to psychiatric hospitals have been reduced. While administrators of this initiative acknowledge that these programs are less than optimal, they note that in countries where there are very few trained mental health specialists it may be necessary to enhance primary care practitioner's skills over time rather than aspire to reach a fully integrated system of care prematurely.

In the Kerala State in India medical officers trained in mental health provide diagnostic and treatment services for persons who have mental disorders as a regular part of their general primary care functions. Their work is supplemented by a multidisciplinary district mental health team that offers outreach clinical services. The services may involve direct management of persons with complex situations and provide in-service training to support the trained medical officers and operate mental health clinics with only occasional support from formal mental health professionals. The availability of psychotropic medication in the clinics has allowed patients to remain in their home communities and reduces expenses as well as travel time to hospitals.

The Islamic Republic of Iran has achieved a nationwide integration of mental health into its primary care system. Similar to programs in Belize and India, general practitioners deliver mental health care within their primary health practices. District or provincial health centers, which have mental health specialists on staff, are available to serve patients with complex problems. Through outreach efforts, community health workers identify and refer people in their villages to primary care settings for assessment. The scope of the Iranian integration of mental health is particularly impressive, reaching urban and rural areas. A sizeable portion of the country's citizens now have access to affordable and acceptable mental health care. As cited earlier in this chapter, better integration of behavioral health and primary care in the United States would likely lead to more responsive care, reduced fragmentation of services, and cost savings associated with earlier appropriate intervention and reductions in parallel administrative structures. Similar programs using primary care physicians, nurses, and community outreach workers have shown promising results in South Africa, Uganda, and Australia.

In addition to community- and nation-specific programs to improve mental health care, there have also been broader campaigns to address problems and disparities. The most prominent efforts have been led by the WHO. Recognizing the interdependence of physical and mental health and the importance of positive mental health for the individual, family, and society, the WHO recently developed a Mental Health Gap Action Program (MhGAP) (WHO, 2008). This initiative was established to advance work that produced the original global action program for mental health, endorsed in 2002. MhGAP focuses on reducing the treatment gap of more than 75% that exists between lower- and lower middle-income countries. The program has identified specific evidence-based approaches for mental, neurological, and substance abuse disorders that have been identified as priorities. MhGAP acknowledges the critical need to obtain political commitment at the highest levels of government and has established a structure and process for developing and implementing a comprehensive, coordinated campaign for acquiring funding and providing prevention and treatment services in resource-poor countries (WHO, 2008).

IMPLICATIONS FOR MENTAL HEALTH POLICY AND PRACTICE IN THE UNITED STATES

As in other areas of endeavor, it is apparent that the United States has been a leader in advancing the field of mental health care. Many of the conceptual and empirical discoveries and innovations have occurred here, including the development of diagnostic tools and psychotherapeutic and pharmacological interventions. In addition to being the source of these specific advances, the United States has also contributed significantly at the macro-level. Major paradigm shifts such as the community support and systems of care models cited earlier occurred in this country.

However, in spite of the abundance of its intellectual and financial resources, the United States still has significant deficits in the way in which it deals with mental health issues and could benefit from the progressive approaches used by other nations. Ironically, some of these lessons come from countries with far fewer resources. For instance, many of the best examples of sites that have effectively integrated mental health with primary health care settings happen to be poor areas with few fiscal or technical resources, such as those programs cited earlier. These nations' willingness to cross traditional disciplinary boundaries may be due, in large part, to not having the ability to create separate mental health structures because of scarce resources.

Likewise, some of the exemplary efforts to provide creative, innovative services seem to be spurred by an attitude of providing the best care possible within the constraints of limited resources. Within the United States there is often an expectation that new programs require additional resources. While it is reasonable to assume that additional funding is helpful for improving services, categorically linking innovation to new funding severely limits reform efforts, particularly during periods of economic distress. The willingness of people in other cultures to collaborate across disciplines and sectors to produce improved care within existing resource limitations is a practice Americans should consider emulating.

However, some managed care organizations in the United States, such as the Kaiser Permanente system, use true integration of care, and have been proposed as models to further improve the British system (Feachem, Sekhri, & White, 2002). The Kaiser organization embraces the integration of services through the continuum of care, to ensure that patients are treated at the most appropriate level of care and that their journey through the system is as rapid and efficient as possible. This system integrates all specialties, including primary care, as equal members of a multispecialty team; this team also jointly controls financial resources. Because the financial integration is complete, all parties in the system (primary care doctors, consultants, and hospitals) are jointly responsible for a single bottom line. This ensures that available resources are spent most effectively to achieve good health care outcomes.

Kaiser also emphasizes integration of leadership and management to ensure partnership between clinical governance and administration in achieving shared goals. This integration of culture and vision within a single organizational structure is helpful in moving a vertically integrated system in one clinical direction while providing high-quality, cost-effective care. This model of care, which is reminiscent of the systems of care model referenced in Chapter 8, holds the promise of creating a uniform health delivery system. Unfortunately, such systems are often strongly resisted in a market economy, which thrives on competition among various vendors or agencies. Disparate systems cause poor sharing of information and duplication of services that cannot justify the cost to the consumer based on poor outcomes. We have created a complex model for health care with stakeholders who have disparate missions, significant interdependencies, and the inability to work together to produce an optimal outcome. Simplification of the payor system from the administrative end and pay for performance on the provider end may hold some promise for the consumer of health care.

In addition to poor integration of services, there are two other contextual impediments to adopting a government-supported or single-payor coverage for health care financing in the United States. First, the sociopolitical culture of the United States is complex and well established. Historically, there have been significant tensions in this area, with a high priority placed on privatization of health and other human services while government continues to play a strong role in funding mental health care through Medicaid, Medicare, and other state and federal programs. There is little likelihood that this often inharmonious balance will shift significantly in the foreseeable future.

The second caveat regarding the benefits of other funding models relates to changes in the economy. Countries such as Sweden and Norway, which have provided state-supported health services, have recently experienced problems in delivering high-quality services because of the financial burdens placed on them during the global economic downturn. Perhaps the lesson to be taken from this is that any model of service provision and funding is only as good as the ability and willingness of the political system to provide sufficient support.

Variations in the political, economic, social, and cultural conditions of the countries we have described in this chapter preclude recommending that the United States adopt another nation's system of mental health care. The fact that none of these other systems can claim anything resembling perfection also bolsters the argument against a replication strategy. Still, there are some specific lessons and recommendations that can be culled from the experiences of other countries and applied to our approach to providing mental health care in the United States. Concepts and strategies employed by other nations that are worthy of consideration include the following:

- **Making Mental Health a Priority.** One of the critical requisites of establishing behavioral health as a high priority is to integrate mental health into that nation's mainstream policy agenda. The primary strategies for accomplishing this appear to be public education directed at heightening the awareness of citizens and public officials about the importance and benefits of good mental health, and integrating mental health into the physical health system. In the United States, the responsibility for educating the public about important health and social issues usually resides with advocacy and professional groups associated with the issue.
    - For mental health, consumer-directed groups, such as the National Alliance for the Mentally Ill and Mental Health America, and professional groups, including the American Psychiatric Association, American Psychological Association, and National Association for Social Work, are well positioned to provide this education. Their efforts would be significantly enhanced by government or foundation support that stipulated collaboration among these organizations as a requisite for receiving funding.
    - The importance of integrating mental health and primary care has previously been discussed. Although bringing these typically separate provider systems together represents a significant challenge, progress would be facilitated by offering incentives for co-location, such as favorable reimbursement rates, targeted funding devoted to assisting organizations with developing integrated infrastructure, policy and regulations fostering coordination and co-location, and research funds dedicated to examining the health outcomes and economic impact of integrating mental and physical health.

- **Money Matters.** Changes in public attitude and policy are essential requisites for enhancing mental health care. However, these efforts will not yield significant improvement without sufficient and appropriate financial support. As noted earlier, several European countries with strong mental health systems allocated 10% of their health care budgets to mental health care, in contrast to the United States, which spends only 6% on mental health. Another correlate of successful systems is the involvement of government in funding and operating health care. Compared to health care provision in many industrialized countries, in the United States the private sector provides more than twice as much of the total health care. Likewise, countries that require mandatory health insurance have been more successful in improving health outcomes.

Given the prevailing anti-government sentiment in this country, it is not likely that any group will be able to rally support in the near future for greater government involvement in the mental health system. Even with the attention given to mental health in light of the recent mass shootings in Tucson, Aurora, and Newtown, there is little indication of stronger government support for mental health, other than perhaps attention to gun purchase screening. Other countries have demonstrated, however, that the amount of resources available is not the only critical factor in responding to mental health needs. The way in which those resources are used is also important.

For example, in the United States there are significant disparities between the level of care available to persons in lower-income groups and that available to those with greater fiscal resources. We might use the principles employed by the Mental Health Gap Action Program of WHO, which systematically identified relevant evidence-based approaches, established priorities, and mobilized the political commitment necessary to obtain funding and develop programs to reduce the gap in care between low- and low-middle-income countries. We would also benefit from the experience of countries directing funding to integrated, one-stop centers where individuals can have multiple health and mental health needs addressed in a single location. Aligning financial incentives to support policy and program goals can be a powerful tool for achieving desired outcomes as long as planners realize that effective care requires attention to other factors, such as a well-prepared workforce and a responsive administrative infrastructure.

Unlike some of the countries cited in this chapter, the United States has not established mental health as a national priority. Without a clear vision and strong plan for mental health care, policy-makers tend to make decisions that may do more harm than good. For example, in the current economic downturn, elected officials are inclined to reduce funding for services as a knee-jerk response to budget imbalances. If these officials had a better understanding of and commitment to mental health care, they might also consider measures that would enhance efficiency and improve services while at the same time being responsive to the broader fiscal crisis. Examples of this approach to budget problems include offering incentives for better integration and less duplication of services, and incorporation of evidence-based programs that produce better outcomes.

- **Data Drive Policy**. The European Union and members such as Scotland have demonstrated how establishing and tracking key health status and outcome indicators can focus attention on critical policy concerns and directions. Systematic monitoring efforts have been effectively used to promote nationwide initiatives to prevent and treat mental health disorders, as well as to address labor force issues. While we collect large amounts of data in the United States, some of which is used to justify politically driven decisions, we have not done as well in developing and utilizing highly visible, sustainable data-tracking mechanisms that allow the policy-makers, as well as citizens, to assess progress on important mental health issues and outcomes.

Even today, the Belgian city of Geel's centuries-old effort to reintegrate individuals with severe mental disabilities into their community is seen as the most comprehensive and impressive model of community recovery. Although it would be difficult to replicate this approach anywhere in the United States, one feature of the Geel model bears consideration as we strive to improve our current system of care. The common perception is that the citizens of Geel must have been very compassionate and kind to take these disabled individuals into their homes and community. While there probably was some charitable intent, historians have noted that the primary motivating force behind this movement was economic, as the host families benefited financially from having these individuals in their homes (Goldstein & Godemont, 2005).

In our current political and economic climate, policies based on compassion may be praised but are seldom implemented. Therefore, making a persuasive argument for improving care for persons with mental health challenges will require providing empirical evidence that these reforms will not only produce benefits for behavioral health service recipients but also yield tangible economic benefits for all citizens and communities.

10

TOWARD MORE RESPONSIVE SYSTEMS OF CARE
CHALLENGES AND STRATEGIES

Robert Cohen and Aradhana Bela Sood

Transforming the current mental health system is indeed a daunting task. Individuals with even brief exposure to the existing system of care quickly realize how complex it is and how many obstacles must be overcome in order to create a genuinely responsive and comprehensive mental health service system. If we hope to successfully transform the existing system, it is essential that we develop effective strategies that take into account the multiple factors and forces that have resulted in our current insufficient and fragmented networks of service. In this chapter, we identify some of the key areas requiring serious attention and propose strategies for remediating the dysfunctional manner in which individuals with mental health challenges are currently served.

THE FALSE DICHOTOMY BETWEEN
HEALTH AND MENTAL HEALTH

To begin to improve mental health care in America, we must first acknowledge and address the artificial separation of mental health from physical health in our society. As pointed out in the previous two chapters, these aspects of health are inextricably linked. The impact of stress and mental well-being on recovery from physical illness, lost days from work, and secondary health problems is well studied. The recent report from the CDC, *Health, United States, 2009* (National Center for Health Statistics, 2010), reveals that in the years 2006-2007, mental illness was the second most frequently mentioned condition causing activity limitation among adults 18–44 years of age, and the third most frequently mentioned among adults 45–54 years of age. Mental health problems among adults affected their ability to do important activities, such as work and everyday household chores. Among children ages 5–11, speech problems, learning disabilities, and attention-deficit/hyperactivity disorder (ADHD or ADD) were the most frequently reported causes of activity limitation. Mental health problems interfered with children's ability to engage in major age-appropriate activities, such as play and self-care, and required special education and early intervention activities.

These are not new or surprising findings. More than a decade ago, the U.S. Surgeon General's report on mental health found that mental illnesses are the second leading cause of disability in the nation and affect 20% of all Americans (Murray & Lopez, 1996). Even more startling is the finding that adults with serious mental illness die 25 years earlier than Americans overall, many from preventable conditions (National Association of State Mental Health Program Directors, 2006).

Mental health is essential to overall health, and vice versa. This guiding principle should inform and underlie any transformational efforts.

STRUCTURE OF MENTAL HEALTH CARE DELIVERY

The current structure of our mental health system and its associated problems have been identified in Chapter 8, while concerns about specific components of the service system, such as college campus mental health services, were described in earlier chapters. It is apparent that we currently have multiple systems arranged in a fragmented and often duplicative manner.

As we begin to address the question of how to improve the way we provide mental health services, it may be helpful to restate the complexity of the system by identifying some of the major entities involved in the delivery of services. The primary organizational entities can be classified along the following dimensions.

Private and Public Service Providers

Included within the public domain are locally based services such as community mental health centers as well as mental health services embedded in other human service settings, such as health departments, schools, and criminal justice systems. In the private sector, services are provided by for-profit and not-for-profit entities, with each group providing a wide range of services, including outpatient, day treatment, residential, and inpatient care, as well as a variety of care management and other system of care functions.

In recent years, the private sector has become a stronger force as government policy increasingly favors paying private providers for services formerly delivered by the public sector. This blurring of boundaries between the public and private sectors, and the existence of a de facto or "shadow" mental health system, make the situation even more confusing. As the private sector's role in providing services grows, particularly with their increased reliance on public funding, we are confronted with difficult questions. Who is responsible for ensuring quality? Can we maintain an authentic safety net without strong involvement of government? How do we ensure that mental health care is accessible to all Americans who need it?

Satisfactory resolution of these questions will require comprehensive planning at the local, state, and federal levels. This planning must be inclusive, involving all stake-holders. The input of consumers and their families is particularly important. Although it may be politically unpopular at the moment, it is unlikely that we will be able to achieve the objectives of delivering high-quality services to those most in need unless government plays a prominent role in monitoring all services supported with public funding.

The configuration of how services are delivered and monitored may vary according to the resources and structures of each state and locality, but these arrangements must be accountable for meeting a common set of uniform standards. For example, government is generally viewed as the appropriate entity for providing safety net services, such as inpatient care for individuals with complex and severe psychiatric challenges. It is possible, however, that in some communities, these services might be delivered by private entities as long as appropriate governmental agencies provide necessary oversight. Unfortunately, current economic pressures combined with the inclination to view private service provision as preferable have led some states to eliminate criti-cal state-operated support services and transfer these functions to private providers without ensuring that the contract entities continue to fulfill the intended objectives of the program.

Levels of Government Engaged in Funding, Regulation, and Provision of Services: Local, State, and Federal

The most prominent entities at the local and state levels are the mental health authori-ties, which are now often referred to as departments of behavioral health. At the state level and, to a lesser extent, within local communities, these agencies have gradually reduced their involvement in the direct provision of services and function more as funding and regulatory agencies. State agencies responsible for dispersing medical assistance funds have become increasingly more influential in shaping mental health policy and practice as states have come to rely more heavily on Medicaid and Medicare as primary funding sources for mental health services. Human service agencies at local and state levels, such as education, criminal justice, health, and social services, are also involved in providing, regulating, or funding mental health service.

The federal government also provides and supports mental health services through a variety of mechanisms. In addition to its role in funding service systems through Medicaid, Medicare, and other federal funding streams, agencies such as the National Institutes of Health, the Substance Abuse and Mental Health Services Administration, the Centers for Disease Control and Prevention, and the Department of Education support development, service delivery, and research related to mental health care. The Veterans Administration operates a large network of inpatient and outpatient mental health services for individuals involved in the military sector. Table 1 in the Appendix provides a simple flow chart of the funding mechanisms of federal, state, local, and private and military mental health systems (Sood, 2009b).

The trend during the past several decades has been to shift the locus of responsibility for provision of mental health and other human services from central to local levels, that is, federal to state, state to local government. This trend is not likely to be reversed in the near future. However, if we hope to improve care, it is critical that we define more clearly the specific responsibilities and channels for accountability for each participating entity. After the Virginia Tech tragedy there was considerable finger-pointing, with the state faulting the university and local mental health agencies for failing to avert the crisis, while local agencies blamed the state for not providing sufficient resources. Although there may be merit in examining the accuracy of these allegations, we are unlikely see much progress until the key public and private stakeholders engage in a serious discussion that defines the scope of the need, identifies needed resources, and clarifies roles and expectations of all participating entities, including measurable objectives. The success of this endeavor will be dependent upon developing a shared commitment to blending and braiding efforts of all stakeholders in a responsive and efficient manner.

THE NEED FOR PUBLIC AND POLITICAL WILL

In attempting to address the question of why mental health services have been allowed to exist at such an inadequate and dysfunctional level, several major factors become apparent. As noted earlier, the most obvious factor is the uncertainty and complexity of the mental health system. Policy-makers as well as the general public have difficulty understanding this arcane system. Following the Virginia Tech tragedy, conversation among public leaders was couched primarily in terms of public safety. Safety was certainly an issue, but this limited focus does not take into consideration the notion that crises in health care often occur because prevention of the crises was not attempted, or because the attempt made was poor. Primary prevention and early intervention, which have the potential to avert future mass tragedies, are often seen as "soft science" and viewed as less important than immediate short-term solutions. Supporting a primary prevention focus is a challenge for most politicians, whose careers will not last long enough to see the return on investment. Most prevention interventions yield fruit in approximately 15 years. Our current health care system is not in the business of planting trees, but it should be.

When advocates and service providers, who themselves are not unified in their positions, attempt to explain what is needed, they often add to the confusion of those they are addressing. While some of this lack of clarity is due to the incomplete body of existing knowledge about causes, treatment, and prevention of mental health disorders, it is incumbent upon those engaged in garnering support for change to communicate in clear and simple terms, speaking with one voice and advocating for a common set of objectives. Effective reform requires a strong grassroots effort, preferably led by consumers of mental health services and their families, who have direct knowledge of what needs to be done and who, unlike service providers, are less likely to be perceived as having a vested interest. The most powerful advocacy organization in the mental health world is the National Alliance on Mental Illness (NAMI).

The public's perceptions and misperceptions about mental illness represent an even more basic impediment to achieving broad-scale mobilization for reform. In spite of the increased levels of education and sophistication among the general public, considerable fear and prejudice still exist in relation to mental illness and those who suffer from it. A case in point is the public's strong focus on shoring up safety measures after the Virginia Tech event, in contrast to the relatively weak support demonstrated for improving mental health treatment that might prevent future occurrences.

As a nation, we must address the broader issues of health care access. Health care reform legislation has been enacted, but the question remains: Is mental health care a right or a privilege in America? Will everyone who requires care receive it?

COMPREHENSIVE AND COORDINATED LEADERSHIP

The combination of insufficient knowledge, complexity of the issue, and the stigma associated with mental illness creates a formidable barrier to achieving progress. These deficits and negative forces produce inertia and resistance, which significantly hamper efforts to transform the mental health system. Without strong leadership, the probability of overcoming these obstacles is low. Even in crisis situations that have captured the attention of the general public, government leaders have failed to mobilize and exercise the political will necessary to substantively address the serious flaws in the mental health system responsible for precipitating the crisis. The Virginia Tech shootings are a case in point. After the initial public outcry subsided and the panel's recommendations were issued and considered by the governor and the General Assembly, the actions that were taken resulted in some changes in the commitment process, but no substantial improvement in the system of care for persons with mental health challenges.

The failure to pursue this opportunity to bolster important prevention and intervention programs can be attributed to several factors. First, once the visibility of and emotional response to the Virginia Tech tragedy subsided, the accompanying political attention was diverted to other headline-grabbing issues. Second, while changing statutes is not easy, enacting legislation conveys an immediate sense that constructive action has been taken regardless of what the long-term impact of the legislation may be. Conversely, developing programs that effectively address complex health and social issues is a difficult task, requiring investment of substantial human and fiscal resources over an extended period of time. Finally, because the issues underlying Seung-Hui's aberrant behavior and failed mental health care are complex, it was difficult to communicate to policy-makers and the public in a simple and concise manner what needed to be done to prevent future occurrences. Given the absence of a strong, unified constituency in favor of behavioral health prevention and intervention solutions, it was difficult to muster sustained support for promoting these types of programs.

When one examines the isolated examples of the implementation of successful comprehensive responsive service systems, a common factor that emerges is the presence of a strong, unified leadership team comprised of individuals representing multiple sectors and viewpoints (Cohen & Cohen, 2000). The leaders involved in these projects have typically overcome or set aside their differences and established a common set of values and principles-driven goals directed at the best interests of mental health consumers. Their shared purpose, combined with a considerable amount of mundane work focused on understanding and effectively addressing salient operational issues, have enabled visionary groups to achieve surprisingly positive outcomes in spite of significant impediments. The programs described in Chapter 8, such as Wraparound Milwaukee (Kamradt, 2000), the Comprehensive Service Act for At Risk Youth Families in Virginia, The Initiatives for Excellence in Ohio, and the Assertive Community Team program developed initially in Wisconsin, all began with diverse groups of stakeholders forming a unified coalition to achieve a common purpose.

If we hope to make significant progress in improving mental health care, we must develop collaborative teams representing multiple stakeholders who are able to do the following:

(1) Establish a clear public message that enables citizens and policy-makers to understand the need for reform and the benefits of producing change.

(2) Develop a political strategy for mobilizing support from all sectors of the mental health community as well as the general public, and identify effective strategies for obtaining endorsement and support from the various political bodies that impact mental health policy and practice.

(3) Bring together a broad coalition of stakeholders who are willing to work collaboratively within the political structure as well as the mental health community in

order to obtain support and actualize their vision into a responsive, coordinated system of care.

(4) Establish short- and long-term plans for implementing transformation in a practical and cost effective manner.

Some would argue that the current economic climate is not conducive to mobilizing this type of comprehensive effort. The counterargument to this pessimistic perspective is that mental health system reform requires a long-term commitment accompanied by a clear set of short, intermediate, and extended goals and plans. Furthermore, the magnitude of the harm and suffering that currently exists requires action.

A good case can also be made for viewing the potential opportunities that may be found during difficult times. Adverse conditions may sometimes serve as fertile ground for positive change. Rather than focusing exclusively on the negative impact of the budget cuts that are currently being made, one might argue that the current shortage of available fiscal resources provides a good opportunity for agencies and individuals to collaborate, to find new ways to achieve productivity and efficiency.

It is worth noting that the establishment of Virginia's Comprehensive Service Act for At-Risk Youth and Families in the early 1990s occurred during a period in which the state was facing a budget deficit comparable in magnitude to the current crisis. It has been conjectured that the poor economic climate may have been partially responsible for the executive branch's spirited advocacy for this legislation. L. Douglas Wilder, Virginia's governor at that time and the nation's first elected African-American governor, may have exerted such a high level of commitment and effort to this project to provide a legacy for himself in the field of health and human services during this period of fiscal austerity.

RECONCILING SCIENCE AND PRACTICE

The current emphasis on promoting evidence-based treatment and intervention is laudable. If mental health care is to gain legitimacy, it must demonstrate that its tools and strategies have been built on a firm foundation. On the other hand, it is apparent that unraveling the mysteries of mental illness and developing treatment approaches with a sound empirical basis are long-term endeavors. The current focus on translating therapeutic techniques that have been established as efficacious in the laboratory into real-world settings is a worthy goal. Continued support for basic as well as translational research is essential if we are to enhance the legitimacy of this field.

While we continue to support this effort, we must also be cautious about proceeding too rapidly. There is a seductive attractiveness to the notion of developing and implementing treatment approaches that have been manualized to provide clear and simple recipes for how to work with individuals with various disorders. There is also considerable risk in over-simplifying and over-promising evidenced-based approaches. When attempts have been made to replicate laboratory-based interventions in real-world community settings, it has quickly become apparent that the resources allocated for the rigorous and pristine process of scientific investigation are not usually available in typical treatment settings. The amount of training that providers receive, the size of their caseloads, and other mitigating factors present challenges for those who wish to replicate approaches that have proven to be successful in more controlled settings. In addition, we have discovered that one size does not fit all. An intervention that is effective with white, middle-class college graduates may require a considerable adaptation if it is to produce effective outcomes for low-income, single-parent minority families.

A constructive approach to the issue of evidence-based practice is to continue to advocate for the use of sound evidence-based approaches, with the caveat that empirical support must exist for that specific application of that practice, that is, age and ethnic background of population served, and nature of the setting where practice is being used. At the same time, we need to advocate for additional research support to extend the scope of service approaches with empirical support for their effectiveness. In the case of Seung-Hui Cho, if he had been given appropriate attention, it might have been possible to prevent his shooting rampage. However, there is not yet an established treatment protocol that would have had a high probability of successfully remediating his complex set of problems.

Within the field of psychiatry, we have witnessed problems with the use of Preferred Drug Lists (PDLs), which have been established to promote clinically appropriate utilization of prescribed medications while containing costs. While these PDLs may be appropriate for illnesses with established single-agent treatment protocols, such as antibiotic responsiveness of certain conditions, the heterogeneity of psychiatric illnesses suggests that "a one size fits all" approach does not work. No one patient with depression is like the next. At this time, we do not have the evidence to characterize which patient will respond to which psychotropic. Evidence from the Sequenced Treatment Alternatives of Resistant–Depression (STAR*D) (Lin & Chen, 2008), the largest prospective study of depression, indicates that it takes trials of four to six medications from different classes to get 80% treatment response, and even then, remission (virtual absence of depression) is difficult to obtain. Twenty to forty percent of patients will not achieve remission, and more trials with different medicines will be needed. Unfortunately, in some cases, PDLs hinder practitioners in applying good science.

Within the mental health community, as well as among the general public, we need to clarify how we can proceed with developing and implementing evidence-based practice and to acknowledge that this is not a simple or linear process. It will require a high level of tolerance of ambiguity. Efforts to identify and adapt empirically based practice should continue with adequate recognition that we do not yet have a sufficient array of off-the-shelf tools appropriate for all situations. We need to support research that will yield best practice in addressing the context in which services are delivered as well as the actual treatment strategies provided (Kazak et al., 2010).

Often the link between the bench or lab researcher and the clinician appears nonexistent. One avenue to address this may be to invest in at least one center of psychiatric excellence in every geographical region, the prime focus of which should be the development of evidence-based interventions in conjunction with local hospitals, clinics, and private practices. Translational research that provides reliable information swiftly and that is generalizable to real-life patients will galvanize the field and bring clinicians to a point where they themselves pose questions that inform their practice.

WORKFORCE DEVELOPMENT

The gap between supply and demand in mental health care is disturbing. With significant shortages of qualified mental health professionals and inadequate insurance coverage for mental health services, persons seeking assistance are often confronted with long waiting periods to see a psychiatrist or therapist, if they are fortunate enough to obtain an appointment at all. Many persons are forced to seek assistance from primary care physicians and other individuals or agencies not necessarily adequately trained in the field of mental health.

Currently, 80% of specialty child mental health care is provided by pediatricians, family practitioners, or primary care physicians (U.S. Department of Health & Human Services, 1999). They constitute the default child mental health system of the United States. Most practitioners in primary care provide this service because they have no choice. Most of these practitioners are engaged in treatment of children for behavioral problems with very little training in these subspecialized areas. Because mental health problems complicate recovery from comorbid medical problems, these practitioners are forced to practice behavioral health with no formal training. The implications are obvious. Not only are they not using evidence-based or best practice interventions, they may also run the risk of providing less than safe care.

To improve this situation, projects to integrate primary care and pediatrics with psychiatry and child psychiatry should be a focus of public and private agencies. This includes models where specialists are co-located within primary care practices or can be retained on a consultative basis by multiple pediatric practices.

Techniques to expand the technical expertise of specialists into rural areas through telemedicine or telepsychiatry are also promising ways to tackle work force deficits.

The use of physician extenders such as nurse practitioners and physician assistants should be ramped up to meet the need as well.

The primary source for training front-line health care providers is regional community colleges. An examination and revamping of community college curricula to align them with the need of area hospitals for trained mid- and low-level providers should be considered.

REALIGNING INCENTIVES

Given the complexity of the mental health system, efforts to improve services should be informed by a clear and practical set of guidelines. This framework should call for a precise assessment of current obstacles and facilitate the development of remedial actions that will produce positive outcomes. An incentive-based framework may be useful in addressing this challenge. By enhancing our understanding of the forces that currently drive the existing system, including how individual and organizational behavior is rewarded and punished, we will be in a better position to identify which factors impede or facilitate achievement of desired outcomes. With this knowledge, it will be possible to develop a plan for insuring that the incentive structure supports the stated goals of the system, that is, responsive care for persons with mental health disorders, rather than operates at cross purposes with these goals.

While financial incentives are central to achieving an effective service system, money is by no means the only critical resource necessary for achieving an effective system of care. If we wish to modify the current dysfunctional system, we also need to understand what motivates consumers, providers, administrators, and policy-makers at all levels and what kind of changes will be required to facilitate individual and organizational change in the desired direction.

The vision for an ideal system of care articulated in this book places great emphasis on coordination among multiple health and human service agencies. While collaboration is frequently touted as desirable, the behavior of those in charge of such agencies often does not reflect this value. Agency personnel are typically held to account for actions, including problems that occur within their organizations, but rarely rewarded or recognized for efforts to work collaboratively with other entities within the human service system.

For example, although Seung-Hui Cho had been diagnosed as having social anxiety and selective mutism while he was in high school, his individual education plan addressed only the social anxiety as it affected his educational performance. His mutism, which had a significant impact on his functioning, did not improve, and no effort was made to work with other mental health resources that might have addressed this serious problem. Even more troubling was the inadequate response at Virginia Tech to the warning signs exhibited by Seung-Hui. Although many individuals and organizations were aware of his aberrant behavior, and despite some efforts by individuals to communicate their concerns to appropriate officials, there was no concerted effort to assess the threat posed by this student and respond appropriately. While some of the impediments to effective action may be attributed to HIPAA and other privacy requirements, a more compelling explanation for this failure is the silo-like structure of the departments and agencies involved, and the low priority given to mental health issues in comparison to other health concerns.

A similar dynamic exists at the consumer level. The prevailing vision of care places considerable emphasis on the empowerment of consumers and their families. Yet service recipients are typically viewed as passive participants in the treatment process and are often given little opportunity for input into their plan of care. Consumers are generally expected to accept the expert opinion of the service provider. Often the insurance carrier has more influence on treatment decisions than does the actual consumer of service.

By understanding how the current incentive structure shapes behavior, we may be able to better align incentives with desired functions and outcomes. Areas in which realignment of incentives would have a significant positive impact on functioning of the mental health system include those discussed next.

Allocation of Funding

There is general consensus that insufficient financial resources are allocated to the care of persons with mental health challenges. There is also agreement that current resources are not necessarily distributed appropriately. The most frequently cited example of misalignment is the imbalance between the high cost of services provided in restrictive settings such as psychiatric hospitals and residential treatment centers, compared to resources allocated for community-based services that enable individuals to function in more normalized settings. There is little argument that services provided in restrictive settings are going to be more expensive. Objections arise because of the disproportionate share of the budget that is allocated to high-end service settings. In recent decades, there has been a shift in the locus of care, with fewer people residing in institutional settings and more individuals being served in the community. Unfortunately, there has not been a commensurate shift of financial resources from restrictive to community-based providers.

In addition to inadequate funding, continuing stigma and prejudice associated with mental illness have made it difficult to gain the widespread acceptance needed to develop an adequate array of community-based services in many localities. Without sufficient availability of community services, consumers and providers have been forced to rely more heavily on services provided in restrictive settings.

Most experts in program reform believe that a shift from the old to a new model of care requires a transition, or "bridge," in which adequate resources are devoted to the established program while also investing in development of the new model. While this approach carries with it some inefficiency, the overlap in services is necessary, to ensure that recipients are not moved from an existing service setting to a situation in which no alternative services are available. Even in times of relative prosperity, this is a difficult concept for policy-makers to grasp. Unfortunately, ignoring the importance of providing bridge funding often leads to poor care that ultimately takes its toll in terms of significant human and financial costs.

Paying for Services

Since the 1960s, when Medicaid and Medicare were established, fee-for-service has been the dominant mechanism for paying for health care. Providers are reimbursed for specific services they give to patients. Sometimes reimbursement is based on time units, that is, per hour, per day, and in other instances payment is linked to specific procedures such as diagnostic tests and surgical interventions. In addition, despite the recognition of community-based or outpatient care as the most optimum venue for care for many patients, the current reimbursement system rewards inpatient care. Primary prevention of crises through outpatient stabilization faces significant challenges because of poor reimbursement for complex outpatient intervention and because of poor access to outpatient specialist care.

Consider this example: If a patient with a history of mental illness is showing signs of instability (hearing voices and is suicidal), it takes more than a 15-minute medication check to determine what may be causing the regression and instability and what can be done, if anything, to stabilize the person without a costly hospitalization. Does the doctor spend the hour to figure out what is wrong and get paid at a fraction of the cost that he or she would be reimbursed if the patient is hospitalized? Generally, the answer is a resounding "no." Providing incentives to ensure regular follow-up care *pre-crisis* for such a patient, while he is doing well, could prevent regression and generate considerable cost savings, as well as reward the doctor for practicing good medicine.

Similarly, if a mental health practitioner has a desire to run parenting groups for first-time parents who have already displayed emotional problems, there is no easy mechanism to pay for this intervention, even though it may be a pivotal low-cost intervention for the entire family, that has the potential to manage or prevent a mother's postpartum depression, mitigate the child's future behavioral problems, and treat a father's worsening stress ulcers and hypertension.

Access to care remains a major issue in rural parts of the country, yet incentives that encourage providers to use telemedicine or teleconferencing remain limited because there are no existing mechanisms in place for reimbursement. These should become standard options for providers.

On a broader level, procedures are paid for at a better rate than time-based modalities. Thus, psychiatry and mental health providers as well as those in other subspecialties such as primary care physicians are paid considerably less than their counterparts whose practices are heavily weighted toward delivery of specific procedures. This is a general failing of our current health system—high-end, poor-yield inpatient and procedure-oriented care is incentivized, while cognitive, low-tech health education–oriented care is reimbursed at such low levels that it makes embracing them insolvent for most health care practices.

With the advent of managed care, there has been an attempt to replace fee-for-service with other mechanisms, such as capitation, which focuses on episodes of care rather than discrete procedures. Some of the motivation for this shift came from the observation that if payment is tied to the amount of service provided, there is an incentive for providers to increase the number of services given to the consumer. Under capitation approaches, the provider is given a specified amount of money for each patient's care, regardless of the amount of time or number of procedures. The specific amount allocated per episode or person is known as the case rate, and is usually based on the nature and severity of the presenting problem. Theoretically, this would encourage providers to deliver only services required to adequately deal with the issue presented by the patient.

Several factors and forces work against successful translation of the capitation model into effective practice. First, in mental health, it is often difficult to identify tangible outcomes, especially in instances where there is a chronic condition. The inability to specify precise outcomes makes it difficult to develop criteria for what constitutes effective service. Second, major changes in funding policies and procedures are often accompanied by modifications in the overall funding base. For example, over the past few decades, the federal government has shifted away from categorical funding in which it paid states for specific programs. Under the newer system, known as block funding, the federal government allocates a lump sum of money to cover an array of services. This change to block funding enabled the state to have greater influence on how it spent funds. To the states' dismay, there was also a concomitant decrease in the total amount of money allocated in the block grant, compared to what had been previously allocated under the categorical funding formula, leaving them with fewer resources to support important programs.

Likewise, many managed care organizations not only shifted their reimbursement paradigm but also reduced the total amount of funding available to mental health providers. In instances where fee-for-service was retained, the payment rates were significantly reduced, causing many providers to stop participating in these insurance programs. Unfortunately, these changes have had a disproportionately negative impact on middle- and low-income families, which were more dependent on third-party payors.

Each funding mechanism has advantages and disadvantages. The capitation approach is more consistent with holistic care, because it focuses on prevention and avoids a narrow definition of service to be provided. However, since the total funding base is insufficient and providers are motivated to keep their costs low, whether for reasons of profit motivation or efficiency, the use of capitation models has often resulted in consumers receiving inadequate services.

Similar problems have occurred with a fee-for-service approach, with some providers offering more frequent or higher cost services in order to generate revenue and other providers refusing to participate when they perceive fees to be inadequate. This has resulted in a diminished supply of qualified practitioners. In many instances, individuals seeking help cannot find anyone to assist them. For those fortunate enough to identify providers, there is often a two- to three-month waiting period to obtain an appointment.

Which funding mechanisms are best suited for designing a truly responsive system of mental health care? Unfortunately, there is not a simple answer to this question. It would be glib to conclude that fee-for-service is at cross purposes with the systems of care approach. When services are adequately funded and appropriately regulated, as with Wraparound Milwaukee, fee-for-service can be used to compensate providers for appropriate delivery of services. Similarly, with an adequate resource base and a good accountability mechanism, capitation is a constructive approach for encouraging prevention and early intervention services and motivating providers to be prudent in figuring out how to meet the needs of consumers in an efficient and appropriate manner.

Engaging and Empowering Consumers as a Strategy for Improving Effectiveness

Consumer empowerment serves as a vehicle for enhancing service recipient self-efficacy, belief in one's ability to perform in a certain manner to attain certain goals, in this case, improved health. Involving consumers in decisions about their care, including payment matters, can also yield positive economic and productivity benefits as well. For example, in Singapore, which is not typically viewed as a liberal or progressive country, citizens are encouraged to save money, including depositing into health savings accounts that receive substantial contributions from employers. The government also plays a significant role by providing 80% of acute care in public hospitals. The system provides many incentives for consumers to be thrifty by establishing premium prices for conveniences such as private hospital rooms. The government also offers substantive incentives for medical students to become family practitioners rather than expensive specialists and promotes healthy life style choices. At the same time, Singapore provides a strong safety net for the poor. By combining liberal and conservative approaches, Singapore has been able to achieve good health outcomes while containing the overall cost of health care (Miller, 2010).

The point of this illustration is not to encourage us to replicate the Singapore approach. Our systems of government and culture are drastically different. Rather, the message is that giving consumers more control over the services they receive can produce a range of positive outcomes, including more responsive care, greater efficiency, and enhancement of consumer self-efficacy. By placing the consumer in the driver's seat it is possible to realign the decision processes in a manner that produces positive mental health service and economic outcomes.

Investing in Prevention

Growing evidence indicates that intervening early with at-risk individuals can reduce later problems and improve functioning for these persons as well as decrease overall treatment costs (Trust for America's Health, 2008). Despite this compelling argument, relatively little funding is allocated for prevention and early intervention. The heavy demand for mental health treatment services and the limited availability of funds accounts for some of the reluctance to invest in prevention programs. The absence of a precise explanation of what causes mental disorders and the field's inability to convince policy-makers and the general public that these programs can actually prevent the occurrence of psychiatric disorders also hamper efforts to obtain additional funding.

In spite of these obstacles, a persuasive argument can be made for increasing our investment in prevention and early intervention programs. One strategy for enhancing prevention support is to allocate a percentage of all mental health funding to support evidence-based practices in prevention and early intervention. While advocates for individuals who are already disabled may object to diverting some of their scarce resources, ensuring that a portion of funding is invested in earlier intervention represents a reasonable compromise and may lead to formation of a stronger coalition of advocates for mental health if prevention and treatment proponents can establish a common agenda.

Incentives for Encouraging Appropriate Provider and Organizational Behavior

Financial incentives that encourage service providers to behave more responsively have been discussed earlier in this chapter. While payment and reimbursement mechanisms are important, these are not the only factors that affect how well services are provided. One of the most daunting challenges in establishing a genuinely holistic system of care is finding ways to encourage and support collaborative, solution-focused behavior among the multiple stakeholders. Engaging leadership within a community such as a college campus has been discussed in detail in Chapter 6. For informed and progressive policies around mental wellness, the recognition and assessment of mental health problems should become an important issue for all stakeholders on campus, including students. The campus environment should support a culture of primary and secondary prevention and have resources for the provision of tertiary care services. At the direct-service level, individuals from different disciplines and agencies often have difficulty working together on behalf of those seeking help and their families. Although some of these problems may be attributed to discipline specific differences in knowledge, perspective, and language, other factors play a role in impeding cooperation.

If we wish to promote teamwork and cooperation, we need to address the personal attitudes and organizational factors, including territorial and bureaucratic impediments that discourage cooperation across disciplines and agencies. At the individual level, performance plans will need to reflect the value of collaboration by specifically identifying cooperation as a measurable objective that is heavily weighted in evaluating and compensating staff performance. In addition, these values should be continually reinforced by the statements and actions of the agency's administration. The inclination to function in a silo or territorial manner is difficult to modify. There are, however, numerous examples of organizations that have overcome this tendency through the values they espouse and the reinforcements they provide.

As we move away from the direct-service level, the barriers to promoting collaboration become even more formidable. Long-standing bureaucratic practices and political divisions make it difficult to overcome "us versus them" mentalities at all levels of government. Intergovernmental conflicts that exist between local, state, and federal levels are particularly entrenched. Because these problems are deeply rooted in our current political system, it is evident that viable solutions must incorporate appropriate political action. In this instance, mental health advocates will need to mobilize sufficient force to persuade the political leadership to exercise the will required to encourage and reinforce collaborative approaches among government and private entities involved in serving individuals with mental disorders.

REDUCING STIGMA THROUGH PUBLIC EDUCATION

All of the challenges described in this chapter, as well as the solutions recommended, are dependent in large part upon convincing policy-makers and the general public of the urgency of these issues. Leaders at all levels of government must believe that improving mental health services is a priority that requires remedial action. Centuries-old fear and prejudice associated with mental illness and the mental health community's inability to articulate its case in a manner that is widely accepted and endorsed represent significant barriers to further progress. In reviewing Seung-Hui Cho's history, it is apparent that stigma associated with mental illness affected the outcome at several levels. Seung-Hui's refusal to acknowledge his personal difficulties probably stemmed in part from the nature of his condition. It is not improbable, however, that the prevailing cultural and societal negative attitudes toward psychiatric issues contributed to his reluctance to seek help for his problems. The failure of the university to respond effectively to the warning signs presented by Seung-Hui and communicated by several of his professors is also likely attributable in part to societal ambivalence about mental illness and the lack of urgency associated with these behaviors.

Sadly, there are no easy remedies. The best hope for changing public opinion is a systematic campaign of public education that addresses the factual basis of mental illness and the considerable body of evidence demonstrating effectiveness of prevention and treatment modalities. Such a public education campaign should also address the economic cost associated with inadequate or inappropriate treatment, and the basic rights of persons with mental health challenges that have been historically curtailed and violated because of misunderstanding and misinformation.

This campaign will need to be comprehensive, providing appropriate knowledge at multiple levels. Education should begin with young children and their parents and continue throughout the developmental cycle. Particular attention should be given to helping policy-makers develop a clear understanding of mental health, including the individual, family, community, and societal consequences of continuing to provide inadequate and inappropriate services for persons with mental health disabilities.

CONCLUSION

The preceding discussion should make it obvious that reforming the current mental health system is a complex and daunting task. Constructive solutions require that we take into account multiple aspects of this challenge, including a philosophical change in the very way we view mental health, scientific and technological advancements, workforce requirements, and funding considerations. In addition, contextual factors, including cultural, social, political, and broader economic influences, must also be considered as new structures are developed.

A central theme that impacts decisions at micro- and macro-levels is the need to balance concerns about individual rights and welfare with concerns about public safety. Both of these concerns are legitimate and deserve serious attention. In addressing the issues of personal well being and public safety, it is important to debunk some of the existing stereotypes that tend to cloud thinking on these matters. Given the fact that only a small percentage of persons with mental illness exhibit violent behavior, there is little evidence to support these destructive contentions. Researchers have struggled with the question of whether violent behavior can be predicted, and to date they have reached very few definitive conclusions. For those individuals who have shown clear signs of tendency to be violent, it is important that safeguards be put in place. However, we should also resist accepting overly simplistic responses, such as incarcerating individuals who exhibit unusual behavior or focusing exclusively on safety aspects, to the exclusion of providing appropriate and adequate treatment.

Tragedies like Virginia Tech focus our attention on constructing policies to rectify identified gaps, but generally we do so out of apprehension. The danger of responding from fear is that once it dissipates, so does our anxious resolve. The other danger is to put a Band-Aid on the problem without addressing its root causes. In the case of Virginia Tech, the focal point has been the overhauling of commitment laws as they relate to mental health. Campus security and threat response have improved nationally post-Tech, but the state of response to mental illness within those communities and in other public places has not. Colleges still struggle with the tension between privacy and public safety.

Articulating clear and reasonable policies on balancing personal rights with public safety concerns is critical. Implementing functional strategies to support these policies is an essential prerequisite to moving forward on developing improved systems of care for individuals with mental disabilities irrespective of venue.

The fundamental nature of American culture presents another significant force that has a pervasive influence on our ability to achieve reform. The French historian Alexis de Tocqueville captured the essential dualism of our culture in the mid-19th century, when he observed that Americans continually struggle to reconcile their competing values of preserving and promoting their disposition toward individualism and the accompanying right to pursue personal gain with their belief in equality and concern for the well-being of others (Tocqueville, 1835, 1840/1969). The tension between these competing perspectives of rugged individualism and caring for those most in need is still apparent today. This dynamic is played out daily in our political discourse, with the most prominent current issue being whether to raise taxes to support social programs or cut spending and services in order to balance the budget. A good example of how this dualism impacts care of persons with mental disorders is found in the current debate about privatizing mental health services versus ensuring that the state provides a safety net for those whose personal and financial conditions preclude them from obtaining help.

So what is the answer? This is a complicated issue that must be approached from a public health perspective with both short-term and, more importantly, longer-term investments that embrace primary, secondary, and tertiary wellness perspectives. The idea that the United States, a country with a reputation of being the richest in the developed world, should struggle with ensuring health care coverage for its population and have health outcome indices that do not make it the *envy* of the developing world, should give us pause.

In this economy it would seem reasonable to consider that systems that employ all three sectors—the private, public, and academic—in the delivery of health care will be most effective in achieving economies of scale and scope. The time is long past gone for a siloed approach to health care. Although suggestions of single-payor systems send alarm signals of impending socialism, there may be a hybrid version that can optimize current systems and leave no American without health care.

Respectful recognition of differing missions of the public, private, and academic sectors, maintaining incentives that are drivers of each system, and a systematic braiding of resources from all three players may produce a solution that will slow the rapid escalation of health care costs and hopefully translate into better outcomes. A system of care that is vertically integrated and operates on the principle of treating a patient's health needs in the most optimized setting is an approach that holds promise. By separating the issue of cost from the setting in which health care is provided and covering preventive care to maintain wellness within a system that covers every aspect of the individuals health, we could begin to move toward a consumer view that his or her care is truly integrated and improves wellness.

Although it is unreasonable to expect that we can achieve rapid or complete resolution of these broad tensions, it is important to take these forces into account when launching any initiatives for reforming mental health services. The rate of progress is dependent on our sophistication about the political and social climate as well as our understanding of the substantive issues and our passion for the cause. The best hope for mobilizing political will may reside with consumers and their families. They carry less extraneous baggage in relation to vested interests, and they have proven to be effective advocates in the past.

As mentioned earlier, the organization with the strongest track record in mobilizing reform efforts on behalf of individuals with mental illness is the National Alliance on Mental Illness (NAMI). This organization has more than 300,000 members and 1,200 local affiliates, and has effectively advocated at federal and state levels for policy changes and additional financial support for services and research that benefit persons with serious mental illness. Given the lack of widespread political support and the large number of competing interests that currently exist, it is not feasible that a single organization, even one as powerful as NAMI, will be able to bring about the sweeping changes needed to achieve comprehensive reform in mental health care.

Achieving substantive improvement in the mental health system will require the development of a well-organized, unified coalition of all concerned stakeholders. This coalition will resemble the dedicated service oriented groups described earlier in this chapter, which created effective, integrated systems of care by establishing a shared vision, common values and goals, and a sound strategic plan. The many stakeholder groups which need to be represented in this coalition—consumers, family members, advocates, service providers, researchers, and civic groups—will need the discipline to set aside nonessential differences and agree to speak with a single voice and the patience to persist in the face of considerable misunderstanding, prejudice and inertia.

Reforming the current mental health system will not be easy, but the need and rationale for change are apparent. We have many of the tools and strategies for improving care, and there is passion for addressing the plight of those who suffer from mental health disorders. With strong leadership and a commitment to persevere, the public can be educated, political will can be influenced, and significant progress can be achieved.

CONCLUSION
CLOSING THOUGHTS

Aradhana Bela Sood

Several years after considering this topic as something to write about, this volume is now finally complete. It has been a strange and curious experience. Deep ambivalence about potentially exploiting the misery of others gave way to the belief that the book might actually contribute in some way to the mental health field: important lessons learned from the Virginia Tech massacre could show us how illness should be recognized and what should be done through intervention to reduce the consequences of illness. The barriers to recognition, assessment, and intervention have to be acknowledged and systematically addressed so that preventable tragedies do not occur. In the past two years, violence in venues beyond college campuses continues to underscore the urgency of this issue.

The events of April 16, 2007, have robbed me of the naïveté about simplistic solutions to a very complex problem. If I have lost some of my optimism, I have also gained important information: I have learned a great deal about health care delivery through my research on the subject. I have come to appreciate that the health care system's multifaceted components—clinical, financial, and administrative—often function at odds with each other. Knowledge of these challenges has made me work a tad harder with patients to facilitate their movement through the various systems, and in doing so I have become a more compassionate physician than I was before. As for this book, why did I decide to write about this subject? I could not pass up the opportunity to share my unique vantage point of an event of such magnitude, one that transfixed the nation, and to combine that experience with my own work as a practicing physician, facing the challenges that hamper the delivery of mental health services in the United States.

We all want to be a part of a system that we can be proud of. Yet there is significant fragmentation in the U.S. health care system. In my 25 years of practicing medicine in the United States, I have seen the successes and failures of the health system. I have watched it do wonders and have watched it fail many. This volume is not so much about the Virginia Tech tragedy as it is an attempt to use the tragedy to understand shortcomings within our system and then to offer possible solutions.

For most patients, irrespective of political persuasions, the one overarching concern is to be in good health. All consumers of health care want to be able to satisfactorily deal with problems that make them feel ill, and they desire interventions that are high quality and timely and restore them to health. In pointing out the problems with the system, I have had to face my own experience as a consumer of health care and my own role as a mid-career practicing physician. I and many of my peers contribute to the problems in our daily practice of medicine; we often are passive participants in a health care system that is very disjointed.

As a doctor with excellent insurance and professional connections, I am often insulated from the challenges faced by the general public. However, as I age and visit doctors' offices more often, I am on the receiving end of both good and bad care. The obstacles that patients face become painfully evident to me as I maneuver through the maze of my own medical appointments. I anticipate four to five hours of missed time from my own work for 30 minutes of face time with my physician. In that encounter I ruminate about how to make the visit worthwhile. Will the doctor know my medical history? Will my lab results be available? The rational side of me is empathetic to the triple-booked internist who makes me wait, half-clothed, while she is examining two other patients simultaneously. I understand she is optimizing time from the business angle. But access to the MD is difficult and I worry: Will I remember to ask her the right questions? If I cannot, will her nurse practitioner allow me to speak with her on the phone later?

In the academic medical center in which I work, where funding cuts and low reimbursement rates make it difficult for us to cover expenses, I am constantly aware of the market side of practicing medicine. In this fiscal environment, how do I maintain the boundary between the craft of practicing medicine, the desire to help the patient, and the reality of a balance sheet? It is an uneasy and complicated equation that health care providers grapple with constantly.

Despite all my protestations of self-righteousness, I am also complicit in contributing to the consumer's woes. Patients knock on my door only to be told there is a four-month waiting list. If they do get to see me, often they are paying out of pocket, as their insurance does not cover my services. The obstacles that patients face when accessing care range from finding a qualified provider whose services are covered by their insurance carrier to finding an appointment that is soon enough and affordable.

Approximately 50% of patients who have a diagnosable illness forgo care (Wang, Berglund, & Kessler, 2000). The severity of the illness may progress, and once intervention is needed it will occur in an emergency room setting instead of a doctor's office, resulting in a more expensive encounter. Ultimately, early and ongoing help-seeking behavior for illness is the balance between the investment of time and resources and the outcome of the visit. Often, the consumer of the mental health care system avoids appointments even if he or she has insurance. Why? Differential co-pays for primary versus specialized care, deductibles, and the ever-present fear of being labeled with a preexisting condition (and the implication for job change) are the impediments to seeking care in a timely manner. This keeps the cost of health care down artificially in the short term but at great cost in the long run by increasing disease burden. The consumer who sits in the middle of this equation receives whatever is doled out, with little influence over the outcome.

Overall, medicine has become a complex interplay of principles derived from the best aspects of the Hippocratic Oath and business principles. Both elements are important for the health care industry to survive. However, health care does not always behave like a market commodity, and pure business principles do not apply to it all the time. This leads to an imbalance in the system, yet the corrective swings of a true market economy are rare.

According to the familiar economic principles of supply and demand, let us take my own specialty of child psychiatry: a profession in high demand with few suppliers of the service. The market economy model would dictate that I could name my price for the work I do. However, that is not the case: I net $36 for a 30-minute medication check (with psychotherapy included) for my non-procedural but complex cognitive decision-making skills; compare this reimbursement to the $150 that my son's insurance pays for a 10-minute physical exam and a 30-second blood draw at the pediatrician's office. These payments are set by the insurance company for the market and do not follow demand-and-supply principles in that prices cannot fluctuate based on availability or scarcity of services. Those who run the business of medicine are governed by strict antitrust laws to set rates that meet costs.

This inequity of payment has other unintended consequences for mental health. Psychologically, the lack of parity in payment adds to the already existing stigma surrounding mental health—"we do not believe mental illness is as serious as physical illness; therefore psychiatrists should be paid less than other physicians." This attitude affects the work force, as it discourages highly debt-ridden newly graduated doctors from joining psychiatry because it is a poorly paid medical specialty. What is the solution? The health care market must set reimbursement rates for cognitive science–based interventions, such as psychotherapy, that are equitable with the rest of medicine so that young physicians are not prevented from choosing psychiatry as a specialty because of their enormous debt burdens. This will improve access to mental health care by increasing the number of mental health care providers, and indirectly improve quality of care by allowing reimbursed time for discussions around mental health issues that often occur in primary care offices. The health care business will have to find other solutions that deemphasize volume of patients as the metric of success and reemphasize quality of patient care.

The discussion does not end at fixing the provider issues as suggested above, as the complex service delivery system in health care has multiple brokers that are responsible for guiding policy. Who are they? Managed care payors, government payor systems, private- and public-sector providers, federal, state, and local levels of health care delivery systems—they all play a part and illustrate the complexity of the system. Very rarely do entities on the national, state, and local levels debate and reach consensus to work cooperatively for the overall good of the system. Fractured relationships, schisms in viewpoints, territorial wars are all factors that contribute to systemic inertia and to the poor health outcome indices for the United States, despite the high dollar investment in overall health care.

As an example, take one of the most powerful players in the health care arena: managed care organizations (MCO), which serve as gatekeepers of health care delivery. Their role in health care has evolved to its current status over the past 30 years. First a historical perspective: The role that health care providers have played in the formation of payor systems such as MCOs has to be acknowledged. The lack of attention to cost and quality of care in the early 1970s, and the profit for providers within a fee-for-service model that had few checks and balances, led to astronomical growth in health care spending. This led to the entry of managed care, which was embraced by the United States as a vehicle for bringing balance and reduction in health care costs. MCOs tantalized the public with the promise of reducing cost of care while the savings would be invested in preventive care. Somewhere midstream in its growth, the managed care industry morphed into a publicly traded enterprise. While the publicly traded status allowed growth for MCOs, the hope for preventive or early intervention focus was forgotten and eventually lost. Allegiance shifted from patients and doctors to stockholders. Not only did we lose that hope of putting resources into prevention and early intervention, but the tension between MCOs and practitioners has grown, as one partner is largely perceived as managing costs by cutting services and plowing the profits into company growth (rather than population health) while the other, that is, the providers, see themselves as losing not only autonomy in clinical decision-making but also their profitability. Whether there are some managed care organizations that have a larger vision than profits is debatable.

To illustrate this tension I offer the familiar example of pharmaceuticals in disease management. A debate currently rages regarding Preferred Drug Lists (PDLs) and their use as a cost-containment measure. If I tailor my prescription of a psychotropic medication to fit a patient's unique medical history (to avoid side effects), the prescription may be rejected if it is not on his insurance plan's PDL. When this rejection is appealed, a clerk at the insurance company informs me that the patient has to fail at X or Y or Z (or sometimes X, Y, *and* Z) medication before the company will approve what I suggest. Never mind that drug X or Y or Z will probably lead to worsening of the clinical presentation even to the extent of requiring a costly hospitalization. The argument from MCOs is that psychotropic drugs are so costly that they have to restrict use to only a few preferred categories so that care is economical.

Practitioners, on the other hand, state that the pharmacogenomics of psychiatric illness are not well delineated and the response to single agents is not predictable. The "one size fits all" and "fail one first" approach to medication choice, bypassing medical opinion and focusing on just cost, paradoxically leads to higher costs. Surely there is something illogical about this approach! Practitioners suggest that creating logical algorithms based on evidence of what works and what does not and utilizing these best practices for treatment will yield better outcomes while individualizing treatment for their patients. The better response and reduced disease burden will help recoup the investment in the higher cost of appropriate pharmaceuticals.

Constantly charged with being fiscally viable, few MCO administrators are willing to look at the larger picture. Apart from a few managed care companies, most use severity of illness as a focus of reimbursement and are diligent in their efforts to keep costs contained. The focus of both the payors and payee has become profit at all costs.

Despite this crisis of trust and the yawning divide between the different interests of stakeholders in health care, we plod along the same path. The bottom line is: the system wears people down until they do not have the energy to continue to struggle with the irrationality of it.

In the past five years as health care reform has been discussed, many have suggested that the health care delivery in the United States is superior to that of other countries and requires no change. As illustrated earlier in this book, the U.S. system is excellent and cutting edge for *emergency care* but *not for preventive, long-term wellness*. The report card for the U.S. health care system from the World Health Organization (Tandon et al., 2000) is an objective measure of our problems. In Seung-Hui Cho's case, if the area services in Blacksburg had been more robust for outpatient care, in all likelihood they would have had the infrastructure to pursue and persuade him to be evaluated and to be followed up after the high-intensity occurrence of his hospitalization.

The Virginia Tech tragedy has pushed the state of Virginia and others to develop better threat assessment teams and build crisis stabilization units. The slow and more prudent approach would be to shift the focus of our health care system away from management of crisis and toward non-emergent care and eventually an emphasis on prevention of illness. Despite the heavily managed care environment, the cost of care continues to escalate and with very little to show for positive outcomes.

After wrestling with the problems of our current health and mental health care systems I have reached the following conclusion: The system has to simplify the way it delivers care. The weight of myriad regulatory agencies (Joint Commission on Accreditation of Health Care [JCAHO], etc.) with differing standards to ensure quality, the sustenance of the rapidly expanding industry of health IT, and the administrative burden to regulate cost are all passed down as "health care" to the consumer: you, me, and others. Should these safeguards and supports exist? Yes. Should they continue to function in this fragmented, duplicative, burdensome and cost-ineffective way? An emphatic no! A business model is essential for sustainability. However, as health care does not behave like a regular market commodity, we require a modified business model for health care. This model must employ sound medical principles of population health to drive the business of health care rather than the other way around. In order to make this happen, we need the political will to develop medically sound policies and give them primacy over the economics of medicine. There also needs to be better alignment of the missions of both providers and payors so that they are not at cross purposes with each other. Strong consumer protection agencies must serve in a watchdog capacity. This will require strong insulation from the lobbying power of business interests.

There must be a concerted attempt at examining what is needed to provide both direct and non-direct care from the consumer's end. Then we need to rebuild and resize the support systems and the direct care system to fit those needs rather than the other way around. Keeping the consumer/patient central to the debate is the only way of solving this gargantuan problem.

So, having made a case for the need to reform our cumbersome and tottering health system on multiple levels, based on both anecdotal and scientific study, and outlining those recommendations in Chapters 8 and 10, let us turn our attention to the questions posed in Chapter 1.

If the events at Virginia Tech in 2007 were a wakeup call, where are we in Virginia and elsewhere in the United States, as far as lessons learned from this tragedy? Did we use that opportunity to wrestle with the thorny issue of the ubiquitous problem of mental illness, illness that touches one in five of us in a tangible way? Have we made a difference in the lives of those individuals and families who struggle with mental illness?

As referenced earlier, it is not surprising that Virginia, where the tragedy occurred, responded with alacrity: as mentioned earlier, in 2008 the Virginia General Assembly enacted the most sweeping reforms in mental health law that had occurred in that state in 30 years. One hundred and twenty bills were introduced during the session and approximately 42 million dollars were appropriated for mental health services. Campus safety and firearm laws relating to the mentally ill were also promulgated.

But did it change the lives of people who suffer from mental illness in a substantive and population-wide way? I am afraid not. Access to care remains a problem, with waiting lists no shorter than they were in 2006. Just as the 42 million dollars were allocated they were also cut substantially in the days of the deepening recession of 2009. Aside from disproportionate cuts to mental health services, the promise of community-based services in lieu of inpatient care has not been fulfilled. The focus in mental health services continues to be on reactive approaches, such as crisis stabilization units, rather than on outpatient care delivery or on prevention and health promotion.

While many persons and organizations, including the state legislature, the governor and his cabinet, which administers the Department of Behavioral Health and Developmental Services, share responsibility for failing to take advantage of this unique opportunity to fix the state's mental health service system, one well-meaning group may have also unwittingly contributed to this failure: the ongoing Commission on Mental Health Law Reform, headed by Professor Richard J. Bonnie, Director of the Institute of Law, Psychiatry and Public Policy at the University of Virginia. The Commission, in my view, had both positive and negative effects following the Virginia Tech tragedy. The positive aspects of the work of the Commission were that it gave the Virginia Tech review panel a head start in looking at commitment laws, it had the expertise of well-established credible professionals, and it supported many of the findings of the panel in pointing out the gaps in mental health services within the commonwealth.

The downside was that the focus of the Commission obfuscated and overlooked the real gaps in mental health service delivery that could have been exposed following the tragedy: the lack of access to specialty care, the paucity of providers, and the absence of follow-up care. The Commission urged the Virginia legislature to focus on a small sliver in the continuum of the mental health needs of the population: commitment to a hospital at the point the individual is in crisis. In reality, Seung-Hui Cho's pre-screener from the community service board had no problem getting him committed to a hospital. His problem was that no one took the commitment to a psychiatric hospital seriously enough within the community where he lived: Virginia Tech.

The Commission, ultimately, offered the legislature relatively low-hanging fruit as a solution to the failures represented by the tragedy—to revamp the high-threshold commitment laws. As such, the focus of the 2008 and 2009 Virginia General Assembly sessions was on bills involving commitment laws (relaxing the commitment criterion in the statute from imminent dangerousness to substantial likelihood of harm), follow-through of recommendations made during the commitment hearing (mandated outpatient treatment), and establishment of crisis intervention teams (CIT). The General Assembly and the Office of the Attorney General did act, believing that they had done what they needed to for mental health. The danger of this approach, however, is that an enormous opportunity for improving services for those at risk of mental disorders may have been lost while maintaining the appearance of substantive progress. The actions that have followed the events at Virginia Tech do not show that Virginia (or the nation) has grasped the fundamental problems plaguing mental health care delivery.

On a positive note, laws have been enacted in Virginia that allow more humanity in the way we transport and treat the mentally ill during their gravest crises. Patients no longer need to be transported to the hospital in police vans, and they can travel with family to be hospitalized. Other constructive efforts are clear mandates to universities about the development of threat assessment teams, sharing of relevant information, and clarity regarding HIPAA and FERPA laws.

But, on balance, the effect of the Commission was hardly transformational—even if considerable weight is to be given to its impact on commitment laws. Why is that not enough? These commitment laws are relevant to merely 10% of the population of persons who are mentally ill. The lack of focus on 90% of the population affected by mental illness is the unwritten tragedy of this event. The Virginia Tech review panel recommended that bridging the gaps in Virginia's mental health service system should include the development of follow-up outpatient services and case management (to prevent costly crises). The small amount of newly appropriated money has gone to community service boards (CSB), Virginia's version of local community mental health centers, which have been mandated to develop crisis intervention teams and to ensure that all commitment hearings have a CSB representative who follows through with directives of the commitment process.

In order to appreciate the regressive (rather than progressive) changes that have occurred in the state after Virginia Tech, it is important to first understand how the public health system in Virginia works. Although the focus of the following passage is on the public–private sectors, the scrutiny is meant as an example to illustrate *one* of the reasons why the U.S. health care delivery system is flawed.

The CSB system in Virginia is responsible for providing public-sector mental health services, connecting patients discharged from hospitals to outpatient services, providing community-based services, allocating federal and state funds to appropriate services, and providing coverage for the population that needs services, simple or complex, irrespective of their insurance status. The state of Virginia has for-profit and not-for-profit private hospital chains not under its control and a rapidly diminishing number of public-sector inpatient beds that the state is directly responsible for. This complex relationship between the public and private provider systems is crucial to understand, as their missions are equally important but different. Each has a place and they are not interchangeable. The private sector within mental health serves a large population of the Commonwealth, but restating the obvious, it is not mandated to provide services to the uninsured. In addition to serving many insured individuals who require complex and multisystem care, the public sector in mental health employs sliding-scale payments and has federal and state grants to manage care for the uninsured and underinsured. The private sector has no such directive and ushers out individuals from its system who cannot pay. When the government allows cuts to public-sector health care or chooses to allow the private sector to manage all care, as has happened in North Carolina (Swartz & Morrisey, 2003) and Georgia, we begin to enter dangerous territory. Although privatization of health care allows the state to reduce operational expenditures, the resulting gate-keeping is burdensome to consumers and reduces access to care. Because there is no legislative mandate for private insurers to provide more than basic care, they may choose to cut out essential care, citing the type of insurance policy that the consumer bought.

Privatization of public mental health leads to (1) reduction in outpatient services as they are low-revenue generators, (2) closure of longer term non-revenue-generating beds, and (3) increased use of emergency rooms (ER) when individuals with mental illness get sick, as basic mental health care is unavailable. On leaving the ER there is no timely outpatient follow-up available, which leads to repeated crises and repeated ER visits. A comparable example in medical care is the individual who does not have a primary care provider and so begins to use the ER as an expensive alternative to primary care—even for minor medical crises. This is not to say that private insurance, private providers, and for-profit hospitals are not essential to the health care system in the United States, but it is essential that public-sector health care be retained. If the private sector begins to manage public-sector plans and funds, then there must be effective oversight, otherwise there will be no system in place to ensure that the provider will serve the public interest rather than its own mission of being profitable.

So how does this apply to Virginia after the Virginia Tech massacre? Logic would dictate that with 42 million new dollars allocated to mental health in the state of Virginia that the public system would begin to infuse money into infrastructure development for state programs. The economic downturn and the state budget deficit altered the landscape. The actions of the state government after 2008 showcased its short memory for the disastrous consequences of the Tech disaster and also the remarkably clouded understanding of decision-makers around public mental health.

What did happen? The state set its sights on developing crisis stabilization units, but no substantive effort was made to develop outpatient services or care for children with mental health problems. Furthermore, in an attempt to balance the budget deficit in 2008 and 2009, a private-sector hospital chain was asked by the state to explore assuming the responsibility for the management of public-sector mental health beds for children. The public safety-net beds serve children with complex psychiatric illness that will not be covered by traditional health care insurance policies that have strict guidelines for care. Upon careful probing, it was discovered that some state health and human services administrators had ties to this private-sector chain. Although the plans were not actualized, even the consideration of a plan to transfer responsibility from the public to the private for-profit sector indicates the failure of the administration to safeguard public safety-net beds (Ress, 2010a, 2010b, 2010c). What stopped this process was vigorous advocacy by child mental health groups and the media coverage of the issue. Although this may not seem relevant to what went wrong after Virginia Tech, this example underscores how policy-makers not only missed an opportunity for change but were supportive of a subversive action that would have worked against the most vulnerable: underinsured children. If publicly elected officials are not able to define and maintain the needs of the public sector, trust in the oversight process erodes.

Finally, some thoughts about the political process. Testifying before the General Assembly over the years has been eye-opening for me. Debates about bills that require technical knowledge, be they medical, engineering, or architectural in nature, occur with or without the presence of those with expertise on the issue. If the expert is present, his or her voice is given equal weight with that of various lobbyists. The implications are frightening. For example, if a bill mandating an insurance company to cover a medical intervention is being considered, the General Assembly might very well hear the debate and rule on the bill without a single medical practitioner being in the room. How can a reasonable conclusion be reached unless scientific reasoning is presented to the lawmakers? Should such far-reaching decisions rest on lobbyists and special interest groups? It has become reasonably clear to me that bureaucratic and political considerations trump technical advice.

In my experience, technical expertise is rarely solicited by lawmakers even when it is obviously needed. State and federal governments must acknowledge and accept the need to get top-notch technical expertise to inform the administrative decisions it makes, otherwise as a nation we will continue to hobble from one administration to another, negotiating what appear to be politically expedient compromises in health and human services.

Political administrations do not tend to build on what the previous administration developed, and they do not consider the price paid to tear down what the previous one had built—particularly in the case of opposing political parties (Patashnik, 2008). The tax payers of this country might ask the following question about physical and mental health care: why do politicians not seek counsel, advice, or policy direction from those whose technical or professional training should inform the bill being considered?

Virginia has squandered an important opportunity to create a transformational change in its mental health delivery system, and by extension to be an example for the nation. This was due in large part to the narrow focus of lawmakers. The politicians did what they considered expedient: they responded to what the Virginia Tech tragedy seemingly highlighted: public safety. This approach has little to do with mental health service reform. Indeed, in Virginia and nationwide the one group of institutions that has responded with alacrity are the institutions of higher learning: our universities. Unfortunately, even within universities the focus has been on public safety and not on mental health. Even after the Virginia Tech tragedy there is little evidence of uniform improvement in the mental health systems of university counseling centers.

Public memory, it seems, is short-lived. In Virginia, bills to trim mental health costs are constantly presented to the General Assembly, in an attempt to reduce the deficit. Children's services are the most vulnerable. Advocacy groups keep a vigilant eye, as no longer can we have confidence that the system will be fair, even as we sit in the shadow of Virginia Tech.

Why does this happen and how do we let it happen? If we recognize that mental illness is a problem that carries the number two disease burden in the country, why are well-intentioned policy-makers averse to developing a logical approach to address this? These are men and women, for the most part, of intelligence and courage.

Given that those we put into power are those in whom we put faith, the next question we need to ask ourselves is why are those *we* put into elected office afraid of taking controversial stands on any issue? Is it that making a sound but politically charged and risky stance might jeopardize their chances of being reelected? Is it because we as the public do not have the common sense or the intelligence to disconnect an individual decision on an issue from the overall performance of the politician? I would propose that *we, the mental health professionals,* are responsible for that short-sighted thinking that makes normally verbal and astute human beings we put into office clearly ineffectual as they wrestle with gridlock born out of fear: *the fear of not being re-elected.*

In view of that, I would propose that any legislation connected to health care must invite mandated technical input. Legislation must not be passed unless it is fully vetted for its technical soundness. When technocrats and bureaucrats begin to take their rightful places in the formulation of policy, politicians will stop being so concerned about the political price of making the right decisions: In other words, the conflict of interest between retaining political power and (a) being beholden to lobbyists or other vested interests and (b) the reduced responsibility of scrutinizing areas beyond their areas of expertise and knowledge will free them up from decisions that are poorly thought out and short-lived. Science will have a better chance of informing policy, and, hopefully, the structures will have greater longevity.

My final reflection is on the status of health care in our collective conscience. Unarguably health care is one of the most important ongoing issues for our country. It impacts our lives on a daily basis, as well as our economy. Yet we are unable to come to a consensus about this central question: is health care a right of all citizens or a commodity that must be purchased by those who have the means? Should health care be part of the market economy and be traded in the free market? My stance is that basic health care such as preventive dental care, immunizations, and physical and mental wellness checkups should be every citizen's right and that this care should be provided at cost and must not be a driver of the market economy. Luxury health care items such as liposuction and cosmetic surgery should be availed according to the purchasing capability of citizens. However, the threshold for necessary versus luxury health care remains debatable. The answers are difficult and complicated and have become divisive not only for lawmakers but also for the general public. This was evident in the health care reform debates witnessed in 2009 and 2010. As common as mental illness is in the population, our urgent tasks are to address work force development and adequate funding for interventions that work and have the science to back them. If the population is not healthy both physically and mentally, the far-reaching economic implications will be felt in this nation for decades to come.

Just as *cancer* is a word that has shed its aura of stigma and has emerged for examination, understanding, and containment with treatment, so should *mental illness*. It should be embraced as a reality that affects even more people than cancer and be treated with parity, equity, and respect. The tragedy at Virginia Tech and the long shadow it has cast should remain a constant reminder that beyond the 32 lives and families it shattered this type of violence can happen anywhere. Not all violence can be prevented, but much of the violence associated with mental illness can be, with appropriate intervention. For me as a child psychiatrist and a participant in the review of the Virginia Tech tragedy, as well as a concerned citizen, I believe we have not made as much progress on this front as we could and should. The fear and prejudice that surround mental illness cloud our collective judgment and impede our ability to act constructively. We have not yet acknowledged or addressed the daunting challenge of developing a comprehensive and responsive system of care for individuals with mental illness. Stigma, ineffective delivery systems, and an understaffed work force are the enemies of progress in mental health.

At the same time I retain a sense of optimism.

Stigma. Science continues to improve our understanding of how our brains function and what types of strategies can aid in preventing, treating, and controlling these disorders. Prejudice recedes with accurate information. With progress relating to the brain sciences, the stigma around mental illness will in all likelihood continue to dissipate, just as it has for cancer over the past 50 years.

Mental Health Delivery System. It cannot be emphasized enough that policy decisions around health care must follow the science. Technical expertise must be integrated into any discussion about a health care issue and must have primacy when decisions are made. Open and authentic discussion about adequate funding for mental illness research in parallel with the development of effective science-backed mental illness intervention programs should be a national agenda priority.

Work Force. The development of a well-trained work force will follow as we place value on the need to address mental illness, fund the field for both research and compensation of services, and chip away at the stigma that makes mental health a second-class issue in health care.

As a society we have demonstrated repeatedly that when the public will is present we can solve difficult problems and create constructive programs to address complex social issues. We must mobilize the support that will persuade the political leadership at all levels that it is in their best interest, as well as ours, to finally get serious about mental illness.

POSTSCRIPT

Between the time this book was first conceived and the date of its publication, the number of horrific, violent tragedies that the world has witnessed seems to have increased. Although the statistics indicate that there really has not been an actual increase in these events, they are laden with so much emotion that they unfailingly elicit the same reactions as those to the tragedy at Virginia Tech. That's simply the way trauma affects us: When we are resensitized, we react as if the tragedy were happening again; we worry it will happen again tomorrow and that it will happen to those close to us. We look for similarities and differences; our mind struggles to find a predictable pattern. We hope that, in finding that common factor, we will find a solution to stop it from happening again. The overwhelming desire is to find the answer and ensure that we personally have done our duty: to express our anger, disgust, and a clearly stated demand for an "event autopsy" and a "psychological autopsy" of the perpetrator.

Just reviewing the number of such events and attempting to categorize them for commonalities is a challenge. It reinforces the widely held view that this is a highly complex subject from start to finish. Even sorting out the manner in which we categorize these events (number of fatalities, motives, age of perpetrator) for the purpose of developing an inventory is a gargantuan task, let alone finding a predictive profile of perpetrators. No clear patterns emerge. The roots of violence remain elusive.

Worldwide, there have been 34 shootings (Infoplease.com, 2013) since the Virginia Tech tragedy. Of these, 27 were in the United States. The involvement of children (Newtown, December 2012) or prominent public figures (Creigh Deeds, November 2013) may not be any different from other violent incidents as far as the personal angst they produce for the survivors and victims' families. However, for obvious reasons they move the discussion of mass violence to a national stage. Adam Lanza, age 20, killed 20 children and 6 others at the Sandy Hook Elementary School after he killed his mother at her home. Lanza committed suicide after the rampage. There were no obvious warning signs here except that he was a loner. We also know that being a loner does not predispose a person to violence. That shooting was the second deadliest in U.S. history, behind the 2007 shooting at Virginia Tech that claimed 32 people.

Former Navy reservist Aaron Alexis, 34, killed 12 people at the Washington Navy Yard, near the U.S. Capitol. He was killed in a shootout with police. Alexis was employed at the base by a military subcontractor and had clearly communicated what he was experiencing: command hallucinations to kill others. In this instance, there were warning signs that were not picked up. Just as with Virginia Tech's Seung-Hui Cho, we struggle to find the link of violence with mental illness, with the access to firearms, exposure to violent video games, or a hint of an unraveling mind. We know that less than 5% of violent acts are connected to mental illness, yet we also know that even when there are clear signs of mental illness with distinct threats being expressed, help may still not be accessible. Prompted by recommendations made by the panel investigating the Virginia Tech tragedy in 2007, the Commonwealth of Virginia allocated 42 million dollars to mental health. One lasting area of improvement that Virginia and the nation saw was in the form of threat assessment teams in public settings such as colleges, schools, and public places. But what about mental illness: How did it fare? According to the Virginia Chapter of the National Alliance of the Mentally Ill (CNN, New York, November 2013), the allocation of resources for mental health by the State decreased by 37.7 million dollars from fiscal year 2009 to fiscal year 2012. The cut was ostensibly because of a tanking economy. So short-lived was the memory of the 32 deaths at Virginia Tech!

It is unfortunate that it took an attempted homicide and subsequent suicide of a Virginia senator's son (Austin "Gus" Deeds), on November 19, 2013, who did not get access to inpatient services for his mental illness, to prompt the formation of a task force to improve Virginia's mental health system. Gripping as the tragedy at Virginia Tech was and extensive as the recommendations of the panel were for systems change in mental health, we have made little progress in getting people the mental health services they require. Although the specific circumstance of not finding a psychiatric bed is the current issue that is garnering the most attention in the Deeds incident, what we really need is not just an immediate targeted response but a full system overhaul. We should not seek to "fix" the problem *du jour* but instead focus on developing a system that takes care of individuals before they get too ill. An example would be outpatient services that are geographically accessible, timely, and outcome driven. Relying on emergency and crisis systems as the mainstay of mental health care does little for wellness. Furthermore, if we do not invest in the primary prevention of illness, we will continue to expend large amounts of money to deal with the complications resulting from mental illness. Examples of this financial burden include the astronomical payment for youth and adults in the justice system, and high-end and expensive emergency room revolving-door care for individuals with no primary care physician or psychiatric care.

We can ill afford to lose another opportunity to move our nation toward a more rational public health approach that considers social determinants of health-seeking behavior as important as illness itself. Even though we may not be capable of profiling an individual with a prediliction for mass violence, we can become more proficient in reducing risk for the individual patient who comes to our attention. Is the memory of our own horror at these larger-than-life tragedies so ephemeral? We must not wait for repeated tragedies to drive rational policy.

APPENDIX

Table 1. Community Systems of Care Principles*

Principle	Annotations for College Mental Health by the Chapter Authors
1. Clinical assessment and treatment approaches should be guided by an understanding of the ecological context of the child and family, incorporating information from all community systems with which they are involved, including formal services as well as natural supports.	Student evaluation should take into account student strengths and liabilities, academic performance, natural support systems already built into the campus community, interpersonal, familial, financial, and cultural stressors. Liaisons with student advisors, for example, could help develop a more informed formulation of the problem.
2. The clinician should develop collaborative and strengths-based relationships with families, emphasizing partnerships at both the case-planning and system-planning levels.	Students within the planning and policy committee can provide input that represents needs unique to the student body. An appointed student ombudsman can serve as a liaison between the counseling center and student body. Clinicians should make the student a partner in the decision-making process in his or her own care. Families and parents should be included in a developmentally appropriate fashion.
3. Mental health interventions should be actively coordinated with services by other providers, including primary care providers, and, whenever possible, integrated with interventions provided by other social agencies.	The counseling center should co-localize and collaborate with the medical clinic and move toward an integration of mental and physical health records. Communication with other entities on campus such as Dean of Student Affairs, and Disabilities Services, and with off-campus providers should be facilitated, if the student authorizes it.

(continued)

Table 1 Continued

Principle	Annotations for College Mental Health by the Chapter Authors
4. Services should be culturally competent and should address the needs of underserved, culturally diverse, at-risk populations.	There should be an attempt to pair students with the most appropriate clinician to maximize cultural understanding and optimize help-seeking behavior and, by inference, improve overall health. Staff should be trained in cultural expression of emotional distress and help-seeking behaviors. Targeted outreach to select groups may be necessary.
5. To achieve individualization of care for children with significant and complex mental health needs, clinicians should consider a wraparound planning process.	Campus services should be a balance of formal and informal supports while keeping privacy concerns in view; consider who the student trusts and would nominate to be part of their "team" on campus. This may be a faculty member, peer, resident assistant, etc. who could function as an advocate. Create a "safety net" to identify problems when they appear and prevent them from escalating.
6. Treatment planning in systems of care should incorporate effective interventions supported by the available evidence.	Interventions should follow evidence-based and best practices that are effective. Deviations must have a rationale.
7. Child and adolescent psychiatrists' roles in systems of care should include triage, provision of direct service, consultation to other service providers, quality improvement, program design, and evaluation and advocacy.	The university counseling centers should incorporate input from psychiatrists who can provide technically sound expertise on major mental illnesses such as major depression and schizophrenia and assist in the development of programs that can effectively address these illnesses.
8. Pharmacotherapy should be performed by a physician or medical practitioner who is integrated into the interdisciplinary process and has completed a biopsychosocial assessment, including interviewing the child and his or her parent(s) or caregiver(s) and reviewing relevant ancillary data.	Communication between the therapist and prescribing psychiatrist should remain a priority. Psychiatric medical practitioners should be easily accessible to students.

(continued)

Table 1 Continued

Principle	Annotations for College Mental Health by the Chapter Authors
9. The clinician should be familiar with the organization and functioning of the system in which he or she is working in order to advocate effectively for adequacy of resources and practices to meet the needs of children and families served.	A counseling center clinician or administrator must be represented in the university leadership group in order to articulate the needs of the counseling center and to understand the organizational structure of the university system. They can serve to educate as well as keep the issues of the counseling center on the radar of the university. Those providers working with students in off-campus settings must also be familiar with campus life, policies, procedures, and administrative structures in order to best evaluate, treat, and advocate for students.
10. The clinician and the family share accountability for treatment success. The system of care, through its component programs, should be accountable for clinical outcomes and be actively involved in quality improvement efforts.	Students, faculty, staff, administrators, parents, and the local community should partner for positive outcomes. Services and programs should be evaluated for effectiveness on a regular basis.
11. Services should be delivered in the most normative and least restrictive setting that is clinically appropriate. Children should have access to a continuum of care with assignment of level of intensity of care determined by clinically informed decision-making.	Students should have access to the full range of mental health treatment services on or near campus. Within this principle is the embedded notion of co-localization of care for both mental and physical health within a university health center.
12. Significant attention should be paid to transitions between levels of care, services, agencies, or systems to ensure that care is appropriate, emphasizing continuity of care.	The transition from high school to college, transitions to and from study abroad programs, the transitions inherent in the academic year calendar, and the transition out of college should be taken into consideration.
13. Systems of care should incorporate prevention strategies in clinical practice and system design.	Resources should be allocated to all levels of prevention intervention.

* Based on Winters and Pumariega (2007).

REFERENCES

Addasi, N., & Shatkin, J. (2008, March/April). The Child & Adolescent Mental Health Studies (CAMS) undergraduate minor at New York University. *AACAP News*, pp. 72–3.

Al-Mateen, C. S. (2002). The effects of witnessing violence on children and adolescents. In D. Schetky & E. Benedek (Eds.), *Principles and Practice of Child and Adolescent Forensic Psychiatry* (pp. 213–24). Washington, DC: American Psychiatric Press.

Alschuler, K., Hoodin, F., & Byrd, M. (2009). Rapid assessment for psychopathology in a college health clinic: Utility of college student specific questions. *Journal of American College Health, 58*(2), 177–9.

Amanda, G. (1999). *Coping with Misconduct in the College Classroom: A Practical Model.* Asheville, NC: College Administration Publications.

American Academy of Child & Adolescent Psychiatry (AACAP). (2007). Practice parameter on child and adolescent mental health care in community systems of care. *Journal of the American Academy of Child & Adolescent Psychiatry, 46*(2), 284–99.

American College Health Association (ACHA). (2009). *American College Health Association National College Health Assessment II: Reference Group executive summary fall 2008.* Baltimore: American College Health Association. Retrieved from http://www.acha-ncha.org/docs/ACHA-NCHA_Reference_Group_ExecutiveSummary_Fall2008.pdf

American College Health Association (ACHA). (2010a). *American College Health Association National College Health Assessment II: Reference Group executive summary spring 2010.* Linthicum, MD: American College Health Association. Retrieved from http://www.acha-ncha.org/docs/ACHA-NCHA-II_ReferenceGroup_ExecutiveSummary_Spring2010.pdf

American College Health Association (ACHA) (2010b). *Considerations for integration of counseling and health services on college and university campuses.* Linthicum, MD: American College Health Association. Retrieved from http://www.acha.org/Publications/docs

American Psychiatric Association. (2000). *Diagnostic and Statistical Manual of Mental Disorders, Fourth Edition—Text Revision (DSM-IV-TR).* Washington, DC: American Psychiatric Association.

American Psychiatric Association. (2013). *Diagnostic and Statistical Manual of Mental Disorders, Fifth Edition (DSM-5).* Washington, DC: American Psychiatric Association.

Americans with Disabilities Act (1990). Pub.L. No.101-336,104 Stat.328.

Anthony, E., & Cohler, B. (Eds.). (1987). *The Invulnerable Child.* New York: Guilford Press.

Arcus, D. (2002). School shooting fatalities and school corporal punishment: A look at the states. *Aggressive Behavior, 28*, 173–83.

Arnett, J. (2000). Emerging adulthood. *American Psychologist, 55*(5), 469–80.

Association for University & College Counseling Center Directors (AUCCCD). (2007). *Statement on parental notification, mandatory counseling and counseling center director status.* Retrieved from http://www.aucccd.org/img/pdfs/Statement_091807.pdf

Barreira, P., & Snider, M. (2010). History of college counseling and mental health services and role of the community mental health model. In J. Kay & V. Schwartz (Eds.), *Mental Health Care in the College Community* (pp. 21–32). West Sussex, UK: Wiley.

Bartels, S. J., Dums, A. R., Oxman, T. E., Schneider, L. S., Areán, P. A., Alexopoulos, G. S., & Jeste, D. V. (2002). Evidence-based practices in geriatric mental health care. *Psychiatric Services, 53*(11), 1419–31.

Beaty, L. A., & Alexeyev, E. B. (2008). The problem of school bullies: What the research tells us. *Adolescence, 43*(169), 1–11.

Belfer, M. L. (2004). Systems of care: A global perspective. In H. Remschmidt, M. L. Belfer, & I. Goodyer (Eds.), *Facilitating Pathways: Care, Treatment and Prevention in Child and Adolescent Mental Health* (pp. 16–26). Berlin: Springer.

Bell, C., & Fink, P. (2000). Prevention of violence. In C. Bell (Ed.) *Psychiatric Aspects of Violence: Issues in Prevention and Treatment* (pp. 37–47). San Francisco: Jossey-Bass.

Bell, C., Flay, B., & Paikoff, R. (2002). Strategies for health behavioral change. In J. Chunn (Ed.), *The Health Behavioral Change Imperative: Theory, Education and Practice in Diverse Populations* (pp. 17–40). New York: Kluwer Academic/Plenum Publishers.

Berg-Cross, L., & Pak, V. (2006). Diversity issues. In P. Grayson & P. Meilman (Eds.), *College Mental Health Practice* (pp. 153–72). New York: Routledge.

Berkowitz, L. (1970). The contagion of violence: An S-R mediational analysis of the effects of observed aggression. *Nebraska Symposium on Motivation, 18*, 9–135.

Blanco, C., Okuda, M., Wright, C., Hasin, D., Grant, B., Liu, S.-M., & Olfson, M. (2008). Mental health of college students and their non-college-attending peers. *Archives of General Psychiatry, 65*, 1429–37.

Bond, G. R., Drake, R. E., Mueser, K. T., & Latimer, E. (2001). Assertive community treatment for people with severe mental illness: Critical ingredients and impact on patients. *Disease Management & Health Outcomes, 9*(3), 141–59.

Borum, R. (1996). Improving the clinical practice of violence risk assessment: Technology, guidelines and training. *American Psychologist, 51*, 945–56.

Borum, R. (2000). Assessing violence risk among youth. *Journal of Clinical Psychology, 56*, 1263–88.

Brener, N., Hassan, S., & Barrios, L. (1999). Suicidal ideation among college students in the United States. *Journal of Consulting and Clinical Psychology, 67*(6), 1004–8.

Brener, N. D., & Krug, E. G. (1997). Nurses' logs as an evaluation tool for school-based violence prevention programs. *Journal of School Health, 67*(5), 171–4.

Breslau, J., Lane, M., Sampson, N., & Kessler, R. (2008). Mental disorders and subsequent educational attainment in a US national sample. *Journal of Psychiatric Research, 42*, 708–16.

Brower, A., & Inkelas, K. (2010). Living-learning programs: One high-impact educational practice we now know a lot about. *Liberal Education, 96*(2), 36–43.

Brown, R. P., Osterman, L. L., & Barnes, C. D. (2009). School violence and the culture of honor. *Psychological Science, 20*(11), 1400–5.

Bruns, E. J., Sather, A., Pullmann, M. D., & Stumbaugh, L. F. (2011). National trends in implementing wraparound: Results from the State Wraparound Survey. *Journal of Child and Family Studies, 20*, 726–35.

Burns, B. J., & Hoagwood, K. H. (2002). *Community Treatment for Youth: Evidence-Based Interventions for Severe Emotional and Behavioral Disorders.* New York: Oxford University Press.

Bustillo, J., Lauriello, J., Horan, W., & Keith, S. (2001). The psychosocial treatment of schizophrenia: An update. *American Journal of Psychiatry, 158*(2), 163–75.

Caley, C., & Thomas, M. (2009). *Optimizing ADHD medication therapy in college health: Evaluating the issues.* American College Health Association Annual Meeting. Retrieved from http://www.acha.org/AnnualMeeting09/docs/ACHA_AM09_FinalProg.pdf

Callahan, C. (2008). Threat assessment in school violence. In Thomas W. Miller (Ed.), *School Violence and Primary Prevention* (pp. 59–77). New York: Springer.

Cameto, R. (2005). *Process reports from the National Longitudinal Transition Study: The transition planning* (NLTS2 Data Brief). Minneapolis, MN: National Center on Secondary Education & Transition. Retrieved from http://www.ncset.org/publications/viewdesc.asp?id=2130

Caplan, G. (1981). Mastery of stress: Psychosocial aspects. *American Journal of Psychiatry, 138,* 413–20.

Card, N. A., & Hodges, E. V. E. (2008). Peer victimization among schoolchildren: Correlations, causes, consequences, and considerations in assessment and intervention. *School Psychology Quarterly, 23*(4), 451–61.

Center for the Study of Collegiate Mental Health (CSCMH). (2009). *2009 pilot study executive summary.* University Park, PA: Penn State. Retrieved from http://www.sa.psu.edu/caps/pdf/2009-CSCMH-Pilot-Report.pdf

Centers for Disease Control & Prevention (CDC). (1999). *Suicide: Risk and protective factors.* Atlanta, GA: Centers for Disease Control & Prevention. Retrieved from http://www.cdc.gov/ViolencePrevention/suicide/riskprotectivefactors.html

Centers for Disease Control & Prevention (CDC). (2008a). *Promoting individual, family, and community connectedness to prevent suicidal behavior.* Atlanta, GA: Centers for Disease Control and Prevention. Retrieved from http://www.cdc.gov/ViolencePrevention/pdf/Suicide_Strategic_Direction_Full_Version-a.pdf

Centers for Disease Control & Prevention (CDC). (2008b). School-associated student homicides—United States, 1992–2006. *Morbidity and Mortality Weekly Report, 57,* 33–36.

Centers for Disease Control & Prevention (CDC). (2009). *Youth violence—Facts at a glance—Summer 2009.* Atlanta, GA: Centers for Disease Control & Prevention (CDC). Retrieved from http://www.cdc.gov/violenceprevention/pdf/YV_DataSheet_Summer2009-a.pdf

Centers for Disease Control & Prevention (CDC), National Institute of Mental Health (NIMH), Office of the Surgeon General, Substance Abuse & Mental Health Services Administration, American Foundation for Suicide Prevention, American Association of Suicidology, and Annenberg Public Policy Center. (2001). *Reporting on suicide: Recommendations for the media.* Retrieved from http://www.sprc.org/library/sreporting.pdf

Chan, V. (2009). *The Delivery of Mental Health Care to College-aged Students: Challenges and Opportunities for Child and Adolescent Psychiatrists. III. Frontlines of ADHD in the University Setting: What Is a Clinician to Do?* Scientific Proceedings of the 2009 Annual Meeting of the American Academy of Child and Adolescent Psychiatry, Volume XXXII. Washington, DC.

CNN. Retrieved from http://www.cnn.com/2013/11/25/politics/creigh-deeds-attack/ (2013, November).

Cohen, D. (1998). Culture, social organization, and patterns of violence. *Journal of Personality & Social Psychology, 75*(2), 408–19.

Cohen, R., & Cohen, J. (2000). *Chiseled in Sand: Perspectives on Change in Human Service Organizations.* Belmont, CA: Wadsworth/Thomson Learning.

Commission on Mental Health Law Reform. (2009). *Progress report on mental health law reform (2009).* Retrieved from http://www.courts.state.va.us/programs/cmh/reports/2009_progress_report.pdf

Cook, J. A., Leff, H. S., Blyler, C. R., Gold, P. B., Goldberg, R. W., Mueser, K. T.,...Burke-Miller, J. (2005). Results of a multisite randomized trial of supported employment interventions for individuals with severe mental illness. *Archives of General Psychiatry 62*(5), 505–12.

Cooper, J. (2008). The federal case for school-based mental health services and supports. *Journal of the American Academy of Child & Adolescent Psychiatry, 47*(1), 4–8.

Cooper, S. (2003). College counseling centers as internal organizational consultants to universities. *Consulting Psychology Journal: Research and Practice, 55*(4), 230–8.

Cornell, D., & Sheras, P. (2006). *Guidelines for Responding to Student Threats of Violence.* Longmont, CO: Sopris West Educational Services.

Crego, C. (1990). Challenges and limits in search of a model. *The Counseling Psychologist, 18*, 608–13.

Critical Incident Response Group. (2000). *The school shooter: A threat assessment perspective.* Quantico, VA: National Center for the Analysis of Violent Crime. Retrieved March 7, 2010, from http://www.fbi.gov/publications/school/school2.pdf

Davar, D. (2010). Psychology and social work training in university mental health. In J. Kay & V. Schwartz (Eds.), *Mental Health Care in the College Community* (pp. 219–46). West Sussex, UK: Wiley.

Davidson, L., Eells, G., Marshall, T., & Silverman, M. (2008). *Campus mental health action planning: Part I. Building momentum.* Retrieved from http://www.jedfoundation.org/professionals/campusmhap-building-momentum

Davidson, L., Hull, M., & Schaefer, P. (2008). *Campus mental health action planning: Part II. Identifying priorities.* Retrieved from http://www.jedfoundation.org/professionals/campusmhap-identifying-priorities

Davidson, L., & Locke, J. (2010). Using a public health approach to address student mental health. In J. Kay & V. Schwartz (Eds.), *Mental Health Care in the College Community* (pp. 267–88). West Sussex, UK: Wiley.

Davidson, L., Moses, K., Silverman, M., & Spencer-Thomas, S. (2009). *Campus mental health action planning: Part III. Developing programs.* Retrieved from http://www.jedfoundation.org/professionals/campusmhap-developing-programs

DeJong, W., Epstein, J. C., & Hart, T. E. (2003). Bad things happen in good communities: The rampage shooting in Edinboro, Pennsylvania, and its aftermath. In M. H. Moore, C. V. Petrie, A. A. Braga, & B. L. McLaughlin (Eds.), *Deadly Lessons: Understanding Lethal School Violence* (pp. 70–100). Washington, DC: National Academies Press.

DeJong, W., Larimer, M., Wood, M., & Hartman, R. (2009). NIAAA's rapid response to college drinking problems initiative: Reinforcing the use of evidence-based approaches in college alcohol prevention. *Journal of Studies on Alcohol and Drugs. Supplement 16*, 5–11.

Delizonna, L., Alan, I., & Steiner, H. A. (2006). Case example of a school shooting: Lessons learned in the wake of tragedy. In S. R. Jimerson & M. J. Furlong (Eds.), *The Handbook of School Violence and School Safety; From Research to Practice* (pp. 617–29). Mahwah, NJ: Lawrence Erlbaum Associates.

DeNavas-Walt, C., Proctor, B. D., & Smith, J. C. (2010). *Income, Poverty and Health Insurance Coverage in the United States: 2009.* Washington, DC: U.S. Department of Commerce.

DeSantis, A., Webb, E., & Naar, S. (2008). Illicit use of prescription ADHD medications on a college campus: A multimethodological approach. *Journal of American College Health, 57*(3), 315–24.

DiFulvio, G., & Rutz, S. (2009). *Campus mental health action planning: Part IV. Measuring impact.* Retrieved from http://www.jedfoundation.org/professionals/campusmhap-measuring-impact

Dinkes, R., Kemp, J., & Baum, K. (2009). *Indicators of school crime and safety: 2009* (NCES 2010-012/NCJ 228478). Washington, DC: National Center for Education Statistics, Institute of Education Sciences, U.S. Department of Education, & Bureau of Justice Statistics, Office of Justice Programs, U.S. Department of Justice.

Division of Student Affairs & Enrollment Services, Virginia Commonwealth University. (2008). *VCU dangerous & disruptive behavior procedures.* Materials presented to faculty of Virginia Commonwealth University.

Dixon, L. (2000). Assertive community treatment: Twenty-five years of gold. *Psychiatric Services, 51*(6), 759–65.

Dixon, L., McFarlane, W. R., Lefley, H., Lucksted, A., Cohen, M., Falloon, I., ... Sondheimer, D. (2001). Evidence-based practices for services to families of people with psychiatric disabilities. *Psychiatric Services, 52*(7), 903–10.

Doll, L. S., Bonzo, S. E., Mercy, J. A., & Sleet, D. A. (2007). *Handbook of Injury and Violence Prevention.* New York: Springer Science & Business Media.

Drum, D., Brownson, C., Denmark, A., & Smith, S. (2009). New data on the nature of suicidal crises in college students: Shifting the paradigm. *Professional Psychology: Research and Practice, 40*(3), 213–22.

Dunkle, J., Silverstein, Z., & Warner, S. (2008). Managing violent and other troubling students: The role of threat assessment teams on campus. *Journal of College and University Law, 34*(3), 585–636.

DuPaul, G. J., Weyandt, L. L., O'Dell, S. M., & Varejao, M. (2009). College students with ADHD: Current status and future directions. *Journal of Attention Disorders, 13*(3), 234–50.

Dwyer, K., Oher, D., & Warger, C. (1998). *Early warning, timely response: A guide to safe schools.* Washington, DC: U.S. Department of Education.

Eichler, R. (2006). Developmental considerations. In P. A. Grayson & P. W. Meilman (Eds.), *College Mental Health Practice* (pp. 21–42). New York: Routledge.

Eisenberg, D., Golberstein, E., & Gollust, S. (2007). Help seeking and access to mental health care in a university student population. *Medical Care, 45*(7), 594–601.

Endsley, S., Kirkegaard, M., Baker, G., & Murcko, A. (2004). Getting rewards for your results: Pay for performance programs. *Family Practice Management, 11*(3), 45–8.

Erikson, E. (1963). *Childhood and Society* (2nd ed.). New York: W.W. Norton.

Family Educational Rights & Privacy Act (FERPA). (2008, December). *Final Rule 34 CFR Part 99. Section-by-section analysis.* Retrieved from http://www2.ed.gov/policy/gen/guid/fpco/pdf/ht12-17-08-att.pdf

Family Educational Rights & Privacy Act (FERPA). (2010). Washington, DC: U.S. Government Printing Office. Retrieved from http://ecfr.gpoaccess.gov/cgi/t/text/text-idx?c=ecfr;sid=6b7e313020dfabb7caa0216830b2a7d8;rgn=div5;view=text;node=34%3A1.1.1.1.34;idno=34;cc=ecfr

Fassler, D. (2008). *A common sense 10-point plan to enhance safety on college campuses.* Retrieved from http://www.aacap.org/cs/root/resources_for_families/a_common_sense_10point_plan_to_enhance_safety_on_college_campuses

Fauman, B., & Hopkinson, M. (2010). Special populations. In J. Kay & V. Schwartz (Eds.), *Mental Health Care in the College Community* (pp. 247–65). West Sussex, UK: Wiley.

Feachem, R., Sekhri, N., & White, K. (2002). Getting more for their dollar: A comparison of the NHS with California's Kaiser Permanente. *British Medical Journal, 324*, 135–41.

Fox, C., & Harding, D. J. (2005). School shootings as organizational deviance. *Sociol Education, 78*, 69–97.

Fox, J. A., & Savage, J. (2009). Mass murder goes to college: An examination of changes on college campuses following Virginia Tech. *American Behaviorial Scientist, 52,* 1465–85.

Francis, P. (2003). Developing ethical institutional policies and procedures for working with suicidal students on a college campus. *Journal of College Counseling, 6,* 114–23.

Frost, H. (2001). First do no harm: Helping students write about difficult topics. *Teachers & Writers Collaborative, 32*(1), 4. Retrieved from http://www.twc.org/resources/techniques/first-do-no-harm

Frymer, B. (2009). The media spectacle of Columbine—Alienated youth as an object of fear. *American Behavioral Scientist, 52*(10), 1387–404.

Gabarino, J., Dubrow, N., & Kostelny, K. (1992). *Children in Danger: Coping with the Consequences of Community Violence.* San Francisco: Jossey-Bass.

Gallagher, R. (2005). *2005 National survey of counseling center directors* (Monograph Series Number 8O). Retrieved from http://www.iacsinc.org/2005%20National%20Survey.pdf

Gallagher, R. (2009). *National survey of counseling center directors 2009.* Monograph Series Number 8R. Alexandria, VA: International Association of Counseling Services, Inc. Retrieved from http://www.collegecounseling.org/pdf/nsccd_final_v1.pdf

Garber, J., Clarke, G. N., Weersing, V. R., Beardslee, W. R., Brent, D. A., Gladstone, T. R.,...Iyengar, S. (2009). Prevention of depression in at-risk adolescents. *Journal of the American Medical Association, 301*(21), 2215–24.

Garnier, L. M., Arria, A. M., Caldeira, K. M.,Vincent. K. B., O'Grady, K. E., & Wish, E. D. (2010). Sharing and selling of prescription medications in a college student sample. *Journal of Clinical Psychiatry, 71*(3), 262–9.

General Accountability Office (GAO). (2000). *Mental Health Parity Act: Despite new federal standards, mental health benefits remain limited.* Retrieved from http://www.gao.gov/archive/2000/he00095.pdf

Giedd, J. N. (2004). Structural magnetic resonance imaging of the adolescent brain. *Annals of the New York Academy of Sciences, 1021,* 77–85.

Girard, K. (2010). Working with parents and families of young adults. In J. Kay & V. Schwartz (Eds.), *Mental Health Care in the College Community* (pp. 179–202). West Sussex, UK: Wiley.

Golberstein, E., Eisenberg, D., & Gollust, S. (2008). Perceived stigma and mental health care seeking. *Psychiatric Services, 59*(4), 392–9.

Goldstein, J. L., & Godemont, J. G. (2005). The legend and lessons of Geel, Belgium: A 1500-year-old legend, a 21st-century model. *Community Mental Health Journal, 39*(5), 441–58.

Gorn, S. (1997). *What Do I Do When... The Answer Book on Special Education Law* (2nd ed.). Horsham, PA: LRP.

Grayson, P. (2006). Overview. In P. A. Grayson & P. W. Meilman (Eds.), *College Mental Health Practice* (pp. 1–20). New York: Routledge.

Grayson, P., & Meilman, P. (Eds.). (2006). *College Mental Health Practice.* New York: Routledge.

Haas, A., Koestner, B., Rosenberg, J., Moore, D., Garlow, S., Sedway, J.,...Nemeroff, C. (2008). An interactive Web-based method of outreach to college students at risk for suicide. *Journal of American College Health, 57*(1), 15–22.

Hahn, R., Fuqua-Whitley, D., Wethington, H., Lowy, J., Crosby, A., Fullilove, M.,...Dahlberg, L., & the Task Force on Community Preventive Services. (2007). Effectiveness of universal school-based programs to prevent violence and aggressive behavior: A systematic review. *American Journal of Preventive Medicine, 33*(2S), S114–S129.

Hansen, M., Litzelman, A., Marsh, D. T., & Milspaw, A. (2004). Approaches to serious emotional disturbance: Involving multiple systems. *Professional Psychology: Research and Practice, 15*(2), 457–65.

Harding, D. J., Fox, C., & Mehta, J. D. (2002). Studying rare events through qualitative case studies—Lessons from a study of rampage school shootings. *Sociological Methods & Research, 31*(2), 174–217.

Harrison, A. G., & Rosenbaum, Y. (2010). ADHD Documentation for students requesting accommodations at the postsecondary level: Update on standards and diagnostic concerns. *Canadian Family Physician, 56*(8), 761–5.

Hart, S. (1995). Psychopathy and risk assessment. *Issues in Criminological and Legal Psychology, 24,* 63–7.

Hasazi, S. B., Furney, K. S., & Destefano, L. (1999). Implementing the IDEA transition mandates. *Exceptional Children, 65*(4), 555–66.

Hayes, T. C., & Lee, M. R. (2005). The Southern culture of honor and violent attitudes. *Sociol Spectrum, 25,* 593–617.

Haynes, N. M., Emmons, C. L., & Woodruff, D. W. (1998). School development program effects: Linking implementation to outcomes. *Journal of Education for Students Placed at Risk [Special Issue: Changing Schools for Changing Times: The Comer School Development Program], 3,* 71–85.

Hefner, J., & Eisenberg, D. (2009). Social support and mental health among college students. *American Journal of Orthopsychiatry, 79*(4), 491–9.

Henry, S. (2000). What is school violence? An integrated definition. *Annals of the American Academy of Political and Social Science, 567,* 16–29.

Henry, S. (2009). School violence beyond Columbine: A complex problem in need of an interdisciplinary analysis. *American Behavioral Scientist, 52,* 1246–65.

Heppner, P., & Neal, G. (1983). Holding up the mirror: Research on the roles and functions of counseling centers in higher education. *The Counseling Psychologist, 11*(1), 81–98.

Herrman, H., Saxena, S., & Moodie, R (Eds.). (2005). *Promoting Mental Health: Concepts, Emerging Evidence and Practice: A Report of the World Health Organization, Department of Mental Health & Substance Abuse in Collaboration with the Victorian Health Promotion Foundation and the University of Melbourne.* Geneva, Switzerland: WHO Press.

Hernandez, T., & Fister, D. (2001). Dealing with disruptive and emotional college students: A systems model. *Journal of College Counseling, 4,* 49–62.

Hiday, V. A., Swartz, M. S., Swanson, J. W., Borum, R., & Wagner, H. R. (2002). Impact of outpatient commitment on victimization of people with severe mental illness. *American Journal of Psychiatry, 159,* 1403–11.

Ho, H., Thomson, L., & Darjee, R. (2009). Violence risk assessment: The use of PCL-SV, HCR-20, and VRAG to predict violence in mentally disordered offenders discharged from a medium secure unit in Scotland. *Journal of Forensic Psychiatry and Psychology, 20,* 523–41.

Hodges, S. (2001). University counseling centers at the twenty-first century: Looking forward, looking back. *Journal of College Counseling, 4,* 161–73.

Hogan, M. F. (1992). New futures for mental health care: The case of Ohio. *Health Affairs (Millwood), 11*(3), 69–83.

Hogarty, G. E., Anderson, C. M., Reiss, D. J., Kornblith, S. J., Javna, C. D., & Madonia, M. J. (1986). Family psychoeducation, social skills training, and maintenance chemotherapy in the aftercare treatment of schizophrenia. I. One-year effects of a controlled study on relapse and expressed emotion. *Archives of General Psychiatry, 43*(7), 633–42.

Hong, M. K., Yamazaki, K., Banaag, C. G., & Yasong, D. (2004). Systems of care in Asia. In H. Remschmidt, M. L. Belfer, & I. Goodyer (Eds.), *Facilitating Pathways: Care, Treatmet and Prevention in Child and Adolescent Mental Health* (pp. 58–70). Berlin: Springer.

Hunt, J., & Eisenberg, D. (2010). Mental health problems and help-seeking behavior among college students. *Journal of Adolescent Health, 46*, 3–10.

Hunt, J., Eisenberg, D., & Kilbourne, A. (2010). Consequences of receipt of a psychiatric diagnosis for completion of college. *Psychiatric Services, 61*, 399–404.

Individuals with Disabilities Education Act, Amendment of 1997. Retrieved from http://thomas.loc.gov/home/thomas.php

Individuals with Disabilities Education Act, Amendment. (2004). In Turnbull, H., Huerta, N., & Stowe, M. (2004). *The Individuals with Disabilities Education Act as Amended in 2004*. Upper Saddle River, NJ: Pearson Education.

Infoplease. (2013). *Timeline of worldwide school shootings. Infoplease.* © 2000–2013, Pearson Education. Retrieved from http://www.infoplease.com/ipa/A0777958.html.

Inkelas, K., Soldner, M., Longerbeam, S., & Leonard, J. (2008). Differences in student outcomes by types of living-learning programs: The development of an empirical typology. *Research in Higher Education, 49*, 495–512.

Institute of Medicine (IOM). (1994). *Reducing risks for mental disorders: Frontiers for preventive intervention research.* Retrieved from http://www.iom.edu/Reports/1994/Reducing-Risks-for-Mental-Disorders-Frontiers-for-Preventive-Intervention-Research.aspx

International Association of Counseling Services, Inc. (IACS). (2000). *Accreditation standards for university and college counseling centers.* Retrieved from http://www.iacsinc.org/Accreditation%20Standards.htm

International Association of Counseling Services, Inc. (IACS). (2010). *Standards for university and college counseling services.* Alexandria, VA: International Association of Counseling Services, Inc. Retrieved from http://www.iacsinc.org/IACS%20STANDARDS%20rev%2010-3-11.pdf

Jackson, R., & Guyton, M. (2008). Violence risk assessment. In R. Jackson (Ed.), *Learning Forensic Assessment* (pp. 153–81). New York: Routledge.

Jed Foundation. (2006). *Framework for developing institutional protocols for the acutely distressed or suicidal college student.* Retrieved from http://www.jedfoundation.org/assets/Programs/Program_downloads/Framework_bw.pdf

Jed Foundation (2007). *Protecting your child's mental health: What can parents do?* Retrieved from http://www.jedfoundation.org/assets/Programs/Program_downloads/parentsguide.pdf

Jed Foundation. (2009). *Transition year: Your guide for emotional health at college—student and parent editions.* Retrieved from http://www.transitionyear.org/

Jed Foundation & mtvU. (2006). *College Mental Health Study: Stress, depression, stigma & students, executive summary.* Retrieved from http://www.halfofus.com/_media/_pr/mtvU-CollegeMentalHealthStudy2006.pdf

Jed Foundation & Suicide Prevention Resource Center (2009). *Comprehensive approach to suicide prevention and mental health promotion.* Retrieved from http://www.sprc.org/collegesanduniversities/comprehensive-approach

Joffe, P. (2008). An empirically supported program to prevent suicide in a college student population. *Suicide & Life-Threatening Behavior, 38(1)*, 87–103.

Johnson, S. A., & Fisher, K. (2003). School violence: An insider view. *American Journal of Maternal Child Nursing, 28(2)*, 86–92.

Kadison, R., & DiGeronimo, T. (2004). *College of the Overwhelmed: The Campus Mental Health Crisis and What to Do About It*. San Francisco: Jossey-Bass.

Kaiser, D. A. (2005). School shootings, high school size, and neurobiological considerations. *Journal of Neurotherapy, 9*(3), 101–15.

Kaiser Permanente of Colorado. (2010). *SBAR technique for communication: A situational briefing model*. Retrieved from http://www.ihi.org/IHI/Topics/PatientSafety/SafetyGeneral/Tools/SBARTechniqueforCommunicationASituationalBriefingModel.htm

Kam, C. M., Greenberg, M. T., & Kusche, C. A. (2004). Sustained effects of the PATHS Curriculum on the social and psychological adjustment of children in special education. *Journal of Emotional and Behavioral Disorders, 12*, 66–78.

Kambam, P., & Thompson, C. (2009). The development of decision-making capacities in children and adolescents: Psychological and neurological perspectives and their implications for juvenile justice. *Behavioral Sciences and the Law, 27*, 173–90.

Kamradt, B. (2000). Wraparound Milwaukee: Aiding youth with mental health needs. *Juvenile Justice—Youth with Mental Health Disorders: Issues and Emerging Responses, 7*(1), 14–23.

Kaplan, G. A., Pamuk, E. R., Lynch, J. W., Cohen, R. D., & Balfour, J. L. (1996). Inequality in income and mortality in the United States: Analysis of mortality and potential pathways. *British Medical Journal, 312*(7037), 999–1003.

Kay, J., & Schwartz, V. (2010). Psychiatry residency training in college mental health services. In J. Kay & V. Schwartz (Eds.), *Mental Health Care in the College Community* (pp. 203–18). West Sussex, UK: Wiley.

Kazak, A. E., Hoagwood, K., Weisz, J. R., Hood, K., Kratochwill, T. R., Vargas, L. A., & Banez, G. A. (2010). A meta-systems approach to evidence-based practice for children and adolescents. *American Psychologist, 65*(2), 85–97.

Kennedy, B. P., Kawachi, I., & Prothrow-Stith, D. (1996). Income distribution and mortality: Cross-sectional ecological study of the Robin Hood Index in the United States. *British Medical Journal, 312*(7037), 1004–7.

Kessler, R., Foster, C., Saunders, W., & Stang, P. (1995). Social consequences of psychiatric disorders, I: Educational attainment. *American Journal of Psychiatry, 152*, 1026–32.

Kessler, R. C., Bergland, P., Demler, O., Jin, R., Merikangas, K. R., & Walters, E. E. (2005). Lifetime prevalence and age-of-onset distribution of DSM-IV disorders in the National Comorbidity Survey Replication. *Archives of General Psychiatry, 62*, 593–603.

Kim, D. (Producer), & Park, C. (Director). (2003). *Oldboy* [motion picture]. South Korea: Egg Films.

Kimmel, M. S., & Mahler, M. (2003). Masculinity, homophobia and violence: Random school shootings, 1982–2001. *American Behavioral Scientist, 46*, 1439–58.

Kitzrow, M. (2003). The mental health needs of today's college students. *NASPA Journal, 41*(1), 167–81.

Klein, J. (2006). An invisible problem: Everyday violence against girls in schools. *Theories in Criminology, 10*(2), 147–77.

Knox, K., Litts, D., Talcott, G., Feig, J., Caine, E., & Romano, J. (2003). Risk of suicide and related adverse outcomes after exposure to a suicide prevention programme in the US Air Force: Cohort study. *British Medical Journal, 327*, 1376–81.

Kognito Interactive. (2009). *The case for gatekeeper training: A white paper*. Retrieved from http://www.iaia.edu/wp-content/uploads/2011/04/Gatekeeper_training.pdf

Komiya, N., & Eells, G. (2001). Predictors of attitudes toward seeking counseling among international students. *Journal of College Counseling, 4*, 153–60.

Kraft, D. (2009). Mens sana: The growth of mental health in the American College Health Association. *Journal of American College Health, 58*(3), 267–75.

Lamb, C. S. (1992). Managing disruptive students: The mental health practitioner as a consultant for faculty and staff. *Journal of College Student Psychotherapy, 7*(1), 23.

Lamb, R. (1984). Deinstitutionalization and the homeless mentally ill. *Hospital & Community Psychiatry, 35*, 899–907.

Langman, P. (2009). *Why Kids Kill—Inside the Minds of School Shooters.* New York: Palgrave Macmillan.

Larkin, R. W. (2009). The Columbine legacy: Rampage shootings as political acts. *American Behavioral Scientist, 52*(9), 1309–26.

Leary, M. R., Kowalski, R. M., Smith, L., & Phillips, S. (2003). Teasing, rejection, and violence: Case studies of the school shootings. *Aggressive Behavior, 29*, 202–14.

Leavitt, M. O., Gonzales, A. R., & Spellings, M. (2007). *Report to the President on issues raised by the Virginia Tech tragedy.* Retrieved from http://www.justice.gov/opa/pr/2007/June/vt_report_061307.pdf

Lee, S., Tsang, A., Breslau, J., Angermeyer, M., Borges, G., Bromet, E.,…Kessler, R. (2009). Mental disorders and termination of education in high-income and low- and middle-income countries: Epidemiological study. *British Journal of Psychiatry, 194*, 411–17.

Lejeune, S. (2009). Special considerations in treating major mental illness: Lessons from bipolar disorder. In *Treating Young Adults: Challenges and Strategies.* Cambridge, MA: Harvard Medical School Department of Continuing Education.

Levin, J., & Madfis, E. (2009). Mass murder at school and cumulative strain: A sequential model. *American Behavioral Scientist, 52*(9), 1227–45.

Lin, E., & Chen, P. S. (2008). Pharmacogenomics with antidepressants in the STAR*D study. *Pharmacogenomics, 9*(7), 935–46.

Locke, J., & Eichorn, M. (2008, Spring). Mental health: What do parents think? *Student Health Spectrum (A Publication of Aetna Student Health)*, pp. 13–17.

Loza, W., & Dhaliwal, G. (2005). Predicting violence among forensic-correctional populations: The past 2 decades of advancement and future endeavors. *Journal of Interpersonal Violence, 20*, 188–94.

Marshall, M., & Lockwood, A. (2000). Assertive community treatment for people with severe mental disorders. *Cochrane Database of Systematic Reviews (2), CD001089.*

Martel, A. (2009, October). The delivery of mental health care to college-aged students: Challenges and opportunities for child and adolescent psychiatrists. I. Introduction to college student mental health. Scientific proceedings presented at the American Academy of Child & Adolescent Psychiatry 56th Annual Meeting, Honolulu, HI.

Martel, A. (2010). *Promoting Autonomy in our Patients Transitioning to College: A Systems Approach.* The Scientific Proceedings of the 2010 Annual Meeting of the American Academy of Child and Adolescent Psychiatry. Volume XXXVII. Washington, DC.

Martel, A., & Namerow, L. (2010). *Promoting Autonomy in Our Patients Transitioning to College: A Systems Approach. IV. Transitioning Adolescents to College: A Framework of Anticipatory Guidance.* The Scientific Proceedings of the 2010 Annual Meeting of the American Academy of Child & Adolescent Psychiatry. Volume XXXIII. Washington, DC.

Martin, R. C. (2001, February). *Zero tolerance policy report.* American Bar Association, Juvenile Justice Policies. Retrieved from http://www.abanet.org/crimjust/juvjus/zerotol-report.html

Mattejat, F., Hirsch, O., & Remschmidt, H. (2003). Value of telephone interview for quality assurance and therapy evaluation in child and adolescent psychiatry. Review of the literature and empirical results of participation quota and possible sampling bias. *Zeitschrift für Kinder- und Jugend-Psychiatrie, 31(1)*, 17–34.

McCloskey, L. A., & Bailey, J. A. (2000). Intergenerational transmission of risk for child sexual abuse. *Journal of Interpersonal Violence, 15*(10), 1019–35.

McCollam, A., O'Sullivan, C., Mukkala, M., Stengard, E., & Rowe, P. (2008) *Mental Health in the EU: Key Facts, Figures and Activities*. Luxembourg: European Commission.

McFarlane, W. R., Dushay, R. A., Stastny, P., Deakins, S. M., & Link, B. (1996). A comparison of two levels of family-aided assertive community treatment. *Psychiatr Services, 47*(7), 744–50.

McInerney, T., Adam, H. M., Campbell, D. E., Kamat, D. M., & Kelleher, K. J. (Eds.). (2008). *American Academy of Pediatrics Textbook of Pediatric Care*. Elk Grove, IL: American Academy of Pediatrics.

McIntosh, P. (1986). *White privilege and male privilege: A personal account of coming to see correspondences through work in women's studies* (Working Paper No. 189). Wellesley, MA: Center for Research on Women, Wellesley College.

McLaughlin, J. R., & Miller, T. W. (2008). Prevention of school violence: Directions, summary and conclusions. In Thomas W. Miller (Ed.), *School Violence and Primary Prevention* (pp. 431–44). New York: Springer Science + Business Media.

McManus, M., Fox, H., O'Connor, K., Chapman, T., & MacKinnon, J. (2008). *Pediatric perspectives and practices on transitioning adolescents with special needs to adult care*. Fact Sheet No. 6. Retrieved from http://www.thenationalalliance.org/facts.html

McPherson, M., Arango, P., Fox, H., Lauver, C., McManus, M., Newachek, P., . . . Strickland, B. (1998) A new definition of children with special health needs. *Pediatrics, 102*(1), 137–40.

Megargee, E. (2009). Understanding and assessing aggression and violence. In J. Butcher (Ed.), *Oxford Handbook of Personality Assessment* (pp. 542–66). New York: Oxford University Press.

Mental Health America (2007). *Guidelines to help students, parents and educators respond and cope with the Virginia Tech shootings*. Alexandria, VA: Mental Health America. Retrieved from http://www.nmha.org/go/coping-virginia-tech

Meyer-Adams, N., & Conner, B. T. (2008). School violence: Bullying behaviors and the psychosocial school environment in middle schools. *Children and Schools, 30*(4), 211–21.

Mihalic, S. W., & Elliott, D. S. (1997). Short and long-term consequences of adolescent work. *Youth and Society, 28*(4), 464–98.

Miller, M. (2010, March 3). What we can learn from Singapore's health-care model. *Washington Post*. Retrieved from http://www.washingtonpost.com/wp-dyn/content/article/2010/03/03/AR2010030301396.html

Milwaukee County Behavioral Health Division. (2009). *Wraparound Milwaukee annual report: 2008*. Milwaukee, WI: Wraparound Milwaukee.

Mueser, K. T., Bond, G. R., Drake, R. E., & Resnick, S. G. (1998). Models of community care for severe mental illness: A review of research on case management. *Schizophrenia Bulletin, 24*(1), 37–74.

Mulvey, E. P., & Cauffman, E. (2001). The inherent limits of predicting school violence. *American Psychologist, 56*(10), 797–802.

Murakami, S., Rappaport, N., & Penn, J. V. (2006). An overview of juveniles and school violence. *Psychiatric Clinics of North America, 29*, 725–41.

Murray, C. J. L., & Lopez, A. D. (Eds.). (1996). *The Global Burden of Disease. A Comprehensive Assessment of Mortality and Disability from Diseases, Injuries, and Risk Factors in 1990 and Projected to 2020.* Cambridge, MA: Harvard School of Public Health.

Murthén, B. O., Brown, C. H., Masyn, K., Jo, B., Khoo, S. T., Yang, C. C., ... Carlin, J. B. (2002). General growth mixture modeling for randomized preventive interventions. *Biostatistics, 3,* 459–75.

Muschert, G. W. (2008). Research in school shootings. *Social and Personality Psychology Compass, 2*(3), 60–80.

Nation, M., Crusto, C., Wandersman, A., Kumpfer, K. L., Seybolt, D., Morrissey-Kane, M., & Davino, K. (2003). What works in prevention: Principles of effective prevention programs. *American Psychologist, 58*(6-7), 449–56.

National Alliance on Mental Illness (NAMI). (2009). *Grading the states: A report on America's health care system for adults with serious mental illness.* Arlington, VA: National Alliance on Mental Illness.

National Alliance on Mental Illness (NAMI). (2010). *Mental health services and choosing a college: Striking a balance.* Retrieved from http://www.nami.org/Template.cfm?Section= Mental_Health_and_Choosing_a_College&Template=/ContentManagement/ ContentDisplay.cfm&ContentID=24725

National Association of School Psychologists. (2002). *Bullying Prevention: What Schools and Parents Can Do.* Bethesda, MD: National Association of School Psychologists.

National Association of State Mental Health Program Directors. (2006). *Morbidity and mortality in people with serious mental illness* (thirteenth in a series of technical reports). Alexandria, VA: National Association of State Mental Health Program Directors (NASMHPD) Medical Directors Council. Retrieved from http://www.nasmhpd.org/ general_files/publications/med_directors_pubs/Technical%20Report%20on%20 Morbidity%20and%20Mortaility%20-%20Final%2011-06.pdf

National Center for Health Statistics. (2010). *Health, United States, 2009: With special features on medical terminology.* Hyattsville, MD: U.S. Department of Health and Human Services. Retrieved from http://www.cdc.gov/nchs/data/hus/hus09.pdf

National Mental Health Association (NMHA) and the Jed Foundation. (2002). *Safeguarding your students against suicide: Expanding the safety net.* Retrieved from http://www. higheredcenter.org/services/publications/safeguarding-your-students-against-suicide -expanding-safety-net

National Research Council and Institute of Medicine. (2009). *Preventing Mental, Emotional and Behavioral Disorders Among Young People: Progress and Possibilities.* Washington, DC: National Academy Press.

New York State Office of Mental Health. (2005, March). *Kendra's Law: Final report of assisted outpatient treatment.* New York: New York Office of Mental Health. Retrieved from http://bi.omh.state.ny.us/aot/files/AOTFinal2005.pdf

Newman, K. S., Fox, C., Roth, W., Mehta, J., & Harding, D. (2004). *Rampage: The Social Roots of School Shootings.* New York: Basic Books.

Norko, M., & Baranoski, M. (2005). The state of contemporary risk assessment research. *Canadian Journal of Psychiatry, 50,* 18–26.

Nutt, D. J., Fone, K., Asherson, P., Bramble, D., Hill, P., Matthews, K., ... Young, S., & British Association for Psychopharmacology. (2007). Evidence-based guidelines for management of attention-deficit/hyperactivity disorder in adolescents in transition to adult services and in adults: Recommendations from the British Association for Psychopharmacology. *Journal of Psychopharmacology, 21*(1), 10–41.

Office for Civil Rights (OCR), U.S. Department of Health & Human Services. (2000). *Understanding health information privacy.* Retrieved from http://www.hhs.gov/ocr/privacy/hipaa/understanding/index.html

Office for Civil Rights (OCR), U.S. Department of Health & Human Services. (2003). *Summary of the HIPAA Privacy Rule.* Retrieved from http://www.hhs.gov/ocr/privacy/hipaa/understanding/summary/privacysummary.pdf

Office of the Inspector General for Mental Health, Mental Retardation & Substance Abuse Services (OIG). (2007). *Investigation of April 16, 2007 critical incident at Virginia Tech* (OIG Report #140-07 [Preliminary Report]). Richmond, VA: Office of the Inspector General. Retrieved from http://www.oig.virginia.gov/documents/VATechRpt-140.pdf

Olds, D. L. (2006). The nurse–family partnership: An evidence-based preventive intervention. *Infant Mental Health Journal, 27*, 5–25.

Pabian, Y. L., Welfel, E., & Beebe, R. S. (2009). Psychologists' knowledge of their states' laws pertaining to Tarasoff-type situations. *Professional Psychology. Research and Practice, 40*(1), 8–14.

Parsons, E. C. (2001). Using power and caring to mediate white male privilege, quality, and equity in an urban elementary classroom: Implications for teacher preparation. *The Urban Review, 33*(4), 321–38.

Patashnik, E. M. (2008). *Reforms at Risk: What Happens after Major Policy Changes Are Enacted* (Princeton Studies in American Politics). Princeton, NJ: Princeton University Press.

Patient Protection and Affordable Care Act. (2010). Pub. L. No. 111-148, §2702, 124 Stat. 119, 318–19.

Piehl, A. M., Kennedy, D. M., & Braga, A. A. (2000). Problem solving and youth violence: An evaluation of the Boston Gun Project. *American Law and Economics Review, 2*(1), 58–106.

Pies, R. (1994). *Clinical Manual of Psychiatric Diagnosis and Treatment: A Biopsychosocial Approach.* Washington, DC: American Psychiatric Association Press.

Professional Risk Management Services, Inc. (PRMS). (2005). Treating college students: Understanding the risks. *Rx for Risk, 13*(4).

Reiman, J. (1990). *The Rich Get Richer and the Poor Get Prison.* New York: Macmillian.

Remschmidt, H., & Belfer, M. (2005). Mental health care for children and adolescents worldwide: A review. *World Psychiatry, 4*(3), 147–53.

Ress, D. (2010a, February 21). Finding on the closing of children's hospital suppressed. *Richmond-Times Dispatch.* Retrieved from http://www2.timesdispatch.com/rtd/news/state_regional/article/HOSP21_20100220-220602/325757/

Ress, D. (2010b, May 31). Mental health commissioner kept center's problems quiet. *Richmond-Times Dispatch.* Retrieved from http://www2.timesdispatch.com/rtd/news/state_regional/state_regional_govtpolitics/article/MENT31_20100530-221407/347972/

Ress, D. (2010c, June 3). Kaine official's promise on children's mental health facilities unfulfilled. *Richmond-Times Dispatch.* Retrieved from http://www2.timesdispatch.com/rtd/news/state_regional/article/MENT03_20100602-222605/348677/

Rhode Island Hospital. (2010). *ISBAR trip tick.* Retrieved from http://www.ihi.org/IHI/Topics/PatientSafety/SafetyGeneral/Tools/ISBARTripTick.htm

Rice, M. J. (2011). Assertive community treatment: Evidence-based hope for the seriously mentally ill. *Journal of American Psychiatric Nurses Association, 17*(1), 13–15.

Rinehart-Thompson, L. A. (2009). Amendments to FERPA regulations: New changes attempt to balance safety and privacy in student records. *Journal of AHIMA, 80*(7), 56–57.

Robertson, B., Mandlhate, C., Seif El Din, A., & Seck, D. (2004). Systems of care in Africa. In H. Remschmidt, M. L. Belfer, & I. Goodyer (Eds.), *Facilitating Pathways: Care, Treatment and Prevention in Child and Adolescent Mental Health* (pp. 71–88). Berlin: Springer.

Robison, S. (2009). *Towards a mentally flourishing Scotland: Policy and action plan 2009–2011.* Edinburgh: The Scottish Government.

Rockland-Miller, H., & Eells, G. (2006). The implementation of mental health clinical triage systems in university health services. *Journal of College Student Psychotherapy, 20*(4), 39–51.

Roosens, E. (1979). *Mental Patients in Town Life: Geel—Europe's First Therapeutic Community.* Beverly Hills, CA: Sage Publications.

Roth, D., Lauber, B. G., Crane-Ross, D., & Clark, J. A. (1997). Impact of state mental health reform on patterns of service delivery. *Community Mental Health Journal, 33*(6), 473–86.

Roy, L. (2009). *No Right to Remain Silent: The Tragedy at Virginia Tech.* New York: Harmony Books.

Rydelius, P. (2004). Systems of care in Europe. In H. Remschmidt, M. L. Belfer, & I. Goodyer (Eds.), *Facilitating Pathways: Care, Treatment and Prevention in Child and Adolescent Mental Health* (pp. 27–34). Berlin: Springer.

Scott, C., & Resnick, P. (2009). Risk Assessment. In R. Kocsis (Ed.), *Applied Criminal Psychology—A Guide to Forensic Behavioral Sciences* (pp. 69–94). Springfield, IL: C. Thomas Publisher.

Scheyett, A. (2009, November). *Planning ahead: Student views on using psychiatric advance directives.* Paper presented at the Annual Program Meeting, Council on Social Work Education, San Antonio, TX.

Schiele, J. H., & Stewart, R. (2001). When white boys kill: An Afrocentric analysis. *Journal of Human Behavior in the Social Environment, 4*(4), 253–73.

Schleimer, K. (2002). International perspectives on the economics of mental health care for children and adolescents: Economic policies and the Swedish experience. In G. J. Young, & P. Ferrari (Eds.), *Designing Mental Health Services and Systems for Children and Adolescents: A Shrewd Investment* (pp. 291–94). Philadelphia: Brunner/Mazel.

Schwartz, V. (1996). *An overview of strategies to reduce school violence. ERIC/CUE Digest No. 115.* New York: ERIC Clearinghouse on Urban Education. Retrieved from http://www.ericdigests.org/1998-1/overview.htm

Schwartz, V., & Kay, J. (Eds.). (2010). *Mental Health Care in the College Community: A Review of Mental Health Care in the College Community.* West Sussex, UK: Wiley-Blackwell.

Schweinhart, L. J., Montie, J., Xiang, Z., Barnett, W. S., Belfield, C. R., & Nores, M. (2005). *The HighScope Perry Preschool Study Through Age 40* (Monographs of the HighScope Educational Research Foundation, 14). Ypsilanti, MI: HighScope Press.

Scott, C., & Resnick, P. (2009). Risk Assessment. In R. Kocsis (Ed.), *Applied Criminal Psychology—A Guide to Forensic Behavioral Sciences* (pp. 69–94). Springfield, IL: C. Thomas Publisher.

Seaman, B. (2005). *Binge: What Your College Student Won't Tell You.* Hoboken, NJ: John Wiley & Sons.

Seaton, E. (2007). Exposing the invisible: Unraveling the roots of rural boys' violence in schools. *Journal of Adolescent Research, 22,* 211–18.

Shah, P. (2010). Transitioning youth with special needs to adult care. *Journal of Children's Memorial Hospital, Chicago, 27*(2), 2–7.

Sham, P. C., MacLean, C. J., & Kendler, K. S. (1994). A typological model of schizophrenia based on age at onset, sex and familial morbidity. *Acta Psychiatrica Scandinavica, 89*(2), 135–41.

Shatkin, J. (2010). *Transition to college: Separation and change for parents and students.* New York: NYU Child Study Center. Retrieved from http://www.aboutourkids.org/articles/transition_college_separation_change_parents_students

Shaw, J. (2000). Assessing the risk of violence in patients: Risks can be assessed, but the results still pose ethical and political dilemmas. *British Medical Journal, 320,* 1088–1089.

Silverman, M. (2008). Campus security begins with caring. *Chronicles of Higher Education, 54*(32), A51–A52.

Silverman, M., Meyer, P., Sloane, F., Raffel, M., & Pratt, D. (1997). The Big Ten Student Suicide Study: A 10-year study of suicides on Midwestern university campuses. *Suicide & Life-Threatening Behavior, 27*(3), 285–303.

Singh, S., Paul, M., Ford, T., Kramer, T., Weaver, T., McLaren, S.,...White, S. (2010). Process, outcome and experience of transition from child to adult mental health care: Multiperspective study. *British Journal of Psychiatry, 197,* 305–12.

Skiba, R., Reynolds, C. R., Graham, S., Sheras P., Conoley, J. C., & Garcia-Vazquez, E. (2006). *Are Zero Tolerance Policies Effective in the Schools? An Evidentiary Review and Recommendations.* American Psychological Association Zero Tolerance Task Force. Washington, DC: American Psychological Association.

Smith, L., Baluch, S., Bernabei, S., Robohm, J., & Sheehy, J. (2003). Applying a social justice framework to college counseling center practice. *Journal of College Counseling, 6,* 3–13.

Snyder, T. D., & Dillow, S. A. (2010). *Digest of education statistics 2009* (NCES 2010-013). Washington, DC: National Center for Education Statistics, Institute of Education Sciences, U.S. Department of Education. Retrieved from http://nces.ed.gov/pubsearch/pubsinfo.asp?pubid=2010013

Sood, B. (2009a, October). *The delivery of mental health care to college-aged students: Challenges and opportunities for child and adolescent psychiatrists. V. Best practices for strengthening mental health on campus.* Scientific proceedings presented at the American Academy of Child & Adolescent Psychiatry 56th Annual Meeting, Honolulu, HI.

Sood, B. (2009b). *Systems-based practice: Organizational and financial structures in mental health systems of care.* American Association of Child and Adolescent Psychiatrists (AACAP) Systems of Care Workgroup's Systems Based Toolkit. Retrieved from http://www.aacap.org/galleries/PracticeInformation/j%20-%20Systems%20Based%20Practice%20Module%20-%20Org%20and%20Fin%20Structures%20for%20Web.pdf

Stambaugh, H. (2008). *U.S. Fire Administration/Technical Report Series: Northern Illinois University shooting, February 14, 2008, DeKalb, Illinois.* USFA-TR-167. Retrieved from http://www.usfa.dhs.gov

Stein, L. I., & Santos, A. B. (1998). *Assertive Community Treatment of Persons with Severe Mental Illness.* New York: W.W. Norton.

Stein, L. I., & Test, M. A. (1980). Alternative to mental hospital treatment: Conceptual model, treatment program and clinical evaluation. *Archives of General Psychiatry, 37*(4), 392–97.

Stier, A., & Hinshaw, S. P. (2007). Explicit and implicit stigma against individuals with mental illness. *Australian Psychology, 42*(2), 106–17.

Stone, G., & Archer, J. (1990). College and university counseling centers in the 1990s: Challenges and limits. *The Counseling Psychologist, 18,* 539–607.

Strawhacker, M. A. T. (2002). School violence: An overview. *Journal of School Nursing, 18*(2), 68–72.

Stroul, B. A., & Friedman, R. M. (1986). *A system of care for severely emotionally disturbed children and youth.* Washington, DC: Georgetown University Child Development Center.

Sturgeon, J. (2009, December 8). Parents file suit over Va. Tech son's suicide. *The Roanoke Times.* Retrieved from http://hamptonroads.com/2009/12/parents-file-suit-over-va-tech-son%E2%80%99s-suicide

Suicide Prevention Resource Center (SPRC). (2004). *Promoting mental health and preventing suicide in college and university settings.* Newton, MA: Education Development Center, Inc. Retrieved from www.sprc.org/library/college_sp_whitepaper.pdf

Svendsen, D. P., Cutler, D. L., Ronis, R. J., Herman, L. C., Morrison, A., Smith, M. K., & Munetz, M. (2005). The Professor of Public Psychiatry Model in Ohio: The impact on training, program innovation, and the quality of mental health care. *Community Mental Health Journal, 41*(6), 775–84.

Swartz, M., & Morrisey, J. (2003). Mental health care in North Carolina: Challenges on the road to reform. *North Carolina Medical Journal, 64*(5), 205–11.

Tandon, A., Murray, C. J. L., Lauer, J. A., & Evans, D. B. (2000). *Measuring overall health system performance for 191 countries* (GPE Discussion Paper Series: No. 30). EIP/GPE/EQC), World Health Organization. Retrieved from www.who.int/entity/healthinfo/paper30.pdf

Task Force of the National Advisory Council on Alcohol Abuse and Alcoholism. (2002). *A call to action: Changing the culture of drinking at U.S. colleges.* (NIH Publ. No. 02–5010). Bethesda, MD: National Institute on Alcohol Abuse and Alcoholism (NIAAA). Retrieved from http://www.collegedrinkingprevention.gov/media/TaskForceReport.pdf

Texas Governor's Fact Finding Committee. (1966). *Report to the Governor: Medical aspects— Charles J. Whitman catastrophe.* Retrieved from http://alt.cimedia.com/statesman/specialreports/whitman/findings.pdf.

Thomas, C. R., & Holzer, C. E. 3rd. (2006). The continuing shortage of child and adolescent psychiatrists. *Journal of the American Academy of Child and Adolescent Psychiatry, 45*(9), 1023–31.

Tierney, J. P., Grossman, J. B., & Resch, N. L. (1995). *Making a Difference: An Impact Study of Big Brothers/Big Sisters.* Philadelphia: Public/Private Ventures.

Ting, J., & Hwang, W-C. (2009). Cultural influences on help-seeking attitudes in Asian American students. *American Journal of Orthospsychiatry, 79*(1), 125–32.

Tocqueville, A. D. (1969). *Democracy in America* (J. P. Mayer, Ed., G. Lawrence, Trans.). Garden City, NY: Anchor Books. (Original work published 1835 and 1840).

Torrey, W. C., Drake, R. E., Dixon, L., Burnd, B. J., Flynn, L., Rush, J. A., Clark, R. E., & Klatzker, D. (2001). Implementing evidence-based practices for persons with severe mental illnesses. *Psychiatric Services, 52*(1), 45–50.

Trust for America's Health. (2008). *Prevention for a healthier America: Investments in disease prevention yield significant savings, stronger communities.* Washington, DC: Trust for America's Health. Retrieved from http://healthyamericans.org/reports/prevention08/Prevention08.pdf

Turner, J. C., & TenHoor, W. J. (1978). The NIMH Community Support Program: Pilot approach to a needed social reform. *Schizophrenia Bulletin, 4*(3), 319–49.

U.S. Department of Education. (2005). *Students with disabilities making great strides, new study finds.* Retrieved from http://www.ed.gov/news/pressreleases/2005/07/07282005.html

U.S. Department of Education, Office for Civil Rights. (2011). *Students with disabilities preparing for postsecondary education: Know your rights and responsibilities.* Washington, DC. Retrieved from http://www2.ed.gov/about/offices/list/ocr/transition.html

U.S. Department of Health & Human Services. (1999). *Mental health: A report of the Surgeon General.* Retrieved from http://www.surgeongeneral.gov/library/mentalhealth/home.html

U.S. Department of Health and Human Services. (2001). *National strategy for suicide prevention: Goals and objectives for action.* Retrieved from http://download.ncadi.samhsa.gov/ken/pdf/SMA01-3517/SMA01-3517.pdf

U.S. Surgeon General. (2001). *Youth violence: A report of the Surgeon General.* Rockville, MD: Office of the Surgeon General. Retreived from http://www.ncbi.nlm.nih.gov/books/NBK44294/

VA Code § 9.1-187 (2001 through Reg Session).

VA Code § 23-9.2:10 (2001 through Reg Session).

VA Code § 23-9.2:11 (2001 through Reg Session).

VA Code § 32.1-127.1:03 (2001 through Reg Session).

Vanbergeijk, E., Klin, A. & Volkmar, F. (2008). Supporting more able students on the autism spectrum: College and beyond. *Journal of Autism and Developmental Disorders, 38*(7), 1359–70.

Veltkamp, L. J., & Lawson, A. (2008). Impact of trauma in school violence on the victim and the perpetrator: A mental health perspective. In T. W. Miller (Ed.), *School Violence and Primary Prevention* (pp. 185–200). New York: Springer Science + Business Media.

Villarreal, A. (2008). *International students a growing force in US colleges, universities.* Retrieved from http://www1.voanews.com/english/news/a-13-2008-02-20-voa22-66741352.html?CFID+30456

Virginia Tech Review Panel. (2007a). Appendix A: Executive order 53 (2007). In *Mass shootings at Virginia Tech: Report of the review panel presented to Governor Kaine, Commonwealth of Virginia* (pp. A-1–A-9). Retrieved from http://www.scribd.com/doc/265874/Virginia-Tech-Shootings-Complete-Report-of-the-Governors-Review-Panel

Virginia Tech Review Panel. (2007b). Appendix B: Individuals interviewed by research panel. In *Mass shootings at Virginia Tech: Report of the review panel presented to Governor Kaine, Commonwealth of Virginia* (pp. B-1–B-11). Retrieved from http://www.scribd.com/doc/265874/Virginia-Tech-Shootings-Complete-Report-of-the-Governors-Review-Panel

Virginia Tech Review Panel. (2007c). Chapter IV: Mental health history of Seung-Hui Cho. In *Mass shootings at Virginia Tech: Report of the review panel presented to Governor Kaine, Commonwealth of Virginia* (pp. 31–62). Retrieved from http://www.scribd.com/doc/265874/Virginia-Tech-Shootings-Complete-Report-of-the-Governors-Review-Panel

Virginia Tech Review Panel. (2007d). Chapter XI: Immediate aftermath and the long road to healing. In *Mass shootings at Virginia Tech: Report of the review panel presented to Governor Kaine, Commonwealth of Virginia* (pp. 135–47). Retrieved from http://www.scribd.com/doc/265874/Virginia-Tech-Shootings-Complete-Report-of-the-Governors-Review-Panel

Voelker, R. (2003). Mounting student depression taxing campus mental health services. *Journal of the American Medical Association, 289*(16), 2055–6.

Volkmar, F., & Wiesner, L. (2009). *A Practical Guide to Autism: What Every Parent, Family Member, and Teacher Needs to Know.* Hoboken, NJ: John Wiley & Sons.

Vossekuil, B., Fein, R. A., Reddy, M., Borum, R., & Modzeleski, W. (2002). *The final report and findings of the safe school initiative: Implications for the prevention of school attacks in the United States.* Washington, DC: U.S. Department of Education, Office of Elementary & Secondary Education, Safe & Drug-Free Schools Program, and U.S. Secret Service, National Threat Assessment Center.

Wang, C-C., & Castaneda-Sound, C. (2008). The role of generational status, self-esteem, academic self-sufficiency, and perceived social support in college students' psychological well-being. *Journal of College Counseling, 11*, 101–18.

Wang, P. S., Berglund, P., & Kessler, R. C. (2000). Recent care of common mental disorders in the United States: Prevalence and conformance with evidence-based recommendations. *Journal of General Internal Medicine, 15*(5), 284–92.

Webster-Stratton, C., Reid, M. J., & Stoolmiller, M. (2008). Preventing conduct problems and improving school readiness: Evaluation of the incredible years teacher and child training programs in high-risk schools. *Journal of Child Psychology and Psychiatry, 49(5)*, 471–88.

Wellford, C. F., Pepper, J. V., & Petrie, C. V. (Eds.), Committee on Law and Justice, National Research Council. (2005). *Firearms and Violence: A Critical Review.* Washington, DC: National Academy Press.

Westphal, A., & Volkmar, F. (2008). An update on autism. *Focus, 6*, 284–92.

Wilcox, H. C., Kellam, S. G., Brown, C. H., Poduska, J. M., Ialongo, N. S., Wang, W., & Anthony, J. (2008). The impact of two universal randomized first and second grade classroom interventions on young adult suicide ideation and attempts. *Drug and Alcohol Dependence, 95*(Suppl. 1), 560–73.

Williams, B. B. W. (2006). *Culturally Competent Mental Health Services in the Schools: Tips for Teachers.* Bethesda, MD: National Association of School Psychologists.

Wilson, S., & Lipsey, M. (2007). School-based interventions for aggressive and disruptive behavior. *American Journal of Preventive Medicine, 33*(2 Suppl), S130–43.

Winters, N., & Pumariega, A. (2007). AACAP Practice Parameters on child and adolescent mental health care in community systems of care. *Journal of the American Academy of Child and Adolescent Psychiatry, 46*(2), 284–99.

Wolf, L., Thierfeld, J., & Bork, R. (2009). *Students with Asperger Syndrome: A Guide for College Personnel.* Shawnee, KS: Autism Asperger Publishing Co.

World Health Organization (WHO). (2000, June 21). World Health Organization assesses the world's health systems. WHO Press Releases, WHO/44. Retrieved from http://www.photius.com/rankings/who_world_health_ranks.html

World Health Organization (WHO). (2003). *Caring for Children and Adolescents with Mental Disorders.* Geneva, Switzerland: WHO Press.

World Health Organization (WHO). (2005). *Mental Health Atlas: 2005.* Geneva, Switzerland: WHO Press.

World Health Organization (WHO). (2008). *Mental Health Gap Action Programme (mhGAP): Scaling Up Care for Mental, Neurological, and Substance Use Disorders.* Geneva, Switzerland: WHO Press.

World Health Organization (WHO) and World Organization of Family Doctors (Wonca). (2008). *Integrating Mental Health into Primary Care: A Global Perspective.* Geneva, Switzerland: World Health Organization Press. Retrieved from http://www.who.int/mental_health/resources/mentalhealth_PHC_2008.pdf

Yannacci, J., & Rivard, J. C. (2006). *Matrix of Children's Evidence-Based Interventions.* Alexandria, VA: National Association of State Mental Health Program Directors Research Institute.

Yoo, S-K., & Skovholt, T. (2001). Cross-cultural examination of depression expression and help-seeking behavior: A comparative study of American and Korean college students. *Journal of College Counseling, 4*, 10–19.

Yorgason, J., Linville, S., & Zitzman, B. (2008). Mental health among college students: Do those who need services know about and use them? *Journal of American College Health, 57*(2), 173–81.

Zivin, K., Eisenberg, D., Gollust, S., & Golberstein, E. (2009). Persistence of mental health problems in a college student population. *Journal of Affective Disorders, 117*, 180–5.

INDEX

Page numbers followed by italicized "f" and "t" indicate figures and tables.

academic performance
  factors impacting, 94f
  Seung-Hui, 18
accommodations, high school, 55–56
acne, minocycline, 56
Active Minds, Inc., 109
admission process, mental health, 92
admissions staff, Virginia Tech, 18
advocates, mental health services, 198–99
Africa, mental health services, 181–82, 183
aggression, 129
Air Force, suicide prevention program, 102
alcohol programs, suicide, 101
Alexis, Aaron, 229–30
American Academy of Child and Adolescent
    Psychiatry, 112
American Association of Suicidology, 114
American College Counseling Association,
    71
American College Health Association
    (ACHA), 73, 94
American Foundation for Suicide
    Prevention (AFSP), 106, 114
American Psychiatric Association (APA), 8,
    112, 191
American Psychological Association, 191
Americans with Disabilities Act of 1990,
    78, 84
ammunition stockpiling, Cho, 50, 51
Annenberg Public Policy Center, 114
anticipating treatment, 119–20
antisocial personality disorder (APD),
    59–60
anxiety
  campus, 74, 78, 117
  Cho's childhood, 52–53
  college students, 76f

suicide, 101
Argentina, mental health, 187–88
art therapy, 16, 17
Asperger's syndrome, 53
Assertive Community Treatment (ACT)
    program, 163, 176, 200
assessment
  campus counseling centers, 85
  frameworks for assessing mental health
    services, 158–60
  mental health care in Europe, 185–86
  suicide prevention mandated, 108
  system of care principle, 231
assisted outpatient treatment (AOT), 141,
    142
Association of University and College
    Counseling Center Directors
    (AUCCCD), 71–72, 108
Ativan, 24
attention-deficit/hyperactivity disorder
    (ADHD), 74, 78, 112, 113, 117, 195
Austria, mental health, 184
autism, 17, 53, 113
autonomy, 99

Bean, Carl, 50
behavior
  college campus environments, 149–50
  Seung-Hui Cho's strange, 16, 20–28,
    204–5
Belgium, Geel program, 184–85, 193
Belize, mental health, 188
Beltway sniper shootings, 5
beneficence, 98–99
best practices. See wellness program
    development
Big Ten Suicide Study, 100

255

Binge, Seaman, 95
bipolar disorder, 74
Bonnie, Richard, 9, 221
Boston Gun Project (BGP), 174
British Association for Psychopharmacology, 112
British National Health Service (NHS), 187
Brower, Aaron, 105
Buckley amendment. *See* Family Educational Rights and Privacy Act (FERPA)
bullying
  mild, 55, 58
  school violence, 150–52
Bush, George W., 4, 28

campus culture, 95–96
CAMPUS LIFE mnemonic, college transition, 119–21, 124
campus mental health systems. *See also* lessons from Virginia Tech; mental health systems; wellness program development
  age of vulnerability, 66–69
  anxiety disorders, 76*f*
  case examples, 67, 68, 71
  Center for the Study of Collegiate Mental Health (CSCMH), 77
  changing campus culture, 95–96
  circles of care, 96*f*
  clients referred for psychiatric evaluation, 73*f*
  clients taking medication, 73*f*
  demographics, 69–71
  depression, 75*f*, 76*f*
  Healthy Minds Study (HMS), 76–77
  hopelessness, 75*f*
  impact on campuses, 94–95
  mental health issues, 71–78
  personal counseling focus, 80
  possible reasons for trends, 78–79
  students coming for counseling already on medication, 72*f*
  students diagnosed with depression, 74*f*
  students with severe psychological problems, 72*f*
  substance abuse, 76*f*
  suicide attempts and consideration, 75*f*
  top five disorders, 74
  wellness planning, 93
  work of counseling centers, 79–81
cancer, 175, 226
Care Team, 21–22, 23, 43, 82
Carillion Hospital, 48, 49, 57, 60, 90, 111
Carillion New River Valley Medical Center, 24
Case Western University, 167
Center for Mental Health Services, 169
Center for Multicultural Human Services, 13
Center for Student Studies, 76–77, 105
Center for the Study of Collegiate Mental Health (CSCMH), 77
Centers for Disease Control and Prevention (CDC), 105, 114, 147, 195, 198
Child and Adolescent Mental Health Studies (CAMS), 109
child psychiatry, 217
China, mental health, 181
Cho, Seung-Hui, 3, 6, 12, 128, 202, 219, 230
  art therapy, 16
  behavior invoking privacy law exceptions, 88, 90
  childhood: baseline anxiety, 52–53
  communication, 14–16, 25–26
  denial of mental health problems, 17, 24–25
  development, 7–8, 13
  family of, 7, 10, 13–14, 39, 166
  interview with family of, 39, 51–52
  middle school: suicidal and homicidal thoughts, 53
  order to outpatient treatment, 143
  panel directive, 6–7
  play foreshadowing attack, 26
  premeditated plan, 26, 27
  psychiatric evaluation, 16–17
  psychological autopsy, 45–46
  psychological profile of, 49–52
  psychosis, 53–54
  school years: threats and buffers, 54–61
  speculative psychological profile of, 52–61
  suicide threat, 23–24, 25, 53
Clark, Ryan, 34
Clarke Cognitive–Behavioral Prevention Intervention, 173
clinical interview, violence assessment, 144*t*
code of conduct, enforceable campus culture, 96

collaboration, college transition, 119
college environments
    bullying, 150–52
    depression, 150
    disruptive behaviors, 149–50
College Mental Health Committee,
    American Psychiatric Association, 8
College of Liberal Arts, 21
College of the Overwhelmed, Kadison and
    DiGeronimo, 94
College Student Mental Health Special
    Interest Study Group, 119
college transition from high school, 115–25,
    233
    CAMPUS LIFE mnemonic, 119–21, 124
    care principles, 118
    case examples, 115–16, 122–23, 123–24
    diagnosis and treatment of mental health
        issues, 117
    evidence-based literature on planning,
        117–19
    students as young adults in transition,
        121–22
Columbine massacre, 16, 53, 54, 55, 56, 86,
    135, 136, 166
command hallucinations, 48, 58
Commission on Mental Health Law Reform,
    8, 9, 221
commitment laws, 9, 221–22
Commonwealth of Virginia, mental health
    services, 168–69, 230
communication
    administration's response to events, 42–43
    college transition, 119
    lessons from Virginia Tech, 82–85
    Seung-Hui Cho, 14–16, 25–26
community
    mental health approach, 171
    mental health services, 160
    school violence, 153
    substance abuse, 174–75
    systems of care principles, 231–33
community-based care, mental health, 160–62
community service boards (CSBs), 10, 222
community support system (CSS), mental
    health, 162–63
comprehensive model of care, mental health,
    162–63

Comprehensive Service Act (CSA) for At Risk
    Youth and Families, 168–69, 200, 201
consumer and family empowerment, mental
    health, 160, 208–9
contagion effect, violence, 132
Cook Counseling Center, 21, 22–23, 23, 25,
    40–42, 49, 60, 82, 90, 92, 111, 128
Cornell University, suicide prevention, 105
crime scene, debriefing panel, 9–10
crisis intervention teams (CITs), 221
crisis management procedures, suicide
    prevention, 113–14
crisis mode, mental health services, 159
crisis stabilization units (CSUs), 87, 223

Davies, Gordon, Ph.D., 5
Dean of Faculty, communication model,
    96, 97*f*
Dean of Student Affairs, communication
    model, 96, 97*f*
death notifications, 34
Deeds, Austin "Gus," 230
delusional disorders, 58–59
demographics, student populations, 98
Denmark, 180
depression, 53
    campus disorders, 74
    college environments, 150
    college students, 74*f*, 75*f*, 76*f*
    Seung-Hui Cho, 16
Depue, Roger, 5, 10, 45
detention, 48, 57
developmental orientation, campus mental
    health wellness plan, 98
diagnosis, antisocial personality disorder
    (APD), 59–60
*Diagnostic and Statistical Manual of Mental
    Disorders* Fifth Edition (DSM-5), 47,
    80, 112
diversity, increasing demand for services,
    78, 81

economy
    funding models, 190–91
    health care, 212, 213
    status of health care, 225–26
    supply and demand for health care,
        217–18

education, reducing mental health stigma, 210–11
education plan, Seung-Hui Cho, 18
Eisenberg, Daniel, 76
Ellis, Carroll Ann, 5, 9, 39
emergency
  parental notification, 83
  psychiatric illness, 47
  Virginia Tech, 37–39
Emory University, 106
English department (Virginia Tech)
  faculty, 40–42, 128
  Seung-Hui Cho, 19–20, 26, 50, 51
erotomanic type, delusional disorder, 59
ethical issues, campus mental health
    wellness plan, 98–99
ethnicity, student mental health, 70
EU Labor Force Survey (LFS), 185
Europe, mental health approach, 183–84
European Union
  mental health care, 185–86
  tracking health data, 193
evaluation, college transition, 121
evidence-based intervention, mental health, 172, 201–3

Facebook, 20
faculty of Virginia Tech, interviews with, 40–43
Fairfax County Police's Victim Assistance
    Program, 39
fairness
  health care spending, 179
  mental health services, 158
family
  college transition, 121
  interview with, of Cho, 39, 51–52
  mental health services, 160
  system of care principle, 231, 233
  of Virginia Tech shooter, 7, 10, 13–14, 39, 166
Family Educational Rights and Privacy Act
    (FERPA), 11–12, 28, 84, 87, 89t, 90, 111, 222. See also privacy laws
Federal Bureau of Investigation (FBI), 5, 39, 140
federal government, mental health, 197–98
female student, harassing, 22, 26, 27

financing
  allocation of funding, 205–6
  European vs. American mental health, 186–87
  funding models and economy, 190–91
  government involvement, 197–98
  health care, 164, 179, 216
  incentives for mental health care, 204, 206–8
  investing in prevention, 209
  mental health services, 159, 192–93
  mental health services by income, 182–83
Finland, 184
First Amendment, 40
follow-up, campus counseling centers, 85–86
France, 180
Freedom of Information Act, 7

gatekeeper training, students at risk, 106
Geel, Belgium, 184–85, 193
General Assembly of Virginia (2008), 83, 84, 224, 225
Germany
  funding mental health, 187
  mental health, 184, 186
  social policies, 180
Giovanni, Nikki, 20, 27, 29t, 40, 42
Girard, K., 122
Goldstein, Andrew, 141
Good Behavior Game (GBG), 173–74
government
  comprehensive and coordinated
    leadership, 199–201
  involvement in mental health services, 197–98
  need for political will, 198–99
grandiose type, delusional disorder, 59
group pressures, violence, 132
Guide to Community Services, CDC, 147

"Half of Us" campaign, 109
harassment, female students, 22, 26, 27
Head State, 174
Health Behavior in School-age Children
    (HBSC), 185
health care
  alliance of suicide prevention with, 107–8

challenges, 215
consumer concern, 216
dichotomy between mental health care
    and, 195–96
economy, 212, 213
integrating mental health with, 187–89
patients forgoing care, 216–17
status, 219, 225–26
health care reform, 164
health insurance, 165, 216, 217
Health Insurance Portability and
    Accountability Act (HIPAA), 11, 28, 48,
    89*t*, 111, 222. *See also* privacy laws
health management, mental health services,
    159
Healthy Minds Study, 76–77, 97, 105
help-seeking behavior, suicide prevention,
    108–10
High Scope Perry Preschool Project, 173
Hilscher, Emily, 34
Hincker, Larry, 38
Hippocratic Oath, 217
Historical/Clinical/Risk Management-20
    (HCR-20), 144*t*
Hogan, Michael, 167
Holocaust, 50
hospitalization, 17, 24, 26, 48
Human Resources, communication model,
    96, 97*f*
hypervigilance, school years, 54, 55

identity, Seung-Hui, 20, 22
immigration, Cho family, 13–14
imposter syndrome, 4
income inequality, mental health care, 165–66
independence, college transition, 121
India, 188
individualized educational plan (IEP), 120
Individuals with Disabilities Education Act
    (IDEA), 78, 117
inhibitions, violence, 131
Initiatives for Excellence in Ohio, 200
Inkelas, Karen, 105
The Inn at Virginia Tech, 34–35
insomnia, campus disorders, 74
Institute of Medicine (IOM), 102
International Association of Counseling
    Services (IACS), 71

intervention
    evidence-based treatment and, 201–3
    mental health approach, 171–75, 176, 177
    system of care principle, 231
interviews
    Cho family, 39, 51–52
    faculty at Virginia Tech, 40–43
    families of victims, 33–34
    The Inn at Virginia Tech, 34–35
    media and unauthorized volunteers,
        36–37
    medical examiner's office, 35–36
involuntary hospitalization, 17, 24, 26
Iran, 188
ISBAR protocol, 111–12, 118

Jed Foundation, 103, 104*f*, 109, 113,
    114, 119
justice, 99

Kaine, Timothy, 3, 4, 5–7, 10
Kaiser Permanente, 190
Kendra's Law, 141
knife, Seung-Hui Cho's behavior, 20, 22, 29*t*

Labour Force Service Centres (LAFOS),
    186
Lamb, Richard, 161
language therapy, 17
Lanza, Adam, 229
learning disorders, 117, 195
legal statutes, campus mental health wellness
    plan, 99
legislation, health care, 225
lessons from school violence, 152–53
    community, 153
    parents, 152
    schools and colleges, 153
lessons from Virginia Tech, 215, 220
    communication, 82–85
    follow-up, 85–86
    outpatient care access, 86–87
    privacy law misinterpretation, 87–92
Level of Service Inventory-Revised (LSI-R),
    144*t*
life skills development, suicide prevention,
    104–5
lifestyle, 120–21

McCoy, Lenwood, 41
maintenance, mental health intervention, 103*f*
major depression: single episode, 16
managed care organizations (MCOs), 164, 207–8, 218, 219
managing treatment, 120
manuscript rejection, 56
Martin, Marcus, 5
Massengill, Colonel Gerald, 5
media, 4, 7
  administration's approach to, 41–42
  coverage of school shootings, 139–40
  interviews with unauthorized volunteers, 36–37
  Seung-Hui Cho's videotape diatribe to, 50–51, 58
Medicaid, 190, 197, 206
medical examiner's office, 35–36
medical-leave policy, mental illness, 114
Medicare, 190, 197, 206
medications
  Ativan, 24
  college campuses, 72*f*, 73*f*
  paroxetine, 16–17
memorandums of understanding (MOUs), 87, 96*f*, 111
mental health
  admission considerations, 92
  Cho's denial of, 17, 24–25
  commitment laws, 9
  data drive policy, 193
  definition, 180
  dichotomy between health care and, 195–96
  financial matters, 159, 182–83, 192–93
  impact of, issues on college campuses, 94–95
  implications for United States, 189–93
  inequity of payment, 217–18
  investing in prevention, 209
  managed care carve-outs, 164–65
  priority, 191
  privatization of, 223
  reform, 159
  Seung-Hui Cho as child, 15
  stigma, 70, 86, 159, 210–11, 226
  system problems, 11–12

mental health care delivery, 6
  balancing rights and public safety, 211–12
  empowering consumers, 208–9
  encouraging provider and organizational behavior, 209–10
  government levels of funding, regulation and provision, 197–98
  paying for services, 206–8
  policy following science, 226–27
  private and public service providers, 196–97, 223–24
  realigning incentives, 204–10
  reconciling science and practice, 201–3
  simplifying, 220
  structure, 196–98
  supply and demand, 203
  workforce development, 203–4
Mental Health Gap Action Program (MhGAP), 189, 192
mental health intervention spectrum, 103*f*
Mental Health Parity Act of 1996, 165
mental health professionals, 99, 203–4, 225, 227
mental health systems. *See also* campus mental health systems
  approaches around the world, 183–84
  brief history of U.S., 160–63
  city and county level, 169–71
  community-based care, 160–62, 171
  community service boards (CSBs), 222–23
  comprehensive and coordinated leadership, 199–201
  comprehensive model of care approach, 162–63
  current state of U.S. system, 163–66
  disparities among nations, 181–83
  early intervention and prevention, 171–75, 176, 177
  European and American funding, 186–87
  frameworks for assessing, 158–60
  integration with primary health care, 187–89
  performance measurement domains, 159–60
  promising approaches, 166–75
  public and political will, 198–99, 213–14
  Seung-Hui Cho, 49–50

service models, 184–86
state level approach, 167–69
system of care approach, 162, 213, 231–33
United States, 157, 183–84, 186
Michigan, High Scope Perry Preschool Project, 173
Middlebury College, 105
Milwaukee County Behavioral Health Division, 169–71
mind-body schism, 181
minocycline, acne, 56
mood disorders, 78, 101, 117
motivations, violence, 131

Nash, Mary Beth, 41
National Alliance on Mental Illness (NAMI), 109, 119, 159, 191, 199, 213, 230
National Association for Social Work, 191
National Center for Education Statistics, 69, 70
National College Health Assessment (NCHA), 73–76, 94
National College Health Risk Behavior Survey, 101
National Epidemiologic Survey on Alcohol and Related Conditions, 101
National Institute of Mental Health (NIMH), 114
National Institutes of Health (NIH), 197
National Study of Living-Learning Programs (NSLLP), 105
National Survey of Counseling Center Directors, 71–72, 81, 110
New River Valley Community Services Board (CSB), 11, 24, 25
No Right to Remain Silent, Roy, 33, 40
Norris Hall, 34, 35, 37, 38
Northeast Ohio University, 167
Northern Illinois University shooting, 114
Norway, 180, 190
Nurse Home Visitation Program, 173

Ohio, 167–68
Oldboy (film), 51
Olds, David, 173
outpatient care, campus counseling centers, 86–87

panel directive, 5–7
panel members, 5, 9–10
panic attacks, 74
paranoid disorder, 58
parental notification, emergency situations, 83
parents, school violence, 152
paroxetine, 16–17, 53
Pataki, George, 141
Patient Protection and Affordable Care Act of 2010, 164
Paul Wellstone Mental Health and Addiction Equity Act of 2008, 165
Pentagon attack, 5
perpetrators of school violence. See also school violence
  characteristics, 136–50
  external factors, 139–40
  internal factors, 136–38
persecutory type, delusional disorder, 59
personal counseling focus, counseling centers, 80
personnel, counseling centers, 79–80
pervasive developmental disorders, 78, 117
pharmacogenomics, 219
pharmacotherapy, system of care principle, 232
play, foreshadowing VA Tech attack, 26
poetry, Cho, 19, 20–21, 29t
political will, mental health services, 198–99, 213–14, 224–25
Preferred Drug Lists (PDLs), 202, 218
premeditation, Cho, 26, 27, 31, 50
prevention. See suicide prevention
  investing in, 209
  mental health approach, 171–75
  mental health intervention, 103f
  suicide, 102–3
  systems of care, 233
primary care. See health care
primary prevention. See suicide prevention
  crisis management procedures, 113–14
  disease, 102
  help-seeking behaviors, 108–10
  life skills development, 104–5
  restricting access to lethal means, 115
  social network promotion, 105

privacy laws, 24–25, 28, 31, 84. *See also*
    Family Educational Rights and Privacy
    Act (FERPA); Health Insurance
    Portability and Accountability Act
    (HIPAA)
  balancing rights and public safety, 211–12
  Cho's behavior and exceptions to, 88, 90
  Family Educational Rights and Privacy
    Act (FERPA), 87, 88, 90, 99
  Health Insurance Portability and
    Accountability Act (HIPAA), 11, 28,
    48, 87, 88, 90, 99
  misinterpretation of, 87–92
  reconciling FERPA and HIPAA, 90–92
  summary of HIPAA and FERPA, 89*t*
private providers, mental health services,
    196–97, 223–24
professional ethics, 7–8
Promoting Alternative Thinking Strategies
    (PATHS), 173
protective factors, long-term risk, 133
psychiatric emergencies, 47
psychiatric illness
  complexity of diagnosis, 46–47
  emergencies, 47
  making a psychiatric diagnosis, 46–47
  risk assessment for danger, 47–48
psychoeducation, 120
psychological problems, college campuses,
    72*f*
psychological profile, Seung-Hui Cho,
    49–52
psychopathology, college campuses, 77–78
psychosis, Seung-Hui Cho, 53–54
public education, reducing mental health
    stigma, 210–11
public health approach, campus mental
    health wellness plan, 99
public information officer, 36
Public Law 94–142, Section 504, 17
public places, violence in, 128–29
public providers, mental health services,
    196–97, 223–24
public will, mental health services, 198–99,
    225
publishing house, manuscript rejection, 56

"question mark," Seung-Hui Cho, 20, 22

rampage school shootings, 134–36. *See also*
    school violence; violence
  bullying, 150–52
  perpetrators, 136, 136–37
  Sandy Hook Elementary, 229
  stages, 138
recruiting, counseling staff, 81
red flags, Seung-Hui Cho, 28, 29*t*, 30*t*
regulation, government involvement in
    mental health, 197–98
responsiveness, mental health services, 158
Ridge, Tom, 5
risk assessment
  challenges in, 48–49
  predicting violence, 140–43
  psychiatric illness and danger, 47–48
risk factors
  bullying, 151–52
  recognizing and reducing influence,
    147–48
  violence, 145, 146*t*
Romeo and Juliet, 23
Roy, Lucinda, 21, 22–23, 27, 29*t*, 33, 40, 42

St. Albans Behavioral Health Center, 24, 30*t*
Sandy Hook Elementary School, 229
schizophrenia, 31, 74
school environment, 147–48, 153
school shootings
  changing campus culture, 95–96
  following Virginia Tech, 229–30
  rampage, 134–36, 138, 150–52
  violence, 125
school violence, 128. *See also* violence
  bullying, 150–52
  cases, 137–38
  characteristics of perpetrators of, 136–40
  community, 153
  defining, 133–36
  external factors, 139–40
  internal factors, 136–38
  lessons learned, 152–53
  parents, 152
  rampage school shooting, 134–36, 150–52
  schools and colleges, 153
  stages of rampage killing, 138
  targeted, 133–34
Scotland, 185–86, 193

screening
   mental health, 92
   students at risk, 106
   suicide, 101–2
Seaman, Garrett, 95
secondary prevention. *See also* suicide
   prevention
   crisis management procedures,
     113–14
   disease, 102
   help-seeking behaviors, 108–10
   identifying students at risk, 106–8
   mental health services, 110–13
selective mutism, 16, 31, 53, 59, 204
selective serotonin reuptake inhibitor,
   paroxetine, 53
Self-Appraisal Questionnaire (SAQ), 144*t*
September 11, 2001, 5
Sequenced Treatment Alternatives of
   Resistant-Depression (STAR*D), 202
Skadden, Arps, Slate, Meagher & Flom, 9
sleep, 120
social anxiety, 53
social anxiety, 53, 76*f*
social network promotion, suicide
   prevention, 105
social networks, 57
Southeast Asia, 182
special needs, Seung-Hui Cho, 15, 17
Stambaugh, Hollis, 10
Steger, Charles, 38, 41–42
stigma, mental health, 70, 86, 159, 210–11,
   226
stress, increasing demand for services, 70,
   78
stressors, Cho in high school, 54–58
Strickland, Diane (Honorable), 5
Student Code of Conduct, 21
students at risk, identifying, 106–8
students of concern teams, 107
substance abuse
   college students, 76*f*
   community mobilizations, 174–75
   suicide, 101
   violence, 131
Substance Abuse and Mental Health
   Services Administration (SAMHSA),
   102, 114, 169

suicide
   Air Force prevention program, 102
   campus mental health programs, 101–2
   college students, 75*f*
   Good Behavior Game (GBG), 174
   Help-seeking and access to care, 101–2
   preventive approach, 102–3
   risk factors, 100–101
   threats of Seung-Hui Cho, 23–24, 25, 27
suicide prevention. *See also* college
   transition from high school
   alliance with primary care, 107–8
   best practices, 103–15
   case examples, 107, 115–16, 122–23, 123–24
   crisis management procedures, 113–14
   gatekeeper training, 106
   identifying students at risk, 106–8
   increasing help-seeking behaviors, 108–10
   ISBAR protocol, 111–12, 118
   Jed Foundation/Suicide Prevention
     Resource Center approach, 104*f*
   life skills development, 104–5
   mandated assessments, 108
   providing mental health services, 110–13
   restricting access to potentially lethal
     means, 115
   social network promotion, 105
   students of concern teams, 107
   web-based screening, 106
Suicide Prevention Resource Center, 104*f*
Survey of Health, Aging and Retirement in
   Europe (SHARE), 185
Susan G. Komen foundation, 175
Sweden
   funding and economy, 190
   funding mental health, 187
   mental health, 184
   social policies, 180
system of care approach
   mental health, 162, 184–86, 213
   principles, 231–33

targeted school violence, 133–34. *See also*
   school violence
tertiary prevention. *See also* suicide prevention
   crisis management procedures, 113–14
   disease, 102
   mental health services, 110–13

threat assessment
 predicting violence, 140–43
 Virginia model for student, 141, 142f
Tocqueville, Alexis de, 212
training, mental health professionals, 99,
 203–4, 227
treatment
 campus counseling centers, 85
 mental health intervention, 103f
 system of care principle, 231, 232
TriData, 9, 10, 41

Ulifeline, 109
Union College, 105
United Kingdom, 179, 180
United States
 financing mental health, 192–93
 health care spending, 179
 health care system, 219
 mental health approach, 157, 183–84, 186
 mental health policy and practice
  implications, 189–93
 mental health system, 163–66
 tracking health data, 193
university counseling centers (UCCs).
  See also campus mental health systems
 assessment and treatment, 85
 college and university, 79–81
 follow-up, 85–86
 institution's responsibility, 81
 outpatient care access, 86–87
 personnel, 79–80
 training professionals, 99
University of Illinois, 108
University of Michigan Comprehensive
 Depression Center, 76
University of Michigan School of Public
 Health, 76
University of Minnesota, 110
University of North Carolina at Chapel Hill,
 106
University of Virginia, 221
utilizing resources, 120

victims
 interviews of families of, 33–34
 medical examiner's office, 35–36

videotape diatribe, Seung-Hui Cho, 50–51,
 58
violence. See also school violence
 aggression and, 129
 biological and physiological factors,
  129–30
 bullying, 150–52
 cases, 127, 130, 134, 137–38
 college campus environments, 149–52
 cultural factors, 132
 dynamic variables, 133
 external factors, 132, 146–48
 group pressures, 132
 individual factors, 145
 inhibitions, 131
 internal factors, 129–31
 long-term risk, 132–33
 long-term strategies for youth, 148
 mental health and intervention, 226
 methods of assessment, 143, 144t
 models and reinforcers, 132
 motivations, 131
 prediction of, 140–43
 prevention, 128–29, 144–48
 psychiatric factors, 131
 psychological factors, 130
 in public places, 128–29
 risk factors for, 145, 146t
 school shootings, 125
 situational factors, 132
 static variables, 132–33
 substance abuse, 131
 threat assessment, 140–43
 Virginia model for student threat
  assessment, 141, 142f
Violence Risk Appraisal Guide (VRAG),
 144t
Virginia, mental health services, 168–69
Virginia Commonwealth University, 4, 97f
Virginia Health Records Privacy statute, 28
Virginia model, student threat assessment,
 141, 142f
Virginia State Police, 34, 39
Virginia Tech. See also lessons from Virginia
 Tech
 admissions staff, 18
 emergency preparedness at, 37–39

fault finding, 198
ignoring aberrant behaviors, 60–61
The Inn at, 34–35
leadership following the shooting,
   199–200
Seung-Hui Cho, 19, 19–22, 27–28
Virginia Tech Police Department (VTPD),
   24
Virginia Tech tragedy, 221, 223, 226
   Commission on Mental Health Law
      Reform, 221
   forcing action in Virginia, 219
   red flags, 29t, 30t
   shootings since, 229–30
   violence, 125
   warning signs, 27–28, 31
volunteers, interviews with unauthorized,
   36–37

warning signs
   rampage school shootings, 139
   red flags, 28, 29t, 30t
   violence, 146t
   Virginia Tech tragedy, 27–28, 31, 205
Washington Navy Yard, 229–30
Webdale, Kendra, 141

wellness program development
   addressing ethical issues, 98–99
   compliant with legal statutes, 99
   culturally competent, 98
   developmentally oriented, 98
   evidence-based, 98
   key principles in, 97–99
   public health approach, 99
   training mental health professionals, 99
West Ambler Johnston dormitory, 33,
   37, 38
Wilder, L. Douglas, 201
workforce development, mental health
   professionals, 99, 203–4, 227
World Health Organization (WHO), 158,
   179, 180, 182, 188–89, 219
World Organization of Family Doctors
   (Wonca), 187
Wraparound Milwaukee, 169–71, 200
Wright State University College of Medicine,
   167

youth violence, 127, 128. See also school
   violence; violence

zero tolerance, schools, 135